the
GET OUT OF DEBT
KIT

Your Roadmap to Total Financial Freedom

Deborah McNaughton

Dearborn™
Trade Publishing
A **Kaplan Professional** Company

Vice President and Publisher: Cynthia A. Zigmund
Editorial Director: Donald J. Hull
Senior Managing Editor: Jack Kiburz
Interior Design: Lucy Jenkins
Cover Design: KTK Design Associates
Typesetting: Elizabeth Pitts

Library of Congress Cataloging-in-Publication Data

McNaughton, Deborah, 1950–
　　The get out of debt kit : your roadmap to total financial freedom /
Deborah McNaughton.
　　　　p.　cm.
Includes index.
　　ISBN 0-7931-6007-3 (8.5 ×11 paperback)
　　1. Consumer credit—United States.　2. Finance, Personal—United
States. I. Title.
　　HG3756. U54　M362 2002
　　332.024′02—dc21
　　　　　　　　　　　　　　　　　　　　　　　　　　　　　2002006184

Dedication

To my wonderful husband, Hal, who has been my strength, my anchor, and my support in all of our financial endeavors, challenges, and growth. You are my greatest cheerleader and my best friend.

Acknowledgments

I consider myself truly blessed by the wonderful people who surround me with their great insight and encouragement on all my books and projects.

A special thank you to Cynthia Zigmund and the team at Dearborn, who have caught my vision to spread the word to help individuals with their finances and to share my story. Cynthia, your words of wisdom and direction are always greatly appreciated.

To Mindy Weinstein, my managing editor for the *Financial Victory* newsletter, who helped put the finishing touches and polish on this book. I couldn't have done it without you. You're the greatest.

To my agent, Chip MacGregor, who is always there to jump in and help me get my projects off the ground. I know I can count on Chip to be there for me and look out for my best interests.

A special thank you for the team at the Debt Relief Clearinghouse, where I am a spokesperson. The passion all of you have to help individuals get out of debt is impressive. To John Puccio, Richard Puccio, Chris Viale, and Thom Fox—thank you for believing in me. You're the best. Keep up the good work.

For my wonderful husband, daughters, sons-in-law, and grandchildren, you are what makes life meaningful to me. I treasure you all.

And last but not least, to all of you readers who have taken your first step to get out of debt and attain financial freedom. You can do it! God bless you.

Contents

Preface   vii

1. Are You Drowning in Debt?   1

2. The Ten Myths of Credit   8

3. Where Did I Go Wrong? Analyzing Your Personal Situation   15

4. SOS! Warning Signs of Debt   28

5. Deciding Who to Pay First: Prioritizing Your Debts   50

6. Increasing Your Income While You're in a Slump   63

7. Tips to Save Money to Pay Off Your Debt   72

8. Setting Up Your Budget   111

9. Stating Your Case to Creditors   133

10. Tips to Get Out of Debt   146

11. Debt Free! Now What?   161

12. What Card Should You Have?   170

13. Breaking the Habits of Debt   181

Appendix A: Cost Savings Converting to a Biweekly Mortgage   186
Appendix B: The Fair Debt Collection Practices Act   199

Glossary   209
Index   211
About the Author   214

Preface

How many of you have learned the hard way by making dumb financial decisions? Why is it we learn things the hard way before we make changes in our life? Is it human nature? Or is it our way of thinking things will get better when we get our big break?

In my life, I was never taught the proper way to manage money. My husband and I owned a real estate franchise business in the 1980s. We had good years and bad years; the real estate business was always feast or famine. The gauge was how the economy was doing.

As our business grew, I saw a need to help some of our potential clients get their credit and spending under control so they could purchase a home. I researched several laws pertaining to credit restoration, and as a result, I founded Professional Credit Counselors. My main intention was not only to help people with their credit needs but also to add to our real estate business. I had knowledge and empathy and a desire to help people.

Never in a million years would I have expected that I would one day become a victim and be nearly bankrupt.

I know from experience that owning a business can give you a false sense of security. There was always that big deal ready to happen that would make all my money dreams come true. Why worry about tomorrow when the big deal was just around the corner? That is why I wanted to write this book for both individuals and business owners.

My friend, I have news for you. The big deal rarely does happen, and if it does, look at the big deal as icing on the cake and not something that will get you out of debt and solve all your money woes.

In the early 1990s, my husband and I decided to sell our real estate franchise and invest the money in another business. As you may have guessed, the new business never got off the ground. The country was in an economic downturn, and we were caught in it. The money we had invested was gone, resulting in a 70 percent drop in our income.

I have to confess that we had been living quite well and had not planned on a business failure. We had not put enough money aside to keep us afloat, and the money we had saved was quickly spent as we tried to keep our creditors happy. The bill collectors and creditors didn't care about our drop in income; they just wanted their money. And the bills kept coming.

Most of the debt was from business loans, credit cards, and taxes. Including all the late fees and penalties, the total was over $300,000. It just kept compounding.

The stress of that debt was awful. We had no peace, and the bill collectors had no sympathy. They called day and night to badger us for money.

At the time bankruptcy wasn't an option. The taxes couldn't be discharged, and we were in a family partnership that we didn't want to have get involved.

Sure, I knew how to deal with the creditors, but I didn't have the money to pay them. Decisions had to be made about what bills we could pay and how we were going to take care of our family.

Now remember that this was not a problem that had happened overnight. The events I am describing went on for several years. When you dig yourself in a hole that deep, it's going to take a long time to crawl out.

As we began to dig our way out of the pit, bad decisions were made, and we listened to bad advisors. When you're desperate and stressed, it's difficult to know right from wrong.

Finally, however, we developed a plan and a budget. It was important that my family's needs be taken care of first. I had three daughters—Tiffany, Christy, and Mindy—living at home, and it was essential to take care of them.

When reviewing ways to save money and cut back on our expenses, I decided to stop paying our medical insurance. I planned to pick it up later when things weren't so tight, and besides, we were all healthy.

Thirty days after letting our medical insurance lapse, my youngest daughter Mindy had to have emergency brain surgery. What appeared as flu symptoms turned out to be hydrocephalus. It seemed that a blockage in the ventricles of her brain caused fluid to build up. Mindy went into a coma and was near death. A neurosurgeon was brought in immediately, and Mindy was rushed into surgery. I didn't know if I would ever see her alive again or in what condition she would be if she survived the surgery. To make matters worse, we had no medical insurance.

The fear of my daughter dying and the recognition that I had no medical insurance were more than I could handle. I was concerned that once the hospital found out we had no insurance, it wouldn't give Mindy the care that she needed. Bankruptcy seemed inevitable.

But miracles still happen! Mindy's surgery was a success. They drained 30 cc's of fluid from her brain and inserted a shunt. She was alive, and all the signs indicated she'd have no side effects. We are a praying family, and I know that God heard our prayers.

The second miracle was that the hospital had a special program for children with traumas, and Mindy fit the profile. The program paid for all medical expenses, totaling over $50,000. Even knowing that we had no insurance, the hospital brought in the best specialists and team to help save my daughter's life.

A week after Mindy's surgery, needless to say the whole family was emotionally drained. To make matters worse, the IRS had taken all our money (the little we had) out of our bank account during the week of Mindy's surgery without our knowing it. When I discovered this, I panicked because I thought I had an arrangement with the agency. My first mistake was not getting the arrangement in writing, which was my fault.

When I contacted the IRS, my nerves were shot and I was a bit emotional trying to describe what had happened during the past week with Mindy's surgery. After realizing the miscommunication that had taken place, the woman I spoke with returned all the money except for $100, and a new arrangement was made. I have no hard feelings about the IRS, especially as all our tax problems are now behind us and everything was paid to the IRS's satisfaction.

With all that said, there is hope for any financial crisis if you do your homework and set a plan in motion to get out of debt when you're able. Of course, it's best not to get into the debt trap to begin with. Even if bad decisions are made, they can be reversed.

Needless to say, my situation changed my life and the life of my family. Career changes took place, because we knew that we would have to have insurance for Mindy who now had a preexisting condition.

We were victims of a poor economy and poor decisions, but we bounced back. My husband and I reevaluated our priorities and made the necessary changes.

Were we able to pay back the $300,000? No. But we negotiated with each of the creditors for a lesser amount. The creditors knew that if we filed for bankruptcy, they would receive nothing. Something was better than nothing in their opinion, and the debts were satisfied without our having to file for bankruptcy. The process took several years because we wouldn't make an offer to a creditor unless we had the money in hand.

It's been many years since our tragedy, and I'm happy to say that all three of my daughters are now married with children. What our tragedy did for me was create a passion to help educate people about the right way to handle their finances so they can avoid the trauma I experienced. When talking to my clients or doing radio or television interviews, I can honestly say I am a better person as a result of my experience. I not only have learned about credit and debt, but I have compassion for those who are looking for ways to remove the burden of debt from their life. I feel what you feel. I've been there.

This book was written to help you get a handle on your debt and be set free of the bondage of debt. It is user friendly. The worksheets will help you position yourself to see all areas of your finances and develop a plan to be debt free.

Don't get discouraged or frustrated if things seem overwhelming. Just pick yourself up, make a plan, get the help or advice you need, make wise decisions, and keep on moving. You'll conquer your debt. It may not be overnight, but you *can* do it. If I could do it, so can you. Now, let's get started.

1

Are You Drowning in Debt?

The eternal optimist! The dreamer! The visionary who knows things will get better! Big "dealitis"!

These are the people who live for the future and never face the present—people who grab what they can now and don't worry about the future. This personality type lives in denial of today's events.

Does this seem a contradiction? Well, it is. This type of person is heading for financial destruction! The person I'm describing will fall into a sea of debt without a life jacket. No realistic vision, no direction, no plan, and no rescuer. Whether you own a business or are employed by someone else, the way you manage your personal finances generally mirrors the way you manage your own business. They go hand in hand.

People without vision can't see what is in front of them. They are people who don't take the time to learn how the credit system works, how to manage personal debt, and what the consequences are for this lack of knowledge. These are people who quickly get into debt and never figure out how they got there.

Without a plan to redeem yourself from the debt you have incurred, it's no wonder you are stressed out and can't sleep at night. Trying to figure out how you are going to get out of the hole you have dug for yourself can be overwhelming. It is important that you formulate a plan for *your* particular situation to get the relief you are looking for. Throughout this book, you will find several different strategies to help you formulate this plan.

Discipline without direction is not only frustrating but also disastrous for your financial well-being. It is through discipline and planning that you will be able to succeed in reaching your financial destination and be free of debt as well as enjoying an inner peace.

When taking a trip, it is important to have a roadmap to your final destination. Without one, you may find yourself going in circles, getting lost, and feeling frustrated. A financial roadmap is a must to get back on track. The following chapters should help you map out your course from the beginning to the end on your road to debt management.

Nothing is more upsetting or disheartening than to feel that all is lost. Being overextended and drowning in debt can make you perceive that there's no end to this vicious cycle. I can tell you that there *is* light at the end of the tunnel. You will be rescued!

Debt is on the rise. When the economy is good, we spend and run up billions of dollars of debt. When the economy turns, many of us are suddenly faced with a mountain of debt but with no plan in place to conquer that mountain. The banks, department stores, and credit card companies all love us. We make money for them.

Let's face it: If it weren't so easy to accumulate debt, we couldn't afford the luxuries we have, the items we simply can't live without. The things we needed to keep up with the Joneses; the meals we had to eat; the clothes we have to have; the big expensive toys like big-screen televisions and state-of-the-art computer packages; and toys for the children we think they can't live without. All these things have led us down the path to excessive debt. Why worry about paying today when you can pay tomorrow? Small monthly payments! Those three words are the beginning of the end. Debt has begun!

We are our own worst enemy. In most areas of our life, we can exercise self-control, but there is little or no will power when it comes to credit cards and other debt.

It's time we overcome our weakness and use self-control. Knowledge about credit and financial issues will empower us to use self-control and stop the credit card industry from enticing us with things we really don't need.

Annie's Story

It was my second consultation with Annie. The first time I spoke to Annie, she and her husband, Ben, were struggling to pay their bills. They had excessive debt and two delinquent credit cards. I had instructed them to contact their creditors and make payment arrangements.

Several months later, Annie phoned me again to tell me that their situation had gotten worse. They had acquired $25,000 in credit card debt, and now all their credit cards had become delinquent. They had no assets and didn't own a home, so an equity loan wasn't a consideration.

Annie explained that both she and Ben were employed and also had a side business. Instead of paying their credit card bills, they were putting any extra money they had into the business. They were waiting for a "big deal" to come in so they could pay off their credit cards.

As soon as I heard about the "big dealitis," I knew they weren't living in the present. This wasn't a new story to me. I had heard the same story over and over again by others who had gotten into side businesses—self-employed people who own a business as well as people not in business for themselves. As a matter of fact, I could relate to this situation because I've been down that road myself and quickly discovered most "big deals" don't happen. If reality doesn't sink in fast, a person hung up with "big dealitis" could end up in bankruptcy, which is exactly what Annie was considering.

Being optimistic in your business is fine as long as you are also being realistic by taking care of the immediate needs of your family and yourself.

Annie said that once the "big deal" came in, they would pay off all their credit cards, but she was having trouble dealing with the calls from creditors demanding payment.

I told Annie to not look at the "big deal" as their ticket to freedom but to look at it as the "icing on the cake." The "big deal" should *add* to their finances and not be used to put out their fire. If the "big deal" never happens, they will be living in a fantasy world with the walls caving in and their life ruined. It was time to face reality and get their debt under control and finances back on track.

I encouraged Annie to make a list of her creditors and make payment arrangements with each of them. Because both Annie and Ben were employed, a steady paycheck was coming in to help them with their plan. I also suggested that if they felt uncomfortable getting in touch with each of the creditors, they should find a debt management company to assist them in working with the creditors.

When the "big deal" does come in, they won't have to use all of it to catch up with bills. There would be enough to put away and save.

Quiz Time

Before we go any further, let's take a short quiz about your knowledge of the credit system. This quiz will show you how responsible you are in handling your finances. Circle your answer(s) and calculate your score before reviewing the correct answers.

KNOWLEDGE OF THE CREDIT SYSTEM QUIZ

1. Before making a decision to apply, when a credit card application arrives in the mail, you should:
   a. Check the annual fees and other charges.
   b. Review the interest rates and the way the interest is calculated.
   c. Read the fine print.
   d. All of the above

2. When a lender is deciding to approve your loan, what is the most important factor it is looking for?
   a. Payment history from your credit report and income
   b. Number of dependents in the household and your marital status
   c. Whether you rent or own your home
   d. An unlisted telephone number

3. When scoring a credit application for a home, automobile, or credit card, the lender is looking for:
   a. Your FICO score.
   b. Your debt-to-income ratio.
   c. Length of employment.
   d. All of the above

4. When determining the cost of your loan, the most important indicator is:
   a. Minimum monthly payment.
   b. Interest rate.
   c. Loan amount.
   d. Number of monthly payments.

5. If you make a partial payment other than the amount due on your credit card statement, your credit report will report:
   a. Delinquent.
   b. Payment is current.
   c. Unrated.
   d. None of the above

6. If you have a credit card balance of $2,000, make the minimum payment each month, and never increase your balance, how long will it take to pay off the balance? (Assume 21 percent interest.)
   a. 2 years
   b. 4 years
   c. 8 years
   d. 16+ years

7. If you are self-employed, how many years does a credit grantor want to know you've been in business?
   a. 2 or more years
   b. 3 or more years
   c. 4 or more years
   d. 5 or more years

KNOWLEDGE OF THE CREDIT SYSTEM QUIZ (Continued)

8. When applying for credit, a red flag is waved and the application instantly denied if your debt-to-income ratio for paying debts (excluding your mortgage/rent payments) is:
   a. 2 to 7 percent of your take-home income.
   b. 8 to 12 percent of your take-home income.
   c. 12 to 19 percent of your take-home income.
   d. 20 percent and higher of your take-home income.

9. If you get a credit card solicitation for a preapproved card or application and don't want to apply for the card, you should:
   a. Toss it in the trash.
   b. Shred or destroy the solicitation.
   c. Call the company making the offer to decline.
   d. None of the above

10. The ideal number of open accounts on your credit report should be:
   a. 0 to 1.
   b. 2 to 3.
   c. 4 to 5.
   d. 6 or more.

Scxoring:

9 to 10 correct: Good job! You are ahead of the game with your credit knowledge.

5 to 8 correct: Be careful! You can easily fall prey to credit card offers without knowing what you are getting into. Examine all solicitations and know what your contracts state. That means reading the fine print. You need to do your homework whenever you apply for credit; and make sure you aren't going to be overextended and have more debt than you can afford.

0 to 4 correct: Watch out! Your financial world may come crashing down on you. It's time to learn all that you can about credit and debt before you make a wrong decision that can result in excessive debt and financial problems.

Reviewing each answer

1. (d) All of the above. Whenever you receive a credit card application, you need to read every word in the application, as well as the disclosures. There can be fees that you will be charged, such as the annual fee, over-the-limit fees, late fees, returned check fees, and so on. Also listed is the interest rate and the way the interest is charged. There may be a grace period from the date of purchase (approximately 20 to 25 days) during which no interest is charged, which enables you to pay off the balance of the new purchases without a finance charge. If there is no grace period, the interest begins at the time of purchase and is calculated daily.

2. (a) A lender will look closely at your payment history from your credit report. From the information taken from your credit report and the monthly income, the creditor can determine if you can afford the new payment on the credit you are applying for.

KNOWLEDGE OF THE CREDIT SYSTEM QUIZ (Continued)

3. (d) The FICO score is a numeric tabulation of several factors listed on your credit report, such as payment history, type of credit you have, balances compared with credit limits, open accounts, number of inquiries, and so forth. How many points are given each factor is top secret. FICO scoring is an important qualification when applying for credit; your FICO score will be low if you are overextended.

    In addition to your FICO score, your debt-to-income ratio is calculated to make sure you can handle the payments. If you have been employed for less than two years, you probably won't qualify for credit.

4. (b) Knowing how high your interest rate is, is the most important factor in determining how much you actually are paying for the use of credit. The higher the interest rate, the more you are paying in finance charges.

5. (a) If you are experiencing problems making your payment, a partial payment will be reported on your credit report as "delinquent." By making a payment less than the minimum amount, the difference in the payment made and the payment owed is rolled into the next month. This is called a "rolling late" and will not become current until the one payment is received. This is a negative mark on your credit report.

6. (d) On a credit card balance of $2,000, making only a minimum payment will take 16 years and 8 months to pay off! You will also pay $2,500 in interest!

7. (a) You must have been self-employed for two or more years to qualify for new credit. Financial statements, such as tax returns, bank statements, and a year-to-date profit and loss statement may be required. A self-employed person is a higher risk for a lender because monthly income isn't stable.

8. (d) An instant denial of credit is made if your debt-to-income ratio is 20 percent or higher. Even 15 percent and above would signal the lender that you may be headed for problems.

9. (b) Whenever you get a credit card solicitation for a preapproved card or application and don't want to apply for the card, SHRED IT! Many people are victimized by their identity being stolen from information listed on the solicitation.

10. (b) The ideal number of open accounts that show payment history are 2 to 3. You don't have to have excessive debt and shouldn't but need only a payment pattern.

By knowing as much as you can about credit and how to avoid the pitfalls of debt, you'll be ahead of the game. You'll become a savvy manager of your finances.

DEBT DESTROYER TIPS

- Learn how the credit system works.

- Establish a plan to get out of debt.

- Be disciplined to avoid frustration.

- Increase your knowledge of credit and financial issues to empower yourself to break your debt.

2

The Ten Myths of Credit

We live in a world filled with information. Some experts claim that we're overwhelmed by our 24/7 media-saturated days. Despite this perpetual buzz, many of us still operate under false financial notions. We somehow manage to look the other way when it comes to learning about handling our money in a manner that enhances our life and ourselves. Because our society is so consumer oriented, we put considerable effort into talking about what we're going to buy, showing off our latest purchases, and perhaps enviously dreaming of all the things we can't have but are absolutely sure would make us completely happy.

Such thinking is dangerous, although it's not unusual for most people to operate under these false assumptions. Many comfort themselves with the assumption that they'll take care of things tomorrow, or that someday a knight in shining armor will come and magically take care of things for them. Perhaps some women think they're not smart enough to learn about handling their own finances. Some may feel they don't make enough money to merit financial planning. The truth is that all of these beliefs are untrue because when it comes to finances, what you don't know can hurt you. Rather than fall prey to false truths, read on and learn how to protect yourself from the pitfalls and perils of bad credit debt and mishandled money.

Myth #1

"Using credit allows me to buy the things I want so I can enjoy my life right now."

Wrong. This is the tried-and-true path to debt and financial trouble. Credit is not free money, nor is it an easy repayment plan with minimum monthly costs. Credit is a serious responsibility. When you accept credit, you are telling a lender that you give your word—you promise—to repay any money loaned to you along with any interest rates incurred.

Credit can be a helpful tool if used wisely. Briefly, what is wise credit use?

- Having credit on hand in case of an emergency.

    Sudden illness or loss of a job can happen to anybody at anytime. Better to have $2,000 to $3,000 worth of credit reserved for such an event. You'll rest better knowing you're covered.
- Purchasing a few items and then paying your account balance off quickly to demonstrate sound payment patterns.

    Just be sure your credit activity is being reported to one of the three credit reporting agencies: Equifax, Experian, or TransUnion.
- Planning for a big-ticket item and using credit to help you cover the costs.

    If you want to buy a car, for example, research the best deals, put as high a down payment as you can afford (even if this means saving for the down payment), and then use a loan to pay off the rest. Make all payments on time; and when you can, add extra money to your payments to avoid further interest costs.
- Using a mortgage loan to help you buy the house of your dreams.

    Costs are high if you're renting, making the move to buy a house wise, because at the end of the term you'll own a house! Just make sure you're getting a good deal (on both the house and the loan) and that you can afford the monthly mortgage payments.
- Not using your credit card for items under $25, impulse purchases, items that immediately begin to devalue, meals, paying off other bills you can't afford, and taking out cash advances that you can't afford.

It's a terrific idea to have your own credit. In fact, I strongly recommend you have two or three open accounts in your own name. But when you use credit, pay off the monthly balance; don't carry over any amount to the following month if possible. Remember the ideal is to have credit without debt.

Myth #2   **"Any type of credit is bad."**

False. There are times when credit is good. Examples of solid credit usage are:

- Emergencies
- Establishing a credit payment history
- Planned big-ticket expenses
- Credit for an automobile or home
- Travel for convenience

It's up to you to use credit for worthwhile purposes. The trick is to ensure you have the money or resources to pay off any debt you incur quickly. Many of us buy an item thinking that it doesn't cost much, you'll get a raise someday, or you simply must have that eye-catching something or else! Retrain your way of thinking. If you see something you think you need to own, wait on it anywhere from one to three days. Consider if you can afford it. If you can't, save for it. By the time you've gathered the money together to make the purchase, you'll definitely know if it's worth it.

Myth #3   **"I'm in financial trouble already. Why should I even bother trying to get myself out of this situation? It's obvious I can't handle finances."**

It's tough to learn the hard way. Rest assured you're not alone in your financial troubles, but you must own up to your actions. You incurred the debt—most likely with the best intentions of paying it off—and now you must find a way to make good on your promise. You'll need to come up with a repayment plan, communicate with your lenders, and seek outside help if you need it.

Most of us never learned much about managing credit and the consequences of being overextended from either our families or our schooling. Now it's up to you to accept your situation, learn from your experience, and then move on. Make it a point to educate yourself about financial management so that you never find yourself in this situation again. You can get yourself out of this mess and you are capable of handling your own finances.

Myth #4   **"I must be very creditworthy because I get all kinds of offers, both online and in the mail, extending me credit."**

Don't believe these offers. Credit is a business. Lenders make money from you through annual fees and finance charges. Credit card companies often make offers based on initial research they've conducted; sometimes, they just use mailing lists.

Always read the fine print on these offers. You'll find a disclosure notice that essentially says you've been "preapproved" based on certain criteria—information in your consumer report among other things. The disclosure notice is typically followed by a disclaimer stating that the offer can be withdrawn subject to continuing qualification. This means that the lender may run a credit check on you before granting your credit application.

It's up to you to know how much credit you can handle. You'll also want to research what credit card company's plan and interest rate—annual percentage rate, or APR—offer the best deal. Sometimes credit card terms can change, and this is detailed in the fine print. Keep only a few credit cards; it's easy to lose track and become overextended if you have too many. You could then acquire too much debt—something you want to avoid!

Should you receive an actual credit card in the mail, cut it up and return it to the lender by certified mail with a return receipt. Specifically inform the sender that you do not want to use its card and that your account should be closed. If you fail to do this, you may be charged the yearly fee or other such costs. Such an oversight could lead to a negative entry on your credit report.

Myth #5   "As long as I pay my monthly minimum payment, everything is fine—right?"

Wrong, wrong, wrong. If you pay only the minimum owed on your account balance, you're increasing both the time to pay back the credit and the amount of interest incurred. You're also carrying over debt from one month to the next. Try to pay off your charges at the end of the month; if you can't, then pay as much as you can. If you've already generated a significant amount of debt, then pay more than the monthly minimum—an additional $5 can greatly reduce your interest charges and help you bring the balance down much more quickly.

Most of us never want to think about loss of employment or sudden illness, but it's important to plan ahead for such situations. If you're constantly creating more debt and an emergency arises, you'll wind up in deep financial trouble. If you're currently just getting by and/or living from paycheck to paycheck, it's time to reassess your finances and come up with a strategic plan. Living off extended credit simply digs you deeper and deeper into serious debt.

Myth #6　**"It's all right if I take out a cash advance to pay off some other debts so I don't fall behind in my payments."**

You could be facing some serious financial difficulties. If you're unable to pay your bills because you're running short, chances are you're living beyond your means. Constantly relying on one credit card to pay off another doesn't help your situation; you're simply postponing an inevitable debt crisis.

You're better off sitting down immediately and reassessing your income and expenses to see where you can cut back. Prioritize your costs and come up with a plan to decrease your debt. If you need to tighten the belt a bit, do so and allocate those extra dollars to paying down your credit card debt. Do not incur any more debt. Stop charging. Take action right away, and to prevent yourself from falling into serious debt and possibly damaging your credit history don't continue relying on old spending and credit habits. Contacting a debt management company is highly recommended.

Myth #7　**"Lenders never go after co-signers when a borrower fails to repay the debt."**

False. When you sign an agreement to co-sign for someone else, you promise to pay back the credit when the borrower cannot. The reason the lender agreed to extend credit to the borrower is your promise that you'll accept responsibility for the borrower's inability to be approved for credit of his own. Basically, you are guaranteeing the line of credit.

In the event that the borrower fails to pay, the failure is reported on both the borrower's and the co-signer's credit report. Likewise, any delinquent payments or account defaults show up on both reports as well. Co-signing is always a risk. Think carefully about co-signing for a credit card. You could have your credit history ruined if you sign for someone who doesn't understand the true responsibility associated with accepting a line of credit.

Myth #8　**"If I have to, I can just take out a home equity loan and pay off all my credit card debts. Plus, I can just deduct the interest on my equity loan from my taxes."**

This is another potentially dangerous myth. When you take out an equity loan, you're offering your house as collateral. Should you be unable to make the payments on your equity loan, you could lose your house!

There are other considerations, too. First, you must have enough equity in the property for a lender to approve a loan. A lender can approve a loan for as much as 100 percent of the appraised property value; and there will also be closing costs. You'll have to calculate whether you'll have enough money to pay off your debts and still manage to make your monthly mortgage payments. You will also be significantly extending the life of your loan. Depending on the loan type, you could be adding 15 to 30 more years to the life of your mortgage.

Do not take out an equity loan or refinance your home if you have an ability to pay off your outstanding credit debt within three years or less. Always keep in mind such unforeseen events as a sudden illness or loss of employment when committing yourself to a second mortgage. No one likes to think of such things, but it could happen. If it does, you'll be grateful that you planned for the proverbial rainy day when you and your home are financially secure.

To find out if you can use your equity loan as a tax write-off, be sure to contact your accountant or the person who prepares your taxes.

Myth #9   "I needn't worry about mishandling my credit because if things get really bad, I'll just declare bankruptcy and that'll take care of everything."

Don't think like this! Bankruptcy is an extremely serious matter that you should only consider when you've exhausted all other possibilities. Filing for bankruptcy is a legal action, one that will show up on your credit reports for up to ten years. Should you file, your bankruptcy will become a matter of public record. And even if you change your mind after filing, the public notice will be listed on your credit report and can affect you for a long time when you apply for certain types of credit, life insurance, or even some employment positions. Bankruptcy is not an easy way out. It is far easier to manage your money and credit wisely from the beginning than to knowingly put yourself in a position where you must resort to bankruptcy and then have to rebuild your finances all over again from scratch.

Myth #10   "No one and nothing can help me. My financial situation is completely hopeless."

It's easy to believe that things are hopeless. More often than not, though, a solution or a way to resolve the situation exists. But it'll require you to be honest and face up to the matter at hand. You may need to get outside help—for support and for gaining a new perspective on your circumstances. You may feel ashamed and depressed and lack the motivation to deal with the reality of your situation. But deal you must. Financial problems don't go away; and the sooner you begin dealing with them, the better.

Research your options. Plenty of resources are available, and most of them cost nothing or very little. You'll need to communicate and figure out a repayment strategy that works for you and that you're comfortable with. The important thing is to take action, gather as much information as possible, consider your options carefully, make your decision, and then begin a repayment program. It will take time, patience, and effort. But your situation is not hopeless. Take heart in the fact that other people have been in your shoes and yet have managed to resolve their financial troubles. You can, too.

DEBT DESTROYER TIPS

- Don't fall victim to false truths about credit and debt. Protect yourself.

- Credit should be used only for emergencies, convenience, and establishing a credit history.

- Balances should be paid off in full at the end of each month.

- Research your options and seek outside advice if you find yourself overextended.

- Read the fine print on any credit card solicitation.

- Don't take cash advances from one credit card to make payment on another credit card.

3

Where Did I Go Wrong? Analyzing Your Personal Situation

If the score wasn't as high as you would have liked it to be on the quiz you took in Chapter 1 (see page 4), don't get discouraged. Most high schools and colleges don't teach us about credit and debt, and few parents teach their children about credit and money management, so you've most likely learned the hard way. I know I did.

Accumulating debt can occur in our late teens with reckless use of credit cards. Credit solicitations are sent to high school seniors, and college halls are filled with vendors offering credit cards.

Without education and proper use of credit, debt quickly rises. The plastic becomes the "Master Blaster." New power! Not real money! Just small payments! The trap's been set—habits begun, control lost, and reality slipped away.

It appears credit-purchasing behavior and financial goals differ according to age. Individuals in their 20s want instant gratification. When they see something they want, they charge it or open a line of credit with no thought given to how long it will take to pay off the purchase or the amount of money being charged in interest. Nor is thought given to possible job lay-offs, illness, divorce, or any other unforeseen emergency that can disrupt their income.

The 30-something age group is starting to realize that it takes longer and longer to pay off their balances by making only minimum payments. This age group seeks larger purchases such as a home, furniture, and automobiles. The children have arrived. More and more charges are being made.

The 40-something age group is getting uncomfortable with their debt. The balances never seem to go down. Most of their money is going toward bills. A saving plan for the future was never started.

The 50-something age group is looking ahead to the golden years of retirement. A plan is initiated to get out of debt, but the 50-somethings are behind in saving for their future.

The 60 and above age group needs to have their finances in order so they can live comfortably during their retirement. Debt should be at a minimum.

Obviously, the above examples are not the perfect picture for proper handling of debt and finances. Depending on the severity of our financial problems, the mistakes with debt management we make at a younger age follow us for many years. It's best to avoid the mistakes before they happen and learn from our mistakes so we don't repeat them.

Bob's Story

Bob's dream was to own his own business. He was employed for several years before he decided to step out on his own. Bob's credit was in good standing, and he had very little debt. He owned his home and had a wife and two children.

During the years of dreaming about his own business, Bob had set aside money to help him get started. A business plan was drawn up and everything looked good, so he took the big step and quit his job to start the business.

The money Bob had saved for the business was spent in no time. He had equipment to buy, rent and utilities to pay, telephones to install, and miscellaneous supplies to purchase. Bob was running low on cash and operating capital, so he took out two small business loans. As the business began to grow, he paid back the two loans.

After three years of operating the business, Bob had done very well financially. The business was making a good profit, and Bob took out another business loan to make improvements. The problem was that rather than setting aside money for savings or a reserve, Bob was spending the money on luxuries for himself and his family. If he didn't have ready cash, he would use his credit cards with the idea he would pay the cards off the following month. Bob had a false sense of security with the money he was making. It felt secure in his hand, but he let it slip through his fingers.

The beginning of the fourth year Bob owned his business, the economy took a turn for the worse. His cash flow was cut in half, and the bills began to pile up. It was so bad that Bob began to use his credit cards for survival. He had to try and keep his business running as well as cover his personal expenses at home. He never told his wife the extent of the financial problems because he didn't want to worry her. She knew things were getting tight but never realized how bad it really was as Bob was in charge of paying the bills.

Bob was taking credit card advances to pay his business and personal expenses. He always intended to pay the credit cards off when his cash flow increased, but it never did. Instead, Bob continued to rob Peter to pay Paul (taking advances from one credit card to pay another card). And then reckoning day arrived! His credit cards were at their limit; the payments were falling further and further behind; and the big deal never happened. Bob had no cash reserves and was sinking fast.

The creditors and collection agencies were calling daily; his mail became a pile of collection notices. Bob would try to explain his situation to the creditors when they called and promise them a payment, but his promises were never kept.

The Negative Effects of Debt

The situation got so bad that when the telephone rang, Bob's heart would start pounding, and many times he didn't take the call. He was $60,000 in debt and lived in fear.

Any debt, including credit card debt, can be more than a financial burden. It can affect your work performance whether you own your own business, are employed, or are a homemaker. Financial overload affects concentration on your job or at home and clouds your ability to make decisions. Furthermore, that cloud follows you wherever you go.

Not only will credit card debt affect your work, but it can also cause mental fatigue. Trying to calculate how you are going to pay the bills plus deal with the creditors would drain anyone.

Stress and physical problems are often related to excessive debt. Even if you are paying on time, too much debt causes stress. The fear of falling behind is very real; and once you fall behind in your payments, the stress is compounded.

An Ohio State University study showed that stress from credit card debt can have a direct correlation with a person's health. There seems to be a correlation between stress-related health problems and financial problems, including a person's income-to-debt ratio that will cause depression and stress. It's no surprise. Look at the symptoms you feel when there are more bills than money. Instant panic! Heart palpitations! Sleepless nights! Depression! Continued stress!

Another area affected by financial problems is your home life. If you and your spouse don't enjoy open communication about finances, disaster is lurking in the shadows. If one of you is in charge of paying the bills without the other one's knowledge about the situation, it's small wonder things blow up when the truth comes out. "Honey! We're in debt up to our eyebrows! We're out of money!"

Many marriages are ruined because of the stress of financial problems. Because two heads are better than one, always keep a line of communication open with your spouse. Financial problems will either bring you closer together or pull you further apart. Arguing won't help, but talking will. Planning together to find a solution brings comfort.

Bob's Solution

When Bob called me at my office, he was very upset. He didn't know how much longer he could continue living the way he was with his debt. His only asset was his house, which he was considering selling to pay off his debts and then move into a cheaper home. Selling his home wasn't really what he wanted to do as he had lived there for 12 years and had a young family.

I instructed Bob to list all of his monthly payments, including his credit card bills and house payments. They totaled $5,600 per month. His house payment had fallen behind twice during the past year, although it was now current.

Lucky for Bob that property values had increased, and he had equity in his home. By refinancing his home, Bob could save $1,200 per month and pay off all his credit card debt as well as his bank loan.

Because the payment on his home had been delinquent as well as many of his credit card accounts, the interest on his mortgage was higher. He still saved money and considered refinancing worth relieving the pressure. This refinancing loan could be a bridge to another loan in a few years with a lower interest rate, and it bought him time to rebuild his credit and get his business and finances back on track.

I suggested that Bob add extra money to his house payment each month so the principal balance would go down more quickly and enable him to pay off the house in less than 30 years. He was instructed to write a note to the lender to apply the extra money to his principal.

Bob was relieved that he didn't have to sell his home and was able to save such a large amount each month.

The pressure was off and the stress gone, so he could get his business back on track. He learned a valuable lesson about money management and where he had gone wrong in handling his finances. The important thing for Bob to remember is to never depend on credit for survival.

Impulse Buying

The problem most individuals have with debt comes from impulse buying. Probably more than half the things we purchase with credit are done on impulse. Having a piece of plastic versus cash makes spending easy. If you had the cash and no credit you probably would think twice before making the purchase.

Picture this: You find something at the mall that you feel you must have, but it costs more than you can afford. Now hold your hands in front of you and picture cash in your right hand and a credit card in your left hand. Which would you use to make the purchase? Probably the credit card, because in your mind you feel as though you are saving your cash. For most people, that's the wrong choice. If you can't afford to spend your cash, don't use your credit card. If you do use your credit card, have an index card in your purse or wallet to record your purchase. Keep track of all your charges for the month using that index card or the sample form. Once you have reached the limit that you can pay off in full for the month, quit charging. For example:

Date	Credit Card (last 4 digits of card)	Item	Cost	Subtotal
Jan. 8	Visa/0298	Dinner	$32.50	$32.50
Jan. 12	Visa/0298	Clothes	29.98	63.48
Jan. 15	MasterCard/8930	Gas	20.00	83.48

As you can see from this example, each entry from the credit card purchase is being subtotaled. That helps you set money aside in your checking account to pay off the balance in full each month. See sample forms to use for tracking your charges at the end of the chapter.

Little thought is typically given to the quality, or a cost comparison, of the item you are purchasing when you use your credit card. One strategy used by many department stores and credit card companies is to offer incentives for opening a charge account. For example, a department store may offer you a 10 percent discount on the merchandise you are purchasing to open a new account with the store. Many people fall for this to get the discount.

What the store is hoping will happen is that you won't pay off the whole balance when the billing statement comes. And by not paying the balance in full, you're charged interest. Most department stores charge 21 percent interest or more. Oops! There go your savings on the purchase. Don't fall for this game. Don't open the account, or if you do, make sure you pay off your balance each month.

Many impulsive shoppers can't control their spending. In fact, shopping and spending can become as addictive as gambling, overeating, or excessive alcohol. If you find yourself in a situation where you feel you have to make a purchase for something you don't really need, leave the store. Go home! Sleep on it! The urge will be gone the next morning.

Some people find power in purchasing on credit because they feel powerless in other areas of their life. It gives them a feeling of control and self-worth, which is obviously a false sense of security.

All of us have power and control over our own life. All of us make choices. Not all of us become addicted to vices that are tempting us; the financial institutions that entice us to use credit, however, know the right things to say and the right enticements to offer. It's time we outsmart the industry and learn how to stay out of debt.

After you complete the following forms, continue to Chapter 4 to discover what you should be on the lookout for.

DEBT DESTROYER TIPS

- Pay cash whenever possible.

- Keep an index card or registry in your purse or wallet for writing down every credit card purchase you make during the month. Charge only what you can pay in full at the end of the month.

- Have a cash reserve.

- Communicate with your spouse about all financial matters.

- Never use credit cards for survival.

- Don't rob Peter to pay Paul. In other words, don't take cash advances from one credit card to pay other credit cards.

- Communicate with your creditors.

- Don't keep charging with the idea that things will get better.

- Don't spend your profits on luxury items unless you have a good cash reserve.

- If you know you are an impulsive buyer and find something you think you must have, go home! Sleep on it! The urge will be gone the next day.

✎ ASSESSING YOUR OWN BEHAVIOR WORKSHEET

Answer each of the following questions.

		TRUE	FALSE
1.	When I shop, I have a hard time walking away from a purchase.	❏	❏
2.	I open charge accounts to get retailers' discounts.	❏	❏
3.	I don't have assets that I can use in case of an emergency.	❏	❏
4.	If I have problems paying my bills, I'm afraid to contact my creditors.	❏	❏
5.	I have no idea what my debt-to-income ratio is.	❏	❏
6.	My spouse and I don't communicate about our financial situation.	❏	❏
7.	I take cash advances from one credit card to pay another credit card.	❏	❏
8.	I don't have a cash reserve for my personal and business accounts.	❏	❏
9.	When I have trouble paying my bills, I keep hoping for the "big deal" to come in.	❏	❏
10.	I don't pay off my balances in full each month.	❏	❏

If you answered "True" to three or more statements, you are headed in the wrong direction.

✏️ **CREDIT CARD TRACKERS**

JANUARY–FEBRUARY

Date	Credit Card (including last 4 digits)	Item	Cost	Subtotal
_____	_____	_____	_____	_____
_____	_____	_____	_____	_____
_____	_____	_____	_____	_____
_____	_____	_____	_____	_____

Date	Credit Card (including last 4 digits)	Item	Cost	Subtotal
_____	_____	_____	_____	_____
_____	_____	_____	_____	_____
_____	_____	_____	_____	_____
_____	_____	_____	_____	_____

Date	Credit Card (including last 4 digits)	Item	Cost	Subtotal
_____	_____	_____	_____	_____
_____	_____	_____	_____	_____
_____	_____	_____	_____	_____
_____	_____	_____	_____	_____

Date	Credit Card (including last 4 digits)	Item	Cost	Subtotal
_____	_____	_____	_____	_____
_____	_____	_____	_____	_____
_____	_____	_____	_____	_____
_____	_____	_____	_____	_____

CREDIT CARD TRACKERS

MARCH–APRIL

Date	Credit Card (including last 4 digits)	Item	Cost	Subtotal
_____	_____	_____	_____	_____
_____	_____	_____	_____	_____
_____	_____	_____	_____	_____
_____	_____	_____	_____	_____

Date	Credit Card (including last 4 digits)	Item	Cost	Subtotal
_____	_____	_____	_____	_____
_____	_____	_____	_____	_____
_____	_____	_____	_____	_____
_____	_____	_____	_____	_____

Date	Credit Card (including last 4 digits)	Item	Cost	Subtotal
_____	_____	_____	_____	_____
_____	_____	_____	_____	_____
_____	_____	_____	_____	_____
_____	_____	_____	_____	_____

Date	Credit Card (including last 4 digits)	Item	Cost	Subtotal
_____	_____	_____	_____	_____
_____	_____	_____	_____	_____
_____	_____	_____	_____	_____
_____	_____	_____	_____	_____

CREDIT CARD TRACKERS

MAY–JUNE

Date	Credit Card (including last 4 digits)	Item	Cost	Subtotal
____	_____	_____	_____	_____
____	_____	_____	_____	_____
____	_____	_____	_____	_____
____	_____	_____	_____	_____

Date	Credit Card (including last 4 digits)	Item	Cost	Subtotal
____	_____	_____	_____	_____
____	_____	_____	_____	_____
____	_____	_____	_____	_____
____	_____	_____	_____	_____

Date	Credit Card (including last 4 digits)	Item	Cost	Subtotal
____	_____	_____	_____	_____
____	_____	_____	_____	_____
____	_____	_____	_____	_____
____	_____	_____	_____	_____

Date	Credit Card (including last 4 digits)	Item	Cost	Subtotal
____	_____	_____	_____	_____
____	_____	_____	_____	_____
____	_____	_____	_____	_____
____	_____	_____	_____	_____

CREDIT CARD TRACKERS

JULY–AUGUST

Date	Credit Card (including last 4 digits)	Item	Cost	Subtotal
_____	_____	_____	_____	_____
_____	_____	_____	_____	_____
_____	_____	_____	_____	_____
_____	_____	_____	_____	_____

Date	Credit Card (including last 4 digits)	Item	Cost	Subtotal
_____	_____	_____	_____	_____
_____	_____	_____	_____	_____
_____	_____	_____	_____	_____
_____	_____	_____	_____	_____

Date	Credit Card (including last 4 digits)	Item	Cost	Subtotal
_____	_____	_____	_____	_____
_____	_____	_____	_____	_____
_____	_____	_____	_____	_____
_____	_____	_____	_____	_____

Date	Credit Card (including last 4 digits)	Item	Cost	Subtotal
_____	_____	_____	_____	_____
_____	_____	_____	_____	_____
_____	_____	_____	_____	_____
_____	_____	_____	_____	_____

✎ CREDIT CARD TRACKERS

SEPTEMBER–OCTOBER

Date	Credit Card (including last 4 digits)	Item	Cost	Subtotal
_____	_____	_____	_____	_____
_____	_____	_____	_____	_____
_____	_____	_____	_____	_____
_____	_____	_____	_____	_____

Date	Credit Card (including last 4 digits)	Item	Cost	Subtotal
_____	_____	_____	_____	_____
_____	_____	_____	_____	_____
_____	_____	_____	_____	_____
_____	_____	_____	_____	_____

Date	Credit Card (including last 4 digits)	Item	Cost	Subtotal
_____	_____	_____	_____	_____
_____	_____	_____	_____	_____
_____	_____	_____	_____	_____
_____	_____	_____	_____	_____

Date	Credit Card (including last 4 digits)	Item	Cost	Subtotal
_____	_____	_____	_____	_____
_____	_____	_____	_____	_____
_____	_____	_____	_____	_____
_____	_____	_____	_____	_____

CREDIT CARD TRACKERS

NOVEMBER–DECEMBER

Date	Credit Card (including last 4 digits)	Item	Cost	Subtotal
_____	_____	_____	_____	_____
_____	_____	_____	_____	_____
_____	_____	_____	_____	_____
_____	_____	_____	_____	_____

Date	Credit CardCredit Card (including last 4 digits)	Item	Cost	Subtotal
_____	_____	_____	_____	_____
_____	_____	_____	_____	_____
_____	_____	_____	_____	_____
_____	_____	_____	_____	_____

Date	Credit Card (including last 4 digits)	Item	Cost	Subtotal
_____	_____	_____	_____	_____
_____	_____	_____	_____	_____
_____	_____	_____	_____	_____
_____	_____	_____	_____	_____

Date	Credit Card (including last 4 digits)	Item	Cost	Subtotal
_____	_____	_____	_____	_____
_____	_____	_____	_____	_____
_____	_____	_____	_____	_____
_____	_____	_____	_____	_____

4

SOS! Warning Signs of Debt

"Debtitis!" The culprit that creeps up on us without our even suspecting how out of control our spending really is. The silent time bomb, when given enough time, will explode.

We have a dream of buying a home, a car, possibly starting a business, paying our bills, living comfortably, and planning for our retirement. A feeling of tranquility and peace can be stolen from us if we don't recognize the warning signs of debt.

We often discover we are in over our heads when it's time to make a major purchase such as a house or car. Reality may strike that we are over-extended when we're trying to pay the monthly bills. Having more bills than money is a sure sign of debtitis. Whenever it hits us, there were usually warning signs before the revelation that our debt was higher than our income.

Here are two quizzes to take to see if you have symptoms of debtitis. One quiz is for your personal finances and the other for your business (see pages 29 and 30). If both apply to you, see how you score.

Janet's Story

Janet came to my office for help with her finances. Janet was a well-educated woman who owned her own business and seemed to be in control of most areas if her life except one: finances. As she began to share with me information about her business and frustration with her finances, her confidence level began to weaken.

DEBTITIS QUIZ

Personal Finances

Let's see if you have any of the warning signs of too much debt. Answer true or false.

	TRUE	FALSE
1. I pay my bills on time; however, I run out of cash between paychecks.	❑	❑
2. I often hide my credit card purchases from my family.	❑	❑
3. I carry more than four Visa and MasterCard cards.	❑	❑
4. I spend money with the expectation that my income will increase.	❑	❑
5. I have to take out cash advances to pay my household bills.	❑	❑
6. Life would be terrible without my credit cards.	❑	❑
7. If it looks as though I'm running low on money, I apply for more credit.	❑	❑
8. This past year I applied for three or more credit cards.	❑	❑
9. I almost always make only the minimum monthly payment.	❑	❑
10. I often fail to keep an accurate record of my purchases.	❑	❑
11. I never review my monthly credit card statements.	❑	❑
12. My credit card payments are more than 20 percent of my income.	❑	❑

Score: If you answered "True" to two or more statements, you need to stop charging. You're headed for problems.

The sinking feeling that Janet feels every month when trying to pay her bills became apparent. She has been living with constant stress and fear, the fear that someone might find out her secret of drowning in debt. Nobody knew her secret; she appeared to have it all together—her own business, a nice car, nice clothes, and a beautiful home. But her secret of poor money management accompanied by an overwhelming amount of debt was slowly destroying her and affecting her business. The creativity and passion for her work was being replaced by worry.

Janet graduated from college owing $45,000 of student loans and $25,000 of credit card debt, not to mention the cost of running her business in addition to house and car payments. She was devastated!

All of Janet's credit cards were charged to the limit. Her payments were always late, resulting in late fees that in turn pushed her balance over the

---

✎ DEBTITIS QUIZ

If You Own a Business

Let's see how you score with your business. Answer true or false to each question.

	TRUE	FALSE
1. When I get a large check, I spend it on luxury items.	❏	❏
2. I feel rich when I can entertain my clients.	❏	❏
3. I have to borrow money from my lines of credit to make the payroll.	❏	❏
4. I don't have a set budget for my business.	❏	❏
5. I'm constantly putting out "fires" with the money I bring in.	❏	❏
6. Putting money in my IRA account is impossible.	❏	❏
7. Setting a reserve account will never happen.	❏	❏
8. I pay myself before I pay creditors.	❏	❏
9. I cut back on necessities in order to pay my creditors.	❏	❏
10. I am constantly late in making my payments.	❏	❏

Score: If you answered "True" to two or more statements, you need to set a budget and stick to it before you go under.

---

credit limit and consequently added another fee. It was a vicious cycle. Janet couldn't seem to get the extra money to pay down the credit cards. Even though she wasn't adding any new charges, the balances were increasing from the finance charges, late fees, and over-the-limit fees. She felt as though she were drowning.

When Janet had gotten the credit cards and student loans, she was young and hadn't taken the time to find out what the fees were and how much the total cost of the debt would cost her.

How often I have heard this same story; how sad it is to learn the hard way. If Janet had read more thoroughly the details on the applications and contracts before signing them and learned how much the total loan was going to cost, she (and perhaps you) may have done things differently.

After reviewing Janet's situation, I showed her how much she was actually paying for the money she had borrowed. She was astonished! Bankruptcy was not an option because a large portion of her debt was student loans that could not be discharged.

I recommended that Janet contact all her creditors to see if they would work with her in reducing her interest and thus reducing the payment. Many creditors were cooperative and agreed to lower the payments. I also suggested that Janet consolidate all her student loans into a single one, which would reduce her payments by lumping all of the loans into one lower payment.

By facing her fears and getting a plan in action, Janet was on the road to recovery. Her finances became more manageable, and she was able to pay off her debt more quickly. She had control over her life; and once her debt was reduced, she could start doing the things she loved to do such as travel.

The Cost of Credit

Do you have any idea how much you are actually paying for the use of your credit cards (making only minimum payments), or for your automobile, home, or other lines of credit? Probably not! If most people calculated how much they would be paying for the life of a loan or line of credit, they would make more of an effort to pay it off as soon as possible—or not get the loan in the first place!

Whenever you make a purchase on the assumption of getting a loan or using your credit card, the lender will charge an APR (annual percentage rate) for the use of the money. To calculate the total cost of a loan, multiply your monthly payments by the total number of months. Subtract the total amount borrowed from the total monthly payments to see how much interest you've paid.

For example: You purchased an automobile costing $9,000 and financed it with a loan for $7,500; your payment is $220 a month for four years (48 months).

$	220	payment per month	$10,560	payments
×	48	months	– 7,500	loan amount
$10,560		total payments made	$ 3,060	interest paid

Based on the above example, you are really paying $10,560 in payments plus the $1,500 down payment, which totals $12,060 for your automobile.

Some banks offering credit cards may calculate interest on a daily basis, whereas other banks calculate it as prorated interest (known as a grace period). Prorated interest means no interest is charged until the billing cycle; that is, if the balance is paid off before the billing cycle, no interest is charged. By paying off the total balance before the billing cycle ends, you have free use of the bank's money. If you don't pay off the balance on a credit card purchase by the end of the billing cycle, the interest (or finance charge) is added to the balance.

Cash advances may result in a higher interest rate than your regular purchases. Review your agreement.

The Sample Credit Card Chart in Figure 4.1 shows you what it is costing you if you pay only the minimum amount each month. Look at the interest you would pay and the total number of months (divide by 12 to see the number of years) it would take to pay off. To make you feel worse, add the total interest paid to the balance. It's disheartening! Think of all the meals, clothes (that are outdated), and other things you bought that you can't even remember.

For example, if you charged $1,000 one month for clothes and eating out but only made the minimum payment each month, it would take you approximately 11½ years to pay it off. Furthermore, you would have paid $1,104.63 in interest and thus a total of $2,104.63 for your food and clothes.

The amounts shown in Figure 4.1 are for balances with no additional charges made.

REMEMBER! As the balance decreases, so does the minimum payment.

Figures are based on a minimum payment of 3 percent of the balance and 1.75 percent interest per month; and figures may vary by bank.

Avoid Becoming Overextended

Before credit is approved when you make an application, the creditor is looking for two main factors. First is your ability to repay your debts. This is determined by your job, the length of your employment and position, and, if applicable, how many years you have owned your own business. The second thing a creditor looks for is your past credit and repayment history, the amount of credit you have, and which creditors you have accounts with.

Credit grantors usually estimate your net income at 80 percent of your gross income (before taxes). Your expenses such as rent and outstanding bills should not exceed 70 percent of your net income. Variable expenses, such as food, fuel, utilities, and the like, are estimated to be about 20 to 25 percent of your net income. Credit grantors prefer that only about 90 to 95 percent of your net income be committed to all expenses. If you exceed these figures, you are probably overextended on your credit.

Most people can afford to pay 10 percent of their net income to installment debt, not including mortgage payments. If you pay more than 15 percent, you need to cut back; if you pay 20 percent, you are in trouble and need to stop using credit immediately; with 25 percent you are in deep trouble and probably need professional help. You must drastically change your lifestyle.

FIGURE 4.1
SAMPLE CREDIT CARD CHART

Balance of Purchases	Number of Payments Until Paid	Total Interest Paid	Total Cost of Purchase + Interest
$3,000	226 (18 yrs, 10 mos)	$3,904.62	$6,904.62
2,900	223 (18 yrs, 7 mos)	3,764.65	6,664.65
2,800	220 (18 yrs, 4 mos)	3,624.64	6,424.64
2,700	217 (18 yrs, 1 mo)	3,484.63	6,184.63
2,600	214 (17 yrs, 10 mos)	3,344.63	5,944.63
2,500	211 (17 yrs, 7 mos)	3,204.64	5,704.64
2,400	209 (17 yrs, 5 mos)	3,064.65	5,464.65
2,300	205 (17 yrs, 1 mo)	2,924.61	5,224.61
2,200	201 (16 yrs, 9 mos)	2,784.65	4,984.65
2,100	197 (16 yrs, 5 mos)	2,644.63	4,744.63
2,000	193 (16 yrs, 1 mo)	2,504.62	4,504.62
1,900	189 (15 yrs, 9 mos)	2,364.62	4,264.62
1,800	185 (15 yrs, 5 mos)	2,224.65	4,024.65
1,700	180 (15 yrs,)	2,084.61	3,784.61
1,600	176 (14 yrs, 8 mos)	1,944.63	3,544.63
1,500	171 (14 yrs, 3 mos)	1,804.61	3,304.61
1,400	165 (13 yrs, 9 mos)	1,664.65	3,064.65
1,300	159 (13 yrs, 3 mos)	1,524.64	2,824.64
1,200	153 (12 yrs, 9 mos)	1,384.64	2,584.64
1,100	146 (12 yrs, 2 mos)	1,244.65	2,344.65
1,000	138 (11 yrs, 6 mos)	1,104.63	2,104.63
900	130 (10 yrs, 10 mos)	964.65	1,864.65
800	121 (10 yrs, 1 mo)	824.62	1,624.62
700	110 (9 yrs, 2 mos)	684.65	1,384.65
600	98 (8 yrs, 2 mos)	544.63	1,144.63
500	83 (6 yrs, 11 mos)	404.64	904.64
400	65 (5 yrs, 5 mos)	264.61	664.61
300	43 (3 yrs, 7 mos)	129.11	429.11
200	25 (2 yrs, 1 mo)	48.32	248.32
100	12 (1 yr)	10.89	110.89

Where the Money Goes

The average American family spends about $35,000 per year. Figure 4.2 shows where the money goes.

To avoid becoming overextended, use the Monthly Debt Worksheets at the end of the chapter to keep a record of your debts: complete it each month to make sure your debt is under control–decreasing rather than increasing. (See the Sample Monthly Debt Worksheet in Figure 4.3.)

It is important not to accept more credit than you need. Unused credit will be used against you when you apply for credit for a home mortgage or automobile. The reason is that the unused credit is viewed by the lender as a risk of your becoming overextended. In addition, the risk associated with unused credit could raise your *debt ratio*–that is, the total amount of your debts (not including your mortgage or rent) divided by your net income (before taxes). For example, if your debts totaled $600 and your income was $3,000 per month, your debt ratio would be 20 percent. Remember that you want to keep your debt ratio at 10 to 15 percent of your income. (See the Sample Debt Ratio Worksheet in Figure 4.4.) Check your debt ratios every month to keep them in check.

Keep a $1,000 to $2,000 reserve of unused credit for emergencies. And don't carry more than three credit cards; if you do, the temptation may be too great to use them. Track all your spending.

When you do use your credit card, never charge an item or meal less than $25 unless you intend to keep track of it and pay it off at the end of the month. It's the many small purchases that add up to large balances and many years to pay back. Why pay interest on a small debt for several years if you could pay cash at the time of your purchase?

Never make a decision for a major purchase with credit until you have analyzed how much it is going to cost you. Go home and sleep on it. Don't make a decision at the lender's office because that's where an impulsive decision may take place.

FIGURE 4.2
WHERE THE MONEY GOES

	0%	5%	10%	15%	20%	25%	30%	35%
Housing							32%	
$939 monthly, $11,268 yearly								
Transportation					19%			
$538 monthly, $6,456 yearly								
Food				15%				
$425 monthly, $5,110 yearly								
Personal Taxes			9%					
$270 monthly, $3,241 yearly								
Family Business			9%					
$269 monthly, $3,223 yearly								
Entertainment		6%						
$165 monthly, $1,977 yearly								
Health Care		5%						
$153 monthly, $1,841 yearly								
Apparel		5%						
$144 monthly, $1,729 yearly								

Notes:
- Housing includes rent/mortgage, utilities, water, fuel, telephone, taxes, maintenance, repair, housekeeping supplies, furnishings, and equipment.
- Transportation includes vehicles purchased or leased, gas, oil, and repairs; and finance charges, insurance, taxes, licenses, and public transportation.
- Food includes meals, beverages, and snacks consumed outside the home plus cereals, bakery products, meats, poultry, fish, eggs, dairy products, fruits, vegetables, and alcoholic and nonalcoholic beverages consumed in the home.
- Personal taxes include federal and state income taxes.
- Family business includes life insurance, pension, and Social Security.
- Entertainment includes concert, movie, and amusement admission tickets; lottery tickets; club dues, books, magazines, and newspapers; toys, sporting supplies, and sporting and photographic equipment; audio, video, and computer equipment; musical instruments; flowers, seeds, and potted plants.
- Health care includes insurance, medical services, drugs and medical supplies, and personal care products and services.
- Apparel includes clothing, shoes, and accessories; and laundry and dry cleaning services.

Source: U.S. Bureau of Labor Statistics, Consumer Expenditures.

FIGURE 4.3
SAMPLE MONTHLY DEBT WORKSHEET

List all your monthly debts, which includes all credit cards, school loans, automobile loans, installment loans, and personal loans. **DO NOT INCLUDE MORTGAGE OR RENT.**

Creditor Name	Balance	Monthly Payment
Credit Cards		
Worldwide Bank Visa	$ 4,162.28	$ 75.00
ABC Bank MasterCard	2,098.31	40.00
America Bank MasterCard	944.38	25.00
Loans		
Auto loan	$12,947.12	$285.00
Student loan	14,533.21	181.20
Personal		
Loan from relative	$ 2,300.00	$200.00
Monthly Total	$36,985.30	$806.20

DEBT DESTROYER TIPS

- Reality checks are essential to avoid excessive debt.
- Calculate how much you are actually paying for an item on credit.
- Most people can afford to pay 10 percent of their net income to installment debt, not including mortgage or rent payments.
- If you pay 20 to 25 percent of your net income to installment debt, not including mortgage or rent payments, you are in trouble and need help.
- It is essential to keep track of your monthly payments.
- Never make a decision for a major purchase at the lender's office. Go home and sleep on it.

FIGURE 4.4
SAMPLE DEBT RATIO WORKSHEET

To determine what your debt ratio is, divide your monthly net income (after taxes) into your total monthly debt. The answer will show your percentage.

Net monthly income $ 4,000

Total monthly debt $ 600

Enter total monthly debt _____$600_____ divided by net monthly

income _____$4,000_____ equals your debt ratio _____15%_____.

CALCULATING YOUR DEBT RATIO

Net monthly income (after taxes) $ _____

Total monthly debt $ _____

(See Monthly Debt Worksheet)

Formula

Use your calculator.

Enter total monthly debt _____ divided by net monthly

income _____ equals your debt ratio _____ .

Remember:

10%: Excellent

15%: Fair

20%: Disaster waiting to happen

25%: Stop! Get help!

MONTHLY DEBT WORKSHEET

JANUARY

Creditor Name	Balance	Monthly Payment
Credit Cards		
_____	_____	_____
_____	_____	_____
_____	_____	_____
_____	_____	_____
_____	_____	_____
Loans		
_____	_____	_____
_____	_____	_____
_____	_____	_____
_____	_____	_____
_____	_____	_____
Personal		
_____	_____	_____
_____	_____	_____
_____	_____	_____
_____	_____	_____
Other		
_____	_____	_____
_____	_____	_____
_____	_____	_____
Monthly Total	_____	_____

MONTHLY DEBT WORKSHEET

FEBRUARY

Creditor Name	Balance	Monthly Payment
Credit Cards		
_____	_____	_____
_____	_____	_____
_____	_____	_____
_____	_____	_____
_____	_____	_____
Loans		
_____	_____	_____
_____	_____	_____
_____	_____	_____
_____	_____	_____
_____	_____	_____
Personal		
_____	_____	_____
_____	_____	_____
_____	_____	_____
_____	_____	_____
Other		
_____	_____	_____
_____	_____	_____
_____	_____	_____
Monthly Total	_____	_____

✎ MONTHLY DEBT WORKSHEET

MARCH

Creditor Name	Balance	Monthly Payment
Credit Cards		
_____	_____	_____
_____	_____	_____
_____	_____	_____
_____	_____	_____
_____	_____	_____
Loans		
_____	_____	_____
_____	_____	_____
_____	_____	_____
_____	_____	_____
_____	_____	_____
Personal		
_____	_____	_____
_____	_____	_____
_____	_____	_____
_____	_____	_____
Other		
_____	_____	_____
_____	_____	_____
_____	_____	_____
Monthly Total	_____	_____

MONTHLY DEBT WORKSHEET

APRIL

Creditor Name	Balance	Monthly Payment
Credit Cards		
_____	_____	_____
_____	_____	_____
_____	_____	_____
_____	_____	_____
_____	_____	_____
Loans		
_____	_____	_____
_____	_____	_____
_____	_____	_____
_____	_____	_____
_____	_____	_____
Personal		
_____	_____	_____
_____	_____	_____
_____	_____	_____
_____	_____	_____
Other		
_____	_____	_____
_____	_____	_____
_____	_____	_____
Monthly Total	_____	_____

MONTHLY DEBT WORKSHEET

MAY

Creditor Name	Balance	Monthly Payment
Credit Cards		
_____	_____	_____
_____	_____	_____
_____	_____	_____
_____	_____	_____
_____	_____	_____
Loans		
_____	_____	_____
_____	_____	_____
_____	_____	_____
_____	_____	_____
_____	_____	_____
Personal		
_____	_____	_____
_____	_____	_____
_____	_____	_____
_____	_____	_____
Other		
_____	_____	_____
_____	_____	_____
_____	_____	_____
Monthly Total	_____	_____

MONTHLY DEBT WORKSHEET

JUNE

Creditor Name	Balance	Monthly Payment
Credit Cards		
_____	_____	_____
_____	_____	_____
_____	_____	_____
_____	_____	_____
_____	_____	_____
Loans		
_____	_____	_____
_____	_____	_____
_____	_____	_____
_____	_____	_____
_____	_____	_____
Personal		
_____	_____	_____
_____	_____	_____
_____	_____	_____
_____	_____	_____
Other		
_____	_____	_____
_____	_____	_____
_____	_____	_____
Monthly Total	_____	_____

MONTHLY DEBT WORKSHEET

JULY

Creditor Name	Balance	Monthly Payment
Credit Cards		
_____	_____	_____
_____	_____	_____
_____	_____	_____
_____	_____	_____
_____	_____	_____
Loans		
_____	_____	_____
_____	_____	_____
_____	_____	_____
_____	_____	_____
_____	_____	_____
Personal		
_____	_____	_____
_____	_____	_____
_____	_____	_____
_____	_____	_____
Other		
_____	_____	_____
_____	_____	_____
_____	_____	_____
Monthly Total	_____	_____

MONTHLY DEBT WORKSHEET

AUGUST

Creditor Name	Balance	Monthly Payment
Credit Cards		
_____	_____	_____
_____	_____	_____
_____	_____	_____
_____	_____	_____
_____	_____	_____
Loans		
_____	_____	_____
_____	_____	_____
_____	_____	_____
_____	_____	_____
_____	_____	_____
Personal		
_____	_____	_____
_____	_____	_____
_____	_____	_____
_____	_____	_____
Other		
_____	_____	_____
_____	_____	_____
_____	_____	_____
Monthly Total	_____	_____

MONTHLY DEBT WORKSHEET

SEPTEMBER

Creditor Name	Balance	Monthly Payment
Credit Cards		
_____	_____	_____
_____	_____	_____
_____	_____	_____
_____	_____	_____
_____	_____	_____
Loans		
_____	_____	_____
_____	_____	_____
_____	_____	_____
_____	_____	_____
_____	_____	_____
Personal		
_____	_____	_____
_____	_____	_____
_____	_____	_____
_____	_____	_____
Other		
_____	_____	_____
_____	_____	_____
_____	_____	_____
Monthly Total	_____	_____

✏️ MONTHLY DEBT WORKSHEET

OCTOBER

Creditor Name	Balance	Monthly Payment
Credit Cards		
_____	_____	_____
_____	_____	_____
_____	_____	_____
_____	_____	_____
_____	_____	_____
Loans		
_____	_____	_____
_____	_____	_____
_____	_____	_____
_____	_____	_____
_____	_____	_____
Personal		
_____	_____	_____
_____	_____	_____
_____	_____	_____
_____	_____	_____
Other		
_____	_____	_____
_____	_____	_____
_____	_____	_____
Monthly Total	_____	_____

MONTHLY DEBT WORKSHEET

NOVEMBER

Creditor Name	Balance	Monthly Payment
Credit Cards		
_____	_____	_____
_____	_____	_____
_____	_____	_____
_____	_____	_____
_____	_____	_____
Loans		
_____	_____	_____
_____	_____	_____
_____	_____	_____
_____	_____	_____
_____	_____	_____
Personal		
_____	_____	_____
_____	_____	_____
_____	_____	_____
_____	_____	_____
Other		
_____	_____	_____
_____	_____	_____
_____	_____	_____
Monthly Total	_____	_____

✏ MONTHLY DEBT WORKSHEET

DECEMBER

Creditor Name	Balance	Monthly Payment
Credit Cards		
_____	_____	_____
_____	_____	_____
_____	_____	_____
_____	_____	_____
_____	_____	_____
Loans		
_____	_____	_____
_____	_____	_____
_____	_____	_____
_____	_____	_____
_____	_____	_____
Personal		
_____	_____	_____
_____	_____	_____
_____	_____	_____
_____	_____	_____
Other		
_____	_____	_____
_____	_____	_____
_____	_____	_____
Monthly Total	_____	_____

5

Deciding Who to Pay First: Prioritizing Your Debts

After evaluating how far in debt you are, it is important to set up a workable plan for paying off your debt. Before you do that, however, you need to prioritize your bills, an exercise that should become standard practice in good times as well as bad.

Ben and Karen's Story

Ben was a salesman who was paid by commission. His wife, Karen, worked part-time so she could be home with the children when they got home from school.

For three consecutive months, Ben's sales quota was down, which affected his income. The couple's bills began to fall behind, and it didn't take long for the creditors to start calling and sending letters requesting payments.

Every time the telephone rang, Ben and Karen would be overcome with dread. The more aggressive the creditor, the more stressed they became. Whichever creditor yelled loudest got paid. Their house payment became delinquent and rolled into the second month of delinquency. When they sent in their late house payment, the mortgage company wouldn't accept it unless both months were paid, but they didn't have two months' payments because they were still trying to satisfy all the creditors, so the house payment rolled into its third month of delinquency. And the same thing happened when Ben and Karen continued to mail in each of the house payments: the payments were returned because the couple never sent in all the back payments to bring the account current. Ben and Karen would soon face foreclosure if they didn't change their payment priorities.

A prioritized list of their debts should have been established before they ever ran into difficulties. Setting good habits and sticking with them is essential.

Once Ben and Karen stepped away from the situation and realized they couldn't pay everyone, they were able to catch up with their mortgage payments. Yes, the other credit card bills fell behind, but they were at least able to keep their home. When Ben's income began to increase, they slowly brought their credit card accounts current, but it was a long and slow process.

Paying your rent or mortgage, having food on the table, and paying your utility bills—gas, electric, water, and telephone—are top priorities. This applies to both your personal finances and your own business. It is important to know what the consequences are of not paying each of your debts, because they may differ from creditor to creditor.

Too often, I hear from clients like Ben and Karen who, when they run into a money problem, pay the creditors who are yelling the loudest. This is not, however, the right way to approach your problems.

Bills should be divided into two categories. Category One contains your essential bills, such as mortgage or rent. Category Two contains bills, such as credit cards, that can be paid at a later date.

Category One Priority: Survival

The first category is composed of debts or expenses that *must* be paid. They are the bills you need to pay to survive and must be included whenever you are structuring your scheduled monthly payment plan as well as your budget. You must protect your home and family's well-being. Here is a list of priorities that you must consider.

Mortgage or rent payments. Having a roof over your head should always be your number one priority. Don't wait too long to analyze your housing situation if financial problems begin to occur.

Utility bills. Water, gas, electricity, and telephone service are necessities. Cable television, an Internet connection, gardeners, and a pool service are not necessities.

Get in touch with your utility company to make payment arrangements. When you get a late notice and a notice of disconnection, call the company immediately. Many companies have special programs that are available for payment assistance.

Food. You obviously have to feed your family and must budget for a monthly food allowance. This is not a debt, however, but a survival essential that should always be a top priority.

Car payments. Most people need transportation to and from work. If you are making a car payment, try to stay current. If you know your payment will be late, call the creditor. Many times it will work with you by deferring a payment for the month or allowing you to make an interest-only payment.

Secured loans. A secured debt is for an item that is guaranteed to be returned to the creditor if the debt is not paid. The item is the security or collateral for the loan. Examples of secured items include a car, a home, furniture, and a boat—in other words, anything pledged as security.

If you are having problems making the payment on a secured loan and it is not a necessity or survival item, sell it or return it. If it is an item you must have, make payment arrangements with the creditor. Late payments will also be reported on your credit report.

Medical insurance. Learn from my experience: medical insurance is a must for most people, even though it can be quite costly. If you have a medical problem and your insurance lapses, you'll have problems getting insurance elsewhere.

Get in touch with your insurance carrier to see if it offers other policies with a higher deductible that would lower your monthly payment. Also shop around—perhaps you belong to an association, such as your credit union or chamber of commerce, that offers its members group rates.

Remember a medical emergency without insurance can bankrupt you!

Child support. There is no excuse not to pay child support if it is due. A court judgment can be filed against you if you don't pay, you can go to jail, your wages may be garnished, and an entry on your credit reports may appear. Child support cannot be discharged through a bankruptcy, so don't wait until further legal action is taken against you.

If your income has dropped, get in touch with an attorney to see if you are eligible for a reduction or call the district attorney's office for assistance.

Unpaid taxes. Don't avoid any communication with the IRS or your state's revenue department if you owe back taxes. The sooner you set up a repayment plan, the less stress you will have.

Category Two Priority: Lower Debts

Debts in this category must be paid, although they may have to be set aside for a later date if you are unable to pay them right now. The consequences of not paying these debts are not as severe as they are for debts in the first category, but you will still suffer negative effects.

Credit and charge cards. Most credit cards are unsecured, so nothing can be repossessed or taken from you if you fall behind in your payments. Creditors will make numerous attempts to collect the debt; the worst that can happen, however, is a negative entry on your credit report, a closed account by creditors, and a possible lawsuit.

Most creditors don't report a late payment on your credit report the first month you are late, although they will if the payment is still delinquent when it comes due in the second billing cycle.

If you need a credit card for your business or personal use, select one card with the lowest interest that is not delinquent. Pay the minimum amount. Don't have more than one account with the same lender. For example, if you have two credit cards, a Visa and MasterCard at ABC Bank, and you pay on only one card, the lender will close both accounts even though one may be current.

If you do keep one card and need it for your home or business, put it into Category One. If you feel your interest rate is too high, call the credit card company and ask it to lower the rate—it just may.

Department store and gasoline charge cards. These charge cards are not secured, so you risk a lawsuit if you stop paying. And the creditors will report a negative entry on your credit report.

If you keep one of your major credit cards active, such as Visa or MasterCard, use that one card for your purchases. Pay on the department store and gasoline charge cards when you can.

Keep in mind that late fees and interest will continue to mount. Many times the late fees will push the credit balance over the credit limit and thus cause an over-the-limit fee. So basically you are paying a late fee and over-the-limit fee each month until the account is paid below the credit limit and brought current. It adds up quickly.

Unsecured loans. These would be issued by a finance company, a bank, a savings and loan association, or a credit union. Nonpayment could result in a negative entry on your credit report and a possible lawsuit.

Attorney, medical, and accounting bills. Pay these when you can set up a payment arrangement. Any one of these bills can be turned over to a collection agency, which would be added to your credit report as a negative entry. In addition, a lawsuit could result.

Other Priorities

The following is a list of debts that must be placed either into Category One or Category Two. Many people are unsure of what is essential to pay, so you have to determine which category of debt fits your situation. By not paying an item listed below, you may or may not suffer severe consequences, but you typically will have to put up with screaming creditors.

When completing your worksheets at the end of the chapter, place each debt from the following list of possible debts in the appropriate category for your specific situation.

Medical insurance. Some people feel that medical insurance is not a necessity, especially if they are healthy. Don't be deceived. I made that mistake and found it's not worth the anguish of wondering if you are getting the proper medical care by not having insurance. Don't depend on Medicare or any state insurance to help you. You may not qualify, but even if you do, there may still be a required deductible.

The purpose of insurance is for the unforeseen. If you drop medical insurance to save money and then are faced with a medical emergency such as I was when my daughter needed emergency brain surgery, you've compounded your problems.

Medical insurance is a necessity if you have any medical problems, in which case don't let your insurance lapse. If you have no medical problems before you let the policy lapse, analyze the consequences and any additional options you may have. You could possibly reduce your premiums by getting a higher deductible or at least by getting catastrophic insurance.

In my opinion, medical insurance should be placed in Category One.

Life insurance. Life insurance is usually the first thing a person will allow to lapse when facing financial difficulties. Age is an important consideration in determining whether to let the insurance lapse.

Unfortunately, the older you are, the harder it is to get a good life insurance policy. You'll have to pay higher premiums and must have no health problems.

If you really don't need life insurance (you have no dependents or your spouse/partner is financially independent), this is a good place to reduce some of your debt.

If you can cash in your policy, you may be able to use the proceeds to pay off additional debt.

Depending on your situation, you have to determine in which category to place life insurance.

Automobile insurance. Most states require you to have automobile insurance if you drive. Without insurance, you risk losing your driver's license as well as legal action if you are ever stopped by the authorities or are in a car accident.

If the car is financed or leased, the loan company will require you to have auto insurance. And if you let the policy lapse, the loan company will add its own insurance to your loan or lease. If this should occur, you must pay the company's insurance, and its premium is usually more expensive than one you could get on your own.

Check the requirements of your state. Get in touch with your insurance agent to get the best possible rates and possibly a higher deductible.

I recommend placing automobile insurance in Category One.

Child care, private schools, and tutoring. If you must work, child care is an issue. You must be secure in knowing that your child is being taken care of properly. If you need child care, make sure you check out all your options.

You may be able to "co-op" with other mothers to watch your children. Another possibility is to hire a baby sitter to come to your home, which may be less costly than placing your children in a day care center.

Private schools or outside tutoring may be unnecessary, depending on whether your child has special needs. However, you may find that your child will have to attend public school (which you already pay for through your tax dollars) rather than a college preparatory school. You need to evaluate whether your local school system is adequate for your child's needs.

Gyms, spas, health clubs, and country clubs. Belonging to any of these facilities or clubs is a luxury, so when you're trying to get out of debt, these must go even if $30 a month seems low. Play at a public golf course; go for a walk with a friend.

When I was cutting back and trying to pay off debt, my friends and I got together to exercise. It's amazing how a cinder block can be used for step aerobics and two 16-ounce cans as weights. Use your imagination to get the exercise you need; and use the money you save to reduce your debt.

Clothing and shopping. Stop being a slave to fashion if you can't afford it. If you must buy something, skip the malls unless you see spectacular sales. Shop at garage sales, yard sales, clothing outlets. Watch the newspapers for sales. Children grow at such a fast rate that you need to continually clothe them, but be smart in your purchases. Give up the expensive designer labels.

Other. If you are making payments on anything not mentioned above, be sure to classify it into the correct category on your worksheets.

Never make a payment in Category Two unless you have made all your payments in Category One. Housing should always be number one, even if you stop making your credit card payments. Never pay a credit card before you have paid mortgage/rent, food, and utilities.

By following this plan, you will maintain good paying habits, always taking care of your home and family first. Many creditors will intimidate you with rude telephone calls and letters, but remain firm with your plan of repayment. Don't ever let a creditor bully you into making a payment unless you have the extra money.

If you can't pay now, pay when you can. Don't promise to pay something on which you can't follow through. If you feel a collection agency or creditor is harassing you, file a complaint with the Federal Trade Commission; visit its Web site at <www.FTC.gov>. Also see Appendix B.

Business Owner's Alert

If you own a business and are trying to prioritize your bills, you should use the same concept of two categories.

Examples of business expenses would be:

- Rent
- Utilities
- Payroll
- Employee taxes
- Equipment
- Advertising
- Supplies
- Accounting
- Legal services
- Other

As you add to the list, place each item into the proper category.

Using Figures 5.1, 5.2, 5.3, and 5.4 as guides, complete the following worksheets.

D E B T   D E S T R O Y E R   T I P S

- Always pay essential survival bills such as mortgage/rent, food, and utilities first.

- The creditor yelling the loudest isn't the one to pay first.

- Don't make promises you can't keep.

- Complete your priority list each month.

FIGURE 5.1
SAMPLE CATEGORY ONE WORKSHEET

Write the names of the creditors whom you owe. Include the amount of the monthly payments. Debt in this category must be paid first.

Creditor	Monthly Payment
Rent/Mortgage	$1,200
Electric	75
Gas	32
Water	40
Telephone	35
Food	250
Automobile	300
Secured loans	120
Medical insurance	200
Unpaid taxes	50
Business	100

CATEGORY ONE WORKSHEET

Creditor	Monthly Payment
Rent/Mortgage	
Electric	
Gas	
Water	
Telephone	
Food	
Automobile	
Secured loans	
Medical insurance	
Unpaid taxes	
Business	
Child support	
Other	

FIGURE 5.2
SAMPLE CATEGORY TWO WORKSHEET

Write the names of the creditors whom you owe. Include the amount of the monthly payments. This category must be paid only after Category One debts have been paid first.

Creditor	Monthly Payment
Credit and charge cards	$160
Department store cards	15
Gasoline cards	10
Unsecured loans	40
Attorney, medical, accounting	50

CATEGORY TWO WORKSHEET

Creditor	Monthly Payment
Credit and charge cards	
Department store cards	
Gasoline cards	
Unsecured loans	
Attorney, medical, accounting	
Other	

FIGURE 5.3
SAMPLE LIST OF OTHER PRIORITIES

Write the names of the creditors whom you owe. Include the amount of the monthly payments. This category must be paid only after Category One debts have been paid first.

Creditor	Monthly Payment
Automobile insurance	$150
Life insurance	50
Child care, private school, or tutoring	300
Club memberships	40
Clothing	30

OTHER PRIORITIES WORKSHEET

Creditor	Monthly Payment
Automobile insurance	
Life insurance	
Child care, private school, or tutoring	
Club memberships	
Clothing	
Medical insurance	
Attorney fees	
Business	
Other	

FIGURE 5.4
SAMPLE BUSINESS PRIORITY WORKSHEET

Category One

Creditor	Monthly Payment
Rent/Mortgage	$1,900
Utilities	350
Payroll	2,000
Employee taxes	500
Equipment	150
Secured loans	200
Supplies	200

Category Two

Creditor	Monthly Payment
Credit and charge cards	$ 300
Advertising	200
Unsecured loans	400
Attorney, medical, accounting	300

BUSINESS PRIORITY WORKSHEET

Category One

Creditor	Monthly Payment
Rent/Mortgage	
Utilities	
Payroll	
Employee taxes	
Equipment	
Secured loans	
Supplies	
Other	

Category Two

Creditor	Monthly Payment
Credit and charge cards	
Advertising	
Unsecured loans	
Attorney, medical, accounting	
Other	

6

Increasing Your Income While You're in a Slump

In trying to determine how you're going to pay off your debts, you need to devise a strategy for increasing your income and cash flow to free up more money to pay off the debts.

Increasing Your Personal Cash Flow

Whether you have a business or not, there are several ways to increase your income to help you pay your bills and get rid of your debt. You have to see what works for you in your particular circumstances. Following are five ways that can help you increase your income:

1. *Holding a garage sale* can be a quick way to make extra money and apply it toward your bills. Take a careful inventory of what you have that you haven't used within the past 12 months; if you haven't used it within that period, you don't need it. Sell it! Make some money and let someone else enjoy your treasure. If you have computer equipment, furniture, jewelry, photography equipment, and the like that you don't need, you'll be able to raise more money that will help you with your debt.

   Some of the items that people love to buy at garage sales are dishes, baby supplies, frames, antiques, and clothes. You'd be surprised how many items you can find to sell just by cleaning out your closets, attic, garage, or basement!

2. *Visit garage sales.* If you find a treasure and know you can resell it for more money, buy it. Resell it at your garage sale for a profit or go to <www.ebay.com> and sell it on the Web.

3. *Getting a part-time job* is another way of earning additional cash to pay off your debts. You must, however, determine if the number of hours you can commit to working part-time is worth the amount of money you'll be earning. For example, if you have to pay for child care, food, clothing, excessive travel time, or other additional expenses, make sure you are coming out ahead with the money you'll bring home. If not, don't waste your time. You want to make sure the money you can contribute to the debt is enough to make a difference in debt reduction.

4. *Working overtime* may also help you increase your cash flow. Ask your employer if there's extra work for you to do. If there is, make sure there are enough overtime hours to make a difference in paying your bills.

5. Many people earn extra money with their *hobbies*. Many of the gifts and talents we have can be used to turn our hobbies into small businesses. For example, if you enjoy photography, you may want to free-lance on the side. You may be employed as a carpet installer and during off-hours can moonlight with your carpet installation business to make extra money. You may enjoy a craft and sell your craft to a craft store or bazaar.

Cassie's Story

Cassie loved going to garage sales. She discovered that many of the items she bought she could sell on eBay's Web site and make money. Cassie paid $25 for a set of china she found and then auctioned it on eBay's site; the set was sold for $75, so Cassie made a profit of $50.

Martin's Story

Martin took an early retirement and was offered a lump sum of money plus a small monthly income. Martin knew he would have to get another job because the money would last only a few months, and the small income was not enough to pay his bills.

One of Martin's hobbies was working with automobiles. While he was looking for another job, many of his friends asked Martin to repair their cars, and they paid him for the work.

The money that Martin earned repairing automobiles plus the small monthly income helped him keep his household running while he looked for a job.

Within two months, Martin found a job and never fell behind making his payments. He was paid for what he loved to do.

Ellen's Story

Ellen was a stay-at-home mother. Her husband, Mark, had a good income that paid the bills each month. When his father became ill, Mark made repeated trips out of state to help his family. The cost of the trips put a financial drain on their finances, and the bills started becoming delinquent.

Ellen had worked as a paralegal for an attorney before getting married. As the pressure of the bills became overbearing, Ellen called her previous employer to ask if she could do work from home. The attorney, in fact, was overloaded with work and was happy to hire Ellen.

Ellen had a computer, telephone, and fax machine at home and scheduled her working hours around the children's schedule. Because of her ability to work from home, Ellen was able to bring in extra money to catch up on the family's bills as well as be at home with the children.

Flexibility in the face of change is important for keeping a clear head about what you have to do to increase your cash flow. If you need to sharpen your skills to improve your job security or launch your own new business, it's better to take necessary classes or read necessary books before you find yourself in a desperate situation.

To discover ways you can increase your cash flow, complete the worksheets on pages 66 and 67.

Ways for Business Owners to Increase Their Cash Flow

Let's suppose you own your own business and your cash flow suddenly started to slow down. What would you do? Would you keep putting money into the advertising you are paying for? Would you continue to operate as you presently are and hope things get better? Or would you jump in and make changes?

Would you review where your money is being spent and see where you can cut back? How about the accounts receivable or the outstanding invoices of customers who bought on credit and have yet to pay? Where would you start?

Take a few minutes to write down your priorities as business owner. You can use the worksheet on page 68.

It's amazing to see the catch-22 you're facing. Without a positive cash flow, your bills become delinquent, and when your customers don't pay, they are delinquent. It seems like the same scenario. Your customers tell you why they can't pay their bills on time just as you tell your creditors the reasons you can't pay.

✏️ WAYS TO INCREASE CASH FLOW WORKSHEETS

Garage Sale Items to Sell

Item	Estimated Amount
_____	_____
_____	_____
_____	_____
_____	_____
_____	_____
_____	_____
_____	_____
_____	_____
_____	_____
_____	_____
_____	_____
_____	_____
_____	_____
Total Amount	_____

Web Site Auction Items

Item	Estimated Amount
_____	_____
_____	_____
_____	_____
_____	_____
_____	_____
_____	_____
_____	_____

✎ WAYS TO INCREASE CASH FLOW WORKSHEETS (Continued)

Web Site Auction Items (Continued)

Item	Estimated Amount
_____	_____
_____	_____
_____	_____
_____	_____
_____	_____
_____	_____
_____	_____

Total Amount _____

Additional Income _____

Part-Time Job

Potential part-time job opportunities:

_____   _____

_____   _____

_____

Estimated amount you can make: _____

Overtime Work

Estimated hours you can work: _____

Estimated amount you can earn: _____

Hobbies

Hobbies or interests that could make money:

_____   _____

_____   _____

_____

Estimated amount you can make: _____

Total additional income: _____

✎ **PRIORITIES FOR THE BUSINESS OWNER**

1. _____
2. _____
3. _____
4. _____
5. _____
6. _____
7. _____
8. _____
9. _____
10. _____

Collection Remedies

In this scenario, you need to devise a plan for collecting the money that is owed you and still keep your customers happy. Remember the Golden Rule: Do unto others as you would have them do unto you. You have to call your creditors soon to let them know your situation. Put yourself in a delinquent customer's position and proceed as you would want that customer to proceed with you in collecting the debt.

If you have customers who have outstanding invoices with you and are slow to pay, call them on the telephone. Find out what the problem is. Many times, customers are afraid to make the call. They are embarrassed or think the bill can wait until they get paid. Most customers don't realize when they are facing a money problem that their nonpayment negatively affects your paying your own bills. They are thinking only about themselves and not the problem they are creating for you.

When you speak to customers on the telephone, ask them when you can expect payment. Have a telephone log ready to write down your notes on all conversations. If a customer indicates you can expect a payment by a specific date, write it down. When that date arrives and you haven't received the payment, call again to remind the customer of the promise.

I don't believe a constant barrage of telephone calls induces a person to pay a bill more quickly if they don't have the money to pay it. Furthermore, a constant barrage of telephone calls puts you at a disadvantage because customers will find a way to cut off all communication with you. They can screen their calls with caller identification, an answering machine, or voice mail; or they can change their telephone number without leaving a forwarding number, or they can get an unlisted number. And you don't want these things to happen.

Follow up by **telephone** only on the days a customer promised to make the payment if it wasn't received. And be consistent with your follow-up. Refer to your telephone log before you make a call to review the notes you took from each of the previous telephone calls.

Letters are another way of communicating with a customer regarding a delinquent debt, but a letter can easily be tossed aside with other bills, so a letter should definitely be followed up with a telephone call.

If all else fails and the promised dates for payment leave you still unpaid, **make a trip** to the customer's home or business. This will be hard for you to do, but the customer may be so surprised and embarrassed to see you that he will find some extra money to settle the bill. A house call should be your last resort, but it may be your most profitable.

You can always contract out the bill to a **collection agency** to try to collect. You definitely would be making an enemy of the customer, but if you have done all that you know how without cooperation from the customer, you may have no choice.

You can handle turning the debt over to a collection agency in two ways. You can contract with the agency to collect the debt, and the agency would keep a certain percentage and pay you the difference. For example, the collection agency might keep 60 percent of what it collects and give you 40 percent. Something is better than nothing.

The second option is to sell the debt to the collection agency, which would purchase the debt at a discount. For example, the debt may be $100, and the collection agency would purchase the debt from you for $30; any money the agency collected would belong to it.

Collection agencies have a bad reputation and are known to engage in aggressive and ruthless tactics. If you do choose to go this route, be sure to check out the collection agency with the Better Business Bureau and the Federal Trade Commission to make sure there are no complaints against the company.

Another approach that is less aggressive is to list all the accounts receivable that are owed you. Categorize each account; list the date the debt is due, the number of days it is past due, and the amount owed. After you have completed the list, total the accounts. Based on the length of delinquency, calculate how large a **discount** on the money owed that you could accept from each of the customers. (See and complete the Business Owner's Cash Flow Worksheet at the end of the chapter.)

Make a **discounted offer** to your delinquent customers. For example, call and let a customer know that if she pays her bill within five days, she will receive a 20 percent discount. That may be enough to get her to pay.

Current customers to whom you are offering credit can be offered **incentives,** such as a 15 percent discount, for paying their bills within ten days of receipt. Many people would be happy to get a discount; it helps them as well as you.

Increasing Your Sales

If you are in a business that offers a service or one that sells product, the way to increase cash revenue is to have a sale or discount on whatever products you have or services you offer.

If you have a service business as a consultant, for example, you might tell potential clients you are offering a special discounted price for the first consultation. You could also offer a special discount consultation for a specific month. By lowering your fee, you may generate more clients and more than make up for the full fee you are giving up. You would be working on volume; and again, something is better than nothing.

If you have product to sell, have an open house and reduce the price of your product. That sounds easy enough but you have to make the public aware of what you're doing. Design flyers and have them delivered. Also, go through your client base and mail letters inviting your past customers to your open house, where they can receive great discounts on your product.

My Story

Many years ago when my children were young, I had joined Mary Kay Cosmetics as a beauty consultant. I loved what I was doing and was a future director. In those days, part of the qualifications for becoming a director was selling a certain quota of product for three consecutive months.

I had several shows booked and decided to take out a bank loan, which was for 90 days, to purchase additional inventory. The first two months, I held my shows with no problems, but I still was a long way from selling the amount of product I needed to repay the loan. My shows dropped off, and I was in a panic; the loan was due within 30 days. I couldn't afford to dip into our personal finances to pay back the loan so I had to come up with a solution.

Two weeks before the loan was due, I decided to hold an open house at my home and display the product. It was near Christmas, so I had additional seasonal items to display. I mailed invitations to all of my former clients to ask them and their friends to the open house. It was a success.

I sold enough items to pay back the bank loan the day it was due. Had I depended on the old way I was doing things, I never would have been able to pay back the loan when it came due given the deadline I had.

Sometimes we have to step aside, analyze a situation, and then make a quick decision.

BUSINESS OWNER'S CASH FLOW WORKSHEET

Customer Name	Due Date	Days Delinquent	Amount Due	Discount Offered

DEBT DESTROYER TIPS

- Carefully analyze your situation to determine which strategies fit your needs.

- Make sure your plan will make money for you—and not cost you money.

- Don't be reactive; be proactive.

7

Tips to Save Money to Pay Off Your Debt

The average household has five or six credit cards with an outstanding balance of approximately $15,000 to $20,000. With that many cards per household, it's not surprising we're all tempted to spend. But financial reckoning day comes when our debt is greater than our income.

Ralph and Lisa's Story

Ralph and Lisa felt as though they were on a sinking ship. For years they had gotten into the habit of borrowing money from family members because their bills were so high. They would run short of money at the end of every month—there never seemed to be enough.

Bankruptcy seemed to be an option, but the couple knew they wanted to try to pay off the credit card companies as well as repay the money they owed family members.

Before our appointment, I instructed Ralph and Lisa to list all their bills, including living expenses and income, for us to review together. As I reviewed the list, I noticed their income seemed enough, but there were missing entries.

When I questioned Ralph and Lisa about their miscellaneous expenses, such as eating out, fast food, clothing, and so on, neither one had a clue as to how much they were spending. And that was the root of their problems: not accounting for incidental expenses.

The first thing I instructed them to do was to each get a journal or note-pad. Then I instructed them to write down every penny that they spent for the next 30 days on a daily basis, listing each item and the amount they spent. At the end of the 30 days, each item was to be put in a specific category. From the totals of each of the categories, it would be apparent where their excess money was going.

Ralph and Lisa were shocked to see how much they were spending each week eating out and going to their favorite coffee houses. By reducing their trips to eat out and brewing their own coffee, they were able to save over $200 a month that they could apply to their debt.

When you're trying to determine where your money is going, it is important that you make a list of *every* penny you spend for at least 30 to 60 days. If you're married, both you and your spouse must track every penny you spend and write it down—and not only your cash spending but also your credit card purchases.

Compose spending categories and be specific; that is, don't just write down "Miscellaneous" as a category. Write down what each item or service is that you spent money on, including what you charged and how much it cost. Also include purchase dates on your list.

Things that people neglect categorizing properly are their ATM purchases, ATM cash withdrawals, and debit card purchases. These must be broken down. If you get $20 from your ATM, list every penny you spend the cash on. ATM withdrawals are the number one problem in letting money slip through your fingers. If asked, most people haven't a clue where the money went. If you're being charged a fee for using your ATM, write that down as well.

If you have a business that is cash and pay, you probably have many incidents where the cash is spent with no recollection by you where it went. "Journalizing" the cash you spend will help you position yourself to save that money and apply it toward your bills.

You'll find several ways you can save money to reduce your debt. It may be painful at first, but it will become habit if you do it long enough. Once you have formed the habit of spending wisely, you'll think twice before you make any purchase.

Using the samples in Figures 7.2 (page 78) and 7.3 (page 91), complete the Cash and Credit Card Expenditures Worksheets at the end of the chapter. Examples of different categories would be meals, fast food, sodas, coffee, clothing, prescriptions, toiletries, gasoline, magazines, books, and so on.

Just by tracking your daily cash and credit card expenditures, you will find ways to cut back your spending and apply the savings to your bills.

Here is a list of different money-saving tips.

Automobile Expenses:

- Buy a used car instead of a new one. You'll save quite a bit of money.
- Pump your own gas rather than going to the full-service island.

Banking:

- Review your business and personal checking account bank statements. Total the monthly service charges plus all the additional charges you are accumulating each time you make ATM withdrawals (outside your bank's network) and/or debit card transactions that incur fees from the merchants. These fees and charges can amount to an additional $20 plus per month.
- To eliminate these charges, find a bank that doesn't charge monthly service fees.
- Go only to the ATM machines that are affiliated with your bank and don't charge fees. This can save you $1 to $2 on each transaction.
- Dump your change daily into a box, bottle, or other container. It adds up quickly.

Credit Cards:

- Review your credit card statements every month. You would be surprised at the amount of errors; charges you never made may be listed on the statement or finance charges you should not have incurred. Compare your monthly statement to the worksheet of your previous charges and receipts.
- Pay your credit card balances off in full each month and eliminate the finance charges and interest from ongoing balances.

Electricity, Gas, Water:

- Change the thermostat by one degree. By doing so, you'll save a significant amount of money on your next bill.
- Cut down on your water use. Don't let the faucet run while you brush your teeth; and take shorter showers.

Entertainment:

- Stop buying lottery tickets.
- Stop subscribing to a cable channel you don't watch. Eliminate extra channels and stick to the basic plan. Better yet, cut out cable altogether.
- Rent videos instead of going out to movies.
- Check out movies and books from the library. Why not rent them— it's free?
- Go to matinees instead of evening movies.

Insurance:

- Examine your medical coverage. See if you can save money by getting higher deductibles.
- Review your car insurance policy. Shop around for cheaper rates and get higher deductibles.

Meals and Beverages:

- Take your own soft drink instead of one from a vending machine. You may be paying $0.60 to $1.00 for the drink from the vending machine. Bringing your own costs only $0.25 but adds up to over $7.00 a month—over $84.00 a year based on one soda a day. How many soft drinks do you drink a day?
- Coffee money. Ouch! Go to a fancy coffee house and you pay approximately $2 a cup or more. Calculated on a five-day workweek, the cost of the coffee totals $10 a week—over $40 a month and over $480 a year! Think about how many cans of coffee you could have purchased at the grocery store and taken brewed coffee with you in a thermos. You could pay off one whole bill with the amount of money you spent on coffee in one year.
- Every time you have the urge to eat out . . . don't! Take the money you would have spent and put it in a fund for money saved. Apply that money to a bill.
- When eating out, split dinners. Order water instead of drinks. Put the money you save into your money-saved fund. When you're debt free, you can celebrate, but until then, every penny counts.

Memberships and Subscriptions:

- Drop your gym and health club membership and invest in video workouts. Use a cinderblock for your step aerobics and cans of vegetables for weights.
- Get your news from the radio or television instead of the newspaper.
- Don't renew your magazine subscriptions. Save money by reading free articles on the Internet.

Shopping:

- Avoid impulsive purchases. When shopping for clothes or a major purchase, go home and think about it. Sleep on it. Many times this will eliminate an impulsive purchase.
- Comparison shop. If there is an item you absolutely need, check the prices at other stores before you make the purchase.
- Clip coupons and shop at grocery stores that double or even triple your coupon's value.

- Take advantage of rebates. If you buy a product that comes with a rebate offer, use it. Even if the amount seems low, money from rebates add up quickly.
- Shop at garage sales and secondhand stores for clothes and toys. Go to discount stores to get your best buys.

Telephone:
- Shop around for a long-distance carrier. You'll be amazed how a just one-cent-a-minute difference in plans can add up.
- Lower your cellular phone bill. Resist the urge to chat, using your cellular phone only for emergencies.
- Cancel call waiting, three-way calling, and caller ID from your telephone.

Here is a fun way to save money while losing weight and inches. The Sample Money Calorie Counter chart in Figure 7.1 shows you how the money you spend on little tasty luxuries, if saved, can make money for you. It also shows you how many calories you can avoid.

This chart is taken from my 2002 book *Financially Secure: An Easy-to-Follow Money Program for Women,* published by Thomas Nelson.

Using the sample worksheet in Figure 7.4 (page 104), complete the Extra Cash Worksheet. When you have completed all the worksheets in this chapter, compare them with each other to see how much money you have saved.

DEBT DESTROYER TIPS

- Carry a journal or notepad to track all your expenditures.
- Look for ways to save money.
- Add the money you save into a special account to pay off your debts and begin saving for your future.

FIGURE 7.1
SAMPLE MONEY CALORIE COUNTER

Based on 5 days a week

10% Int. Compounded

Item	Cost	Calories	Monthly Calories	Yearly Calories	Monthly Cost	Yearly Cost	10-Year Savings	20-Year Savings
Donut	$ .75	170	3,683	44,200 (13 lbs.)	$ 16.25	$ 195.00	$ 3,318.49	$12,339.74
Cream-filled donut	.75	270	5,850	70,200 (20 lbs.)	16.25	195.00	3,318.49	12,339.74
Cookie 2.5 oz.	1.39	325	7,041	84,500 (25 lbs.)	30.17	361.40	6,180.17	22,910.16
Hamburger	.95	270	5,850	70,200 (20 lbs.)	20.58	247.00	4,215.71	15,627.81
Cheeseburger	1.02	320	6,933	83,200 (23 lbs.)	22.10	265.20	4,527.01	16,783.05
Fries (lg.)	2.05	540	11,700	140,400 (40 lbs.)	44.42	533.00	9.099.21	33.731.16
(med.)	1.71	450	9,750	117,000 (33 lbs.)	37.05	444.60	7,589.50	28,134.62
Pizza 1 slice (cheese)	2.50	309	6,695	80,340 (23 lbs.)	54.17	650.00	11,696.45	41,135.00
Mocha/iced with whipped cream 16 oz.	3.35	370	8,017	96,200 (27 lbs.)	72.58	871.00	14,876.65	55,114.99
Mocha frappacino 16 oz.	3.33	290	6,283	75,400 (22 lbs.)	72.15	865.80	14,779.57	54,788.46
with whipped cream		390	8,450	101,400 (29 lbs.)				
Mocha latte 16 oz.	3.05	270	5,859	70,200 (20 lbs.)	66.08	793.00	13,536.16	50,179.09
Chocolate candy bar Lg.	.89	510	11,050	132,600 (38 lbs.)	19.28	231.40	3,949.41	14,640.63
Sm.	.50	230	4,983	59,800 (17 lbs.)	10.83	130.00	2,218.47	8,223.96
Ice cream (chocolate) 4½ oz.	1.89	180	3,900	46,800 (13 lbs.)	40.95	491.40	8,388.40	31,096.15
9 oz.	3.59	360	8,025	93,600 (27 lbs.)	77.78	933.40	15,926.70	59,063.71
13½ oz.	5.19	540	11,700	140,400 (40 lbs.)	112.45	1,349.40	23,039.82	85,391.03

FIGURE 7.2
SAMPLE 30-DAY CASH EXPENDITURES WORKSHEET

List other categories if applicable. Remember every penny must be listed.

Date	ATM	Meals	Beverages	Clothing	Toiletries	Books	Entertainment	Other
9/1/00	20.00		3.23					
9/2/00		25.31					14.00	4.00
9/3/00		7.50			5.99			
9/4/00		33.38		57.76				
9/5/00	40.00		5.87					
9/6/00								7.20
9/7/00					18.94			
9/8/00		14.77	2.50					
9/9/00						12.80		
9/10/00		6.74						9.40
9/11/00			1.00					
9/12/00		13.75					10.76	
9/13/00					31.22			
9/14/00		5.75	3.25					
9/15/00							24.00	
9/16/00	20.00		2.75					
9/17/00				25.53	10.76			
9/18/00		17.03	1.75					10.00
9/19/00								
9/20/00		9.95			6.63			
9/21/00			3.25					
9/22/00		7.95					8.45	
9/23/00	20.00							
9/24/00		5.56	1.50					
9/25/00				39.16				
9/26/00			1.00					10.00
9/27/00		23.00						
9/28/00					3.55	8.93		
9/29/00		4.54	1.50					
9/30/00							14.00	
Total	100.00	175.23	27.60	122.45	77.09	21.73	71.21	40.60

30-DAY CASH EXPENDITURES WORKSHEET

JANUARY

Date	ATM	Meals	Beverages	Clothing	Toiletries	Books	Entertainment	Other

30-DAY CASH EXPENDITURES WORKSHEET

FEBRUARY

Date	ATM	Meals	Beverages	Clothing	Toiletries	Books	Entertainment	Other

30-DAY CASH EXPENDITURES WORKSHEET

MARCH

Date	ATM	Meals	Beverages	Clothing	Toiletries	Books	Entertainment	Other

30-DAY CASH EXPENDITURES WORKSHEET

APRIL

Date	ATM	Meals	Beverages	Clothing	Toiletries	Books	Entertainment	Other

30-DAY CASH EXPENDITURES WORKSHEET

MAY

Date	ATM	Meals	Beverages	Clothing	Toiletries	Books	Entertainment	Other

30-DAY CASH EXPENDITURES WORKSHEET

JUNE

Date	ATM	Meals	Beverages	Clothing	Toiletries	Books	Entertainment	Other

30-DAY CASH EXPENDITURES WORKSHEET

JULY

Date	ATM	Meals	Beverages	Clothing	Toiletries	Books	Entertainment	Other

30-DAY CASH EXPENDITURES WORKSHEET

AUGUST

Date	ATM	Meals	Beverages	Clothing	Toiletries	Books	Entertainment	Other

30-DAY CASH EXPENDITURES WORKSHEET

SEPTEMBER

Date	ATM	Meals	Beverages	Clothing	Toiletries	Books	Entertainment	Other

30-DAY CASH EXPENDITURES WORKSHEET

OCTOBER

Date	ATM	Meals	Beverages	Clothing	Toiletries	Books	Entertainment	Other

30-DAY CASH EXPENDITURES WORKSHEET

NOVEMBER

Date	ATM	Meals	Beverages	Clothing	Toiletries	Books	Entertainment	Other

30-DAY CASH EXPENDITURES WORKSHEET

DECEMBER

Date	ATM	Meals	Beverages	Clothing	Toiletries	Books	Entertainment	Other

FIGURE 7.3
SAMPLE 30-DAY CREDIT CARD EXPENDITURES WORKSHEET

List other categories if applicable. Remember every penny must be listed. Save receipts to compare with your credit card statements and worksheets.

Date	Merchant	Meals	Fast Food	Clothing	Gasoline	Misc.
9/1/00	Mama's Pizza	22.19				
9/5/00	Marty			42.53		
9/8/00	Uno				15.00	
9/14/00	Pete Burger		5.66			
9/16/00	Clothes Inc.			24.89		
9/21/00	Tool Depot					129.32
9/23/00	<www.book.com>					35.00
9/29/00	ABC Station				18.25	
Total		**22.19**	**5.66**	**67.42**	**33.25**	**164.32**

30-DAY CREDIT CARD EXPENDITURES WORKSHEET

JANUARY

Date	Merchant	Meals	Fast Food	Clothing	Gasoline	Misc.

30-DAY CREDIT CARD EXPENDITURES WORKSHEET

FEBRUARY

Date	Merchant	Meals	Fast Food	Clothing	Gasoline	Misc.

30-DAY CREDIT CARD EXPENDITURES WORKSHEET

MARCH

Date	Merchant	Meals	Fast Food	Clothing	Gasoline	Misc.

30-DAY CREDIT CARD EXPENDITURES WORKSHEET

APRIL

Date	Merchant	Meals	Fast Food	Clothing	Gasoline	Misc.

30-DAY CREDIT CARD EXPENDITURES WORKSHEET

MAY

Date	Merchant	Meals	Fast Food	Clothing	Gasoline	Misc.

30-DAY CREDIT CARD EXPENDITURES WORKSHEET

JUNE

Date	Merchant	Meals	Fast Food	Clothing	Gasoline	Misc.

30-DAY CREDIT CARD EXPENDITURES WORKSHEET

JULY

Date	Merchant	Meals	Fast Food	Clothing	Gasoline	Misc.

30-DAY CREDIT CARD EXPENDITURES WORKSHEET

AUGUST

Date	Merchant	Meals	Fast Food	Clothing	Gasoline	Misc.

30-DAY CREDIT CARD EXPENDITURES WORKSHEET

SEPTEMBER

Date	Merchant	Meals	Fast Food	Clothing	Gasoline	Misc.

30-DAY CREDIT CARD EXPENDITURES WORKSHEET

OCTOBER

Date	Merchant	Meals	Fast Food	Clothing	Gasoline	Misc.

30-DAY CREDIT CARD EXPENDITURES WORKSHEET

NOVEMBER

Date	Merchant	Meals	Fast Food	Clothing	Gasoline	Misc.

30-DAY CREDIT CARD EXPENDITURES WORKSHEET

DECEMBER

Date	Merchant	Meals	Fast Food	Clothing	Gasoline	Misc.

FIGURE 7.4
SAMPLE EXTRA CASH WORKSHEET

Create a list of things you can do to save money to be applied toward your bills or savings. Enter the dates, item on which you saved money, and the amount you saved. Don't forget to set the savings aside to put into a special fund. Do this daily.

Date	Item	Cost	Amount Saved
9/14/00	Soda		$ .35
9/14/00	Coffee		1.75
9/14/00	Meal		9.00
		Total Savings	$11.10

EXTRA CASH WORKSHEET

JANUARY

Date	Item	Cost	Amount Saved
		Total Savings	

FEBRUARY

		Total Savings	

EXTRA CASH WORKSHEET

MARCH

Date	Item	Cost	Amount Saved
		Total Savings	

APRIL

Date	Item	Cost	Amount Saved
		Total Savings	

✎ EXTRA CASH WORKSHEET

MAY

Date	Item	Cost	Amount Saved
		Total Savings	

JUNE

		Total Savings	

✎ EXTRA CASH WORKSHEET

JULY

Date	Item	Cost	Amount Saved

Total Savings

AUGUST

Total Savings

✏️ EXTRA CASH WORKSHEET

SEPTEMBER

Date	Item	Cost	Amount Saved
		Total Savings	

OCTOBER

		Total Savings	

✏️ EXTRA CASH WORKSHEET

NOVEMBER

Date	Item	Cost	Amount Saved
		Total Savings	

DECEMBER

		Total Savings	

8

Setting Up Your Budget

Now that you've found hidden money, you should be brave enough to get a budget in place. Many people fall into the debt trap by not following a budget.

Setting up a budget and sticking to it is not easy; it takes discipline and accountability. In the beginning, it is time consuming and sometimes painful. However, the benefits are many, and the goals you wish to accomplish will be reached much more quickly if you have your budget on paper.

When setting up a budget, you must list *all* the debts that you have, including your everyday living expenses. You also need to know how much money you have coming in each month to pay your bills and what assets you have. You need to set a monthly budget to help you stay focused on the whole picture, so you'll see how much money you have to bring in to pay all your bills. A monthly budget will also show why you are short each month and why your debt changes so little.

Setting a yearly budget would be especially helpful if you are self-employed or paid on commission, as you don't know how much you will be making from one month to another.

A word of warning: If you are self-employed or on commission, don't take the large amounts of money you earn in a given month and spend it. This is false security because every month your income can fluctuate. If you spend all your money one month, you may have a low paycheck the following month. You need to determine how much is needed on a yearly basis to pay your bills. Divide that amount by 12, the total being the amount you should put aside each month even in good times. Try to stay ahead by two or three months if your income is higher one month, which will eliminate catch-up when another month is slow.

Planning for expenditures that may have to be paid once a year, quarterly, or monthly must be added into the monthly budget. These expenditures are "budget busters" because most people forget to add them into their monthly budget and come up short when bills are due.

Different categories should be listed on projections for nonmonthly expenses, which I refer to as budget-buster expenses. Examples would be property taxes, home insurance, car maintenance, and the like. Suppose your property tax bill is $1,200 per year; you divide the bill by 12 (number of months in a year) to get a total of $100, which means you must set aside $100 each month so the bill can be paid when due. These expenses would then be added to the monthly budget.

The items listed in the budget-buster categories require a forced savings plan for these expenses, so you won't be caught short when the bills come due. A separate savings account should be opened so you aren't tempted to spend the forced savings.

One of the first things you should do before creating your budget and gaining control of your finances is to calculate your net worth. If you were to apply for a business, home, or automobile loan, you would have to complete an application form that provides the potential lender an idea of your net worth. Your net worth is calculated by subtracting your total liabilities from your total assets. You should calculate your net worth at the beginning of every year to see the progress you are making in accomplishing your goals. See the Sample Net Worth Statement in Figure 8.1.

George and Marie's Story

George and Marie were rapidly losing ground with their finances. Marie worked part-time, and George had a job in which he was paid strictly by commission.

Some years George's annual income was quite high, but in other years his income dropped off, so there was no consistency from year to year.

The problem was that George and Marie were living as though they had high annual incomes every year, and they were spending money recklessly. If you asked them where their money went, neither one could tell you. They had become accustomed to a certain lifestyle and were unwilling to change. Unfortunately, they had no more chances. Reckoning day had arrived.

Every month the two were unable to pay their bills. George had even cashed in his pension and 401(k)s and was now getting cash from his credit cards to pay bills. George and Marie were maxed out and drowning in debt.

After I carefully reviewed their debts, it was apparent the couple were a step away from bankruptcy. They had three children living at home, all of whom were in private schools, and one was soon to start college. Severe

> **FIGURE 8.1**
> ## SAMPLE NET WORTH STATEMENT
>
> ### Assets
>
> | | |
> |---|---:|
> | Cash on hand | $ 125 |
> | Checking account | 653 |
> | Savings account | 4,978 |
> | Money markets | 5,000 |
> | Accounts receivable | 11,740 |
> | Stocks and bonds | 15,000 |
> | Notes receivable | 3,430 |
> | Cash value life insurance | 25,000 |
> | Automobiles (value) | 22,700 |
> | Real estate (value) | 98,000 |
> | Household goods | 9,700 |
> | Business | 210,000 |
> | Inventory | 10,000 |
> | **Total Assets** | **$416,326** |
>
> ### Liabilities
>
> | | |
> |---|---:|
> | Real estate loan | $ 70,000 |
> | Automobile loan | 15,000 |
> | Student loan | 14,000 |
> | Credit card balances | 9,890 |
> | Department stores | 764 |
> | Accounts payable | 4,200 |
> | Taxes payable | 2,900 |
> | Medical expenses | 1,000 |
> | **Total Liabilities** | **$117,754** |
>
> Total Assets minus Total Liabilities = **$298,572** Net Worth

financial consequences would happen unless George and Marie made drastic changes.

The list of debts they had prepared wasn't the whole picture. Because they hadn't broken down all of the listed miscellaneous or annual expenses, they had painted a false picture.

The first thing I advised them to do was write in a journal every dollar they spent for the next 60 days. I told them to categorize each purchase and total the amounts spent at the end of 30 days and then continue this procedure for another 30 days to see where their money was going. This would give them a full 60 days to review their expenditures and determine where they could cut back.

Because George was paid on commission, the couple had to prepare an annual budget to see how much they needed to live; and the annual budget would help them prepare their monthly budget.

NET WORTH STATEMENT

Assets

Cash on hand	$ _____
Checking account	_____
Savings account	_____
Money markets	_____
Accounts receivable	_____
Stocks & bonds	_____
Notes receivable	_____
Cash value life insurance	_____
Automobiles (value)	_____
Real estate (value)	_____
Household goods	_____
Business	_____
Inventory	_____
Other assets	_____
Total Assets	$ _____

Liabilities

Real estate loan	$ _____
Automobile loan	_____
Student loan	_____
Credit card balances	_____
Department stores	_____
Accounts payable	_____
Taxes payable	_____
Medical expenses	_____
Other liabilities	_____
Total Liabilities	$ _____

Total Assets minus Total Liabilities = $ _____ Net Worth

When the total annual budget was completed, George and Marie could calculate exactly how much they needed to set aside each month. If George received a high commission check for one month that was over and above what they needed, I instructed them to set that money aside to add to the following month's commission. It was important that they stay two to three months ahead, setting money aside for bills, so they wouldn't be short when the commissions were low.

By setting a monthly budget and eliminating the excess money they had been spending (after the 60-day review of their spending habits), George and Marie were in a better position to live within their means and know exactly where their money was being spent.

As I've suggested already, you should always strive to have at least three to six months of living expenses saved—three months if you are married and both working and six months if you are single or a one-income household.

FIGURE 8.2
EXAMPLES OF BUDGET-BUSTER NONMONTHLY EXPENSES

Housing
  Property taxes
  Home insurance
  Security systems
  Home repairs/Maintenance (yard)
  Maintenance agreements
Utilities
  Waste management
  Water/Water softener
Automobiles
  Automobile insurance
  Auto registrations (all vehicles)
  Auto maintenance and repairs
Medical
  Medical insurance
  Life insurance
  Disability insurance
  Doctor/Dental
  Orthodontia
  Vision exam/Contacts/Glasses
  Health maintenance
Memberships & Subscriptions
  Church tithing
  Organizations/Clubs
  Professional licenses
  Sports
  Warehouse clubs
  Magazines

Schooling
  School tuition
  Books/Supplies
Office
  Office equipment maintenance
Clothing
  Work clothes
  School uniforms
  Clothes (adult & children's)
  Sport clothes
Recreation
  Recreational hobbies
  Vacations
  Music lessons
Pets
  Pet maintenance
  Training
Miscellaneous
  Accountant
  Taxes
  Savings
  Investments
  Gifts (birthday, anniversary, etc.)
  Holidays
  Other

If you're not sure what you are spending, refer to your check registry and past credit card statements for 12 months. When you grasp this concept and put it into practice, you'll know exactly how much and on what you spend.

From the list of budget-buster nonmonthly expenses in Figure 8.2, determine which items you must pay throughout the year as shown in Figure 8.3. If you have items not listed here, add them to your list.

Take this same approach if you have a business. Now you can complete the Budget-Buster Nonmonthly Expense Worksheet.

With the amount totaled, divide that amount by 12 (months), which is the amount each month that must be set aside in a special fund to pay your bills when they are due. It is also the total that you would enter on your Personal Monthly Budget Worksheet as shown in Figure 8.4. Also, see the Sample Yearly Budget Worksheet in Figure 8.5 before completing your own worksheet.

FIGURE 8.3
SAMPLE BUDGET-BUSTER NONMONTHLY EXPENSE WORKSHEET

Category	Item	Allocated Amount
Housing	Property tax	$1,400
Automobiles	Auto repair	800
Schooling	Books	515
Miscellaneous	Savings	200
Pets	Training	150
	Total =	$3,065
		$3,065 ÷ 12 months = $255.42

DEBT DESTROYER TIPS

- Be sensitive to what you are spending and list your expenditures in your budget.

- List all of your assets and liabilities.

- Include budget busters in your budget.

- Strive to have three to six months of living expenses saved.

BUDGET-BUSTER NONMONTHLY EXPENSE WORKSHEET

Category	Item	Allocated Amount

FIGURE 8.4
SAMPLE PERSONAL MONTHLY BUDGET WORKSHEET

Month: September (Complete each month)

Income

Salaries	3,400.00
Wages (if self-employed)	
Commissions	
Dividends	
Rental income	500.00
Other	
Total Income	**3,900.00**

Fixed Expenses

Mortgage/Rent/Housing	1,125.00
Savings	300.00
Automobile payments	350.00
Automobile insurance	140.00
Medical and dental care	75.00
Education	
Internet	18.95
Cable	
Other	
Total Fixed Expenses	**2,008.95**

Variable Expenses

Utilities	250.00
Groceries	300.00
Telephone	75.00
Tithing/Giving	400.00
Taxes	
Other (take from nonmonthly list)	255.42
Total Variable Expenses	**1,280.42**

Installments

Credit cards	255.00
Credit line	
Other	
Total Installments	**255.00**

Occasional Expenses

Clothing	100.00
Recreation	50.00
Other	
Total Occasional Expenses	**150.00**
TOTAL EXPENSES	**3,694.37**
TOTAL INCOME MINUS EXPENSES	**205.63**

PERSONAL MONTHLY BUDGET WORKSHEET

JANUARY

Income
- Salaries _____
- Wages (if self-employed) _____
- Commissions _____
- Dividends _____
- Rental income _____
- Other _____

Total Income _____

Fixed Expenses
- Mortgage/Rent/Housing _____
- Savings _____
- Automobile payments _____
- Automobile insurance _____
- Medical and dental care _____
- Education _____
- Internet _____
- Cable _____
- Other _____

Total Fixed Expenses _____

Variable Expenses
- Utilities _____
- Groceries _____
- Telephone _____
- Tithing/Giving _____
- Taxes _____
- Other (take from nonmonthly list) _____

Total Variable Expenses _____

Installments
- Credit cards _____
- Credit line _____
- Other _____

Total Installments _____

Occasional Expenses
- Clothing _____
- Recreation _____
- Other _____

Total Occasional Expenses _____
TOTAL EXPENSES _____
TOTAL INCOME MINUS EXPENSES _____

PERSONAL MONTHLY BUDGET WORKSHEET

FEBRUARY

Income
 Salaries   _____
 Wages (if self-employed)   _____
 Commissions   _____
 Dividends   _____
 Rental income   _____
 Other   _____
Total Income   _____

Fixed Expenses
 Mortgage/Rent/Housing   _____
 Savings   _____
 Automobile payments   _____
 Automobile insurance   _____
 Medical and dental care   _____
 Education   _____
 Internet   _____
 Cable   _____
 Other   _____
Total Fixed Expenses   _____

Variable Expenses
 Utilities   _____
 Groceries   _____
 Telephone   _____
 Tithing/Giving   _____
 Taxes   _____
 Other (take from nonmonthly list) _____
Total Variable Expenses   _____

Installments
 Credit cards   _____
 Credit line   _____
 Other   _____
Total Installments   _____

Occasional Expenses
 Clothing   _____
 Recreation   _____
 Other   _____
Total Occasional Expenses   _____
TOTAL EXPENSES   _____
TOTAL INCOME MINUS EXPENSES _____

PERSONAL MONTHLY BUDGET WORKSHEET

MARCH

Income
Salaries   _____
Wages (if self-employed)   _____
Commissions   _____
Dividends   _____
Rental income   _____
Other   _____
Total Income   _____

Fixed Expenses
Mortgage/Rent/Housing   _____
Savings   _____
Automobile payments   _____
Automobile insurance   _____
Medical and dental care   _____
Education   _____
Internet   _____
Cable   _____
Other   _____
Total Fixed Expenses   _____

Variable Expenses
Utilities   _____
Groceries   _____
Telephone   _____
Tithing/Giving   _____
Taxes   _____
Other (take from nonmonthly list)   _____
Total Variable Expenses   _____

Installments
Credit cards   _____
Credit line   _____
Other   _____
Total Installments   _____

Occasional Expenses
Clothing   _____
Recreation   _____
Other   _____
Total Occasional Expenses   _____
TOTAL EXPENSES   _____
TOTAL INCOME MINUS EXPENSES   _____

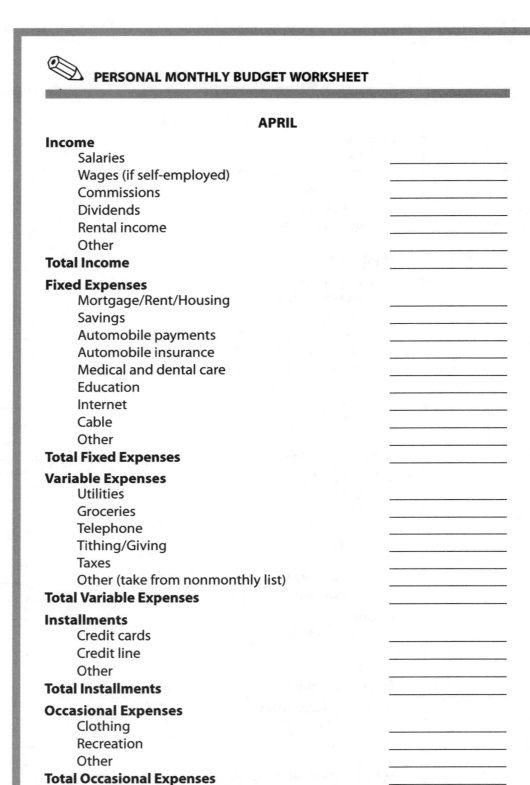

PERSONAL MONTHLY BUDGET WORKSHEET

APRIL

Income
    Salaries   _____
    Wages (if self-employed)   _____
    Commissions   _____
    Dividends   _____
    Rental income   _____
    Other   _____
Total Income   _____

Fixed Expenses
    Mortgage/Rent/Housing   _____
    Savings   _____
    Automobile payments   _____
    Automobile insurance   _____
    Medical and dental care   _____
    Education   _____
    Internet   _____
    Cable   _____
    Other   _____
Total Fixed Expenses   _____

Variable Expenses
    Utilities   _____
    Groceries   _____
    Telephone   _____
    Tithing/Giving   _____
    Taxes   _____
    Other (take from nonmonthly list)   _____
Total Variable Expenses   _____

Installments
    Credit cards   _____
    Credit line   _____
    Other   _____
Total Installments   _____

Occasional Expenses
    Clothing   _____
    Recreation   _____
    Other   _____
Total Occasional Expenses   _____
TOTAL EXPENSES   _____
TOTAL INCOME MINUS EXPENSES   _____

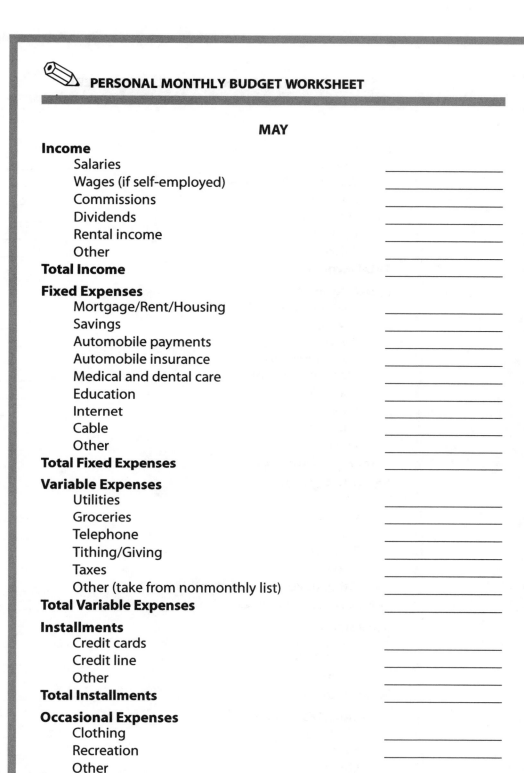

PERSONAL MONTHLY BUDGET WORKSHEET

MAY

Income
    Salaries   _____
    Wages (if self-employed)   _____
    Commissions   _____
    Dividends   _____
    Rental income   _____
    Other   _____
Total Income   _____

Fixed Expenses
    Mortgage/Rent/Housing   _____
    Savings   _____
    Automobile payments   _____
    Automobile insurance   _____
    Medical and dental care   _____
    Education   _____
    Internet   _____
    Cable   _____
    Other   _____
Total Fixed Expenses   _____

Variable Expenses
    Utilities   _____
    Groceries   _____
    Telephone   _____
    Tithing/Giving   _____
    Taxes   _____
    Other (take from nonmonthly list) _____
Total Variable Expenses   _____

Installments
    Credit cards   _____
    Credit line   _____
    Other   _____
Total Installments   _____

Occasional Expenses
    Clothing   _____
    Recreation   _____
    Other   _____
Total Occasional Expenses _____
TOTAL EXPENSES   _____
TOTAL INCOME MINUS EXPENSES _____

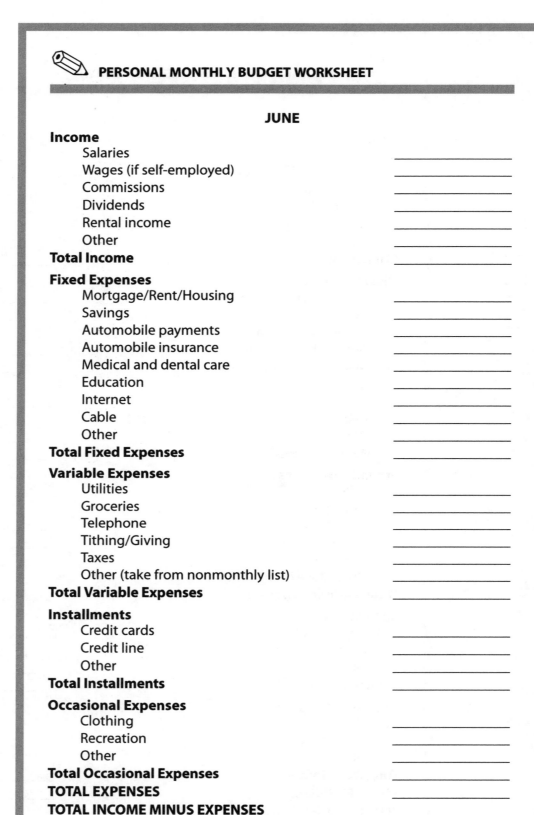

PERSONAL MONTHLY BUDGET WORKSHEET

JUNE

Income
Salaries _____
Wages (if self-employed) _____
Commissions _____
Dividends _____
Rental income _____
Other _____
Total Income _____

Fixed Expenses
Mortgage/Rent/Housing _____
Savings _____
Automobile payments _____
Automobile insurance _____
Medical and dental care _____
Education _____
Internet _____
Cable _____
Other _____
Total Fixed Expenses _____

Variable Expenses
Utilities _____
Groceries _____
Telephone _____
Tithing/Giving _____
Taxes _____
Other (take from nonmonthly list) _____
Total Variable Expenses _____

Installments
Credit cards _____
Credit line _____
Other _____
Total Installments _____

Occasional Expenses
Clothing _____
Recreation _____
Other _____
Total Occasional Expenses _____
TOTAL EXPENSES _____
TOTAL INCOME MINUS EXPENSES _____

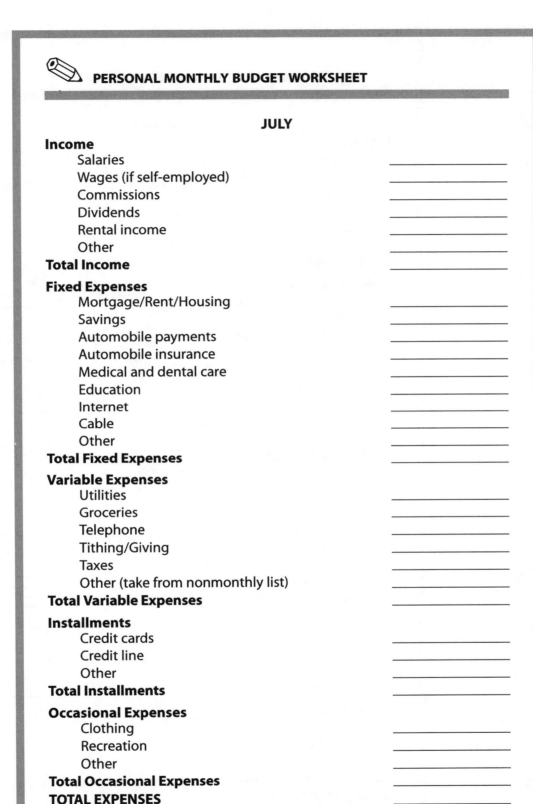

PERSONAL MONTHLY BUDGET WORKSHEET

JULY

Income
　　Salaries _____
　　Wages (if self-employed) _____
　　Commissions _____
　　Dividends _____
　　Rental income _____
　　Other _____
Total Income _____

Fixed Expenses
　　Mortgage/Rent/Housing _____
　　Savings _____
　　Automobile payments _____
　　Automobile insurance _____
　　Medical and dental care _____
　　Education _____
　　Internet _____
　　Cable _____
　　Other _____
Total Fixed Expenses _____

Variable Expenses
　　Utilities _____
　　Groceries _____
　　Telephone _____
　　Tithing/Giving _____
　　Taxes _____
　　Other (take from nonmonthly list) _____
Total Variable Expenses _____

Installments
　　Credit cards _____
　　Credit line _____
　　Other _____
Total Installments _____

Occasional Expenses
　　Clothing _____
　　Recreation _____
　　Other _____
Total Occasional Expenses _____
TOTAL EXPENSES _____
TOTAL INCOME MINUS EXPENSES _____

PERSONAL MONTHLY BUDGET WORKSHEET

AUGUST

Income
- Salaries _____
- Wages (if self-employed) _____
- Commissions _____
- Dividends _____
- Rental income _____
- Other _____

Total Income _____

Fixed Expenses
- Mortgage/Rent/Housing _____
- Savings _____
- Automobile payments _____
- Automobile insurance _____
- Medical and dental care _____
- Education _____
- Internet _____
- Cable _____
- Other _____

Total Fixed Expenses _____

Variable Expenses
- Utilities _____
- Groceries _____
- Telephone _____
- Tithing/Giving _____
- Taxes _____
- Other (take from nonmonthly list) _____

Total Variable Expenses _____

Installments
- Credit cards _____
- Credit line _____
- Other _____

Total Installments _____

Occasional Expenses
- Clothing _____
- Recreation _____
- Other _____

Total Occasional Expenses _____

TOTAL EXPENSES _____

TOTAL INCOME MINUS EXPENSES _____

PERSONAL MONTHLY BUDGET WORKSHEET

SEPTEMBER

Income
    Salaries   _____
    Wages (if self-employed)   _____
    Commissions   _____
    Dividends   _____
    Rental income   _____
    Other   _____
Total Income   _____

Fixed Expenses
    Mortgage/Rent/Housing   _____
    Savings   _____
    Automobile payments   _____
    Automobile insurance   _____
    Medical and dental care   _____
    Education   _____
    Internet   _____
    Cable   _____
    Other   _____
Total Fixed Expenses   _____

Variable Expenses
    Utilities   _____
    Groceries   _____
    Telephone   _____
    Tithing/Giving   _____
    Taxes   _____
    Other (take from nonmonthly list)   _____
Total Variable Expenses   _____

Installments
    Credit cards   _____
    Credit line   _____
    Other   _____
Total Installments   _____

Occasional Expenses
    Clothing   _____
    Recreation   _____
    Other   _____
Total Occasional Expenses   _____
TOTAL EXPENSES   _____
TOTAL INCOME MINUS EXPENSES   _____

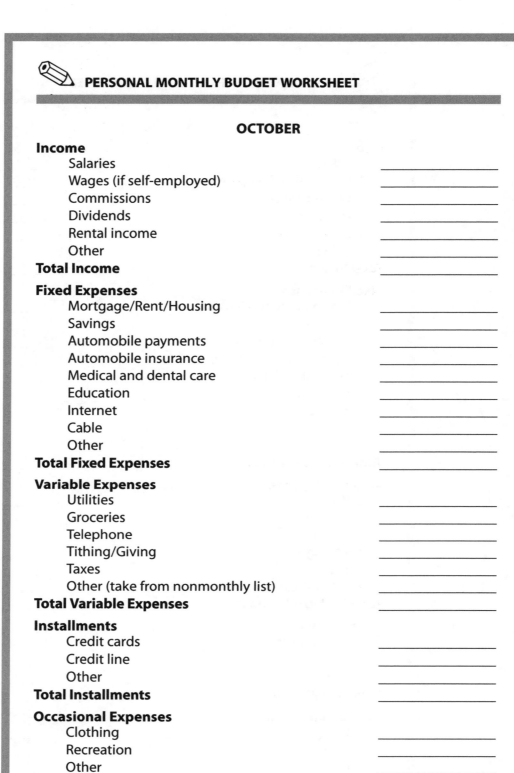

PERSONAL MONTHLY BUDGET WORKSHEET

OCTOBER

Income
- Salaries _____
- Wages (if self-employed) _____
- Commissions _____
- Dividends _____
- Rental income _____
- Other _____

Total Income _____

Fixed Expenses
- Mortgage/Rent/Housing _____
- Savings _____
- Automobile payments _____
- Automobile insurance _____
- Medical and dental care _____
- Education _____
- Internet _____
- Cable _____
- Other _____

Total Fixed Expenses _____

Variable Expenses
- Utilities _____
- Groceries _____
- Telephone _____
- Tithing/Giving _____
- Taxes _____
- Other (take from nonmonthly list) _____

Total Variable Expenses _____

Installments
- Credit cards _____
- Credit line _____
- Other _____

Total Installments _____

Occasional Expenses
- Clothing _____
- Recreation _____
- Other _____

Total Occasional Expenses _____

TOTAL EXPENSES _____

TOTAL INCOME MINUS EXPENSES _____

PERSONAL MONTHLY BUDGET WORKSHEET

NOVEMBER

Income
- Salaries _____
- Wages (if self-employed) _____
- Commissions _____
- Dividends _____
- Rental income _____
- Other _____

Total Income _____

Fixed Expenses
- Mortgage/Rent/Housing _____
- Savings _____
- Automobile payments _____
- Automobile insurance _____
- Medical and dental care _____
- Education _____
- Internet _____
- Cable _____
- Other _____

Total Fixed Expenses _____

Variable Expenses
- Utilities _____
- Groceries _____
- Telephone _____
- Tithing/Giving _____
- Taxes _____
- Other (take from nonmonthly list) _____

Total Variable Expenses _____

Installments
- Credit cards _____
- Credit line _____
- Other _____

Total Installments _____

Occasional Expenses
- Clothing _____
- Recreation _____
- Other _____

Total Occasional Expenses _____

TOTAL EXPENSES _____

TOTAL INCOME MINUS EXPENSES _____

PERSONAL MONTHLY BUDGET WORKSHEET

DECEMBER

Income
    Salaries _____
    Wages (if self-employed) _____
    Commissions _____
    Dividends _____
    Rental income _____
    Other _____
Total Income _____

Fixed Expenses
    Mortgage/Rent/Housing _____
    Savings _____
    Automobile payments _____
    Automobile insurance _____
    Medical and dental care _____
    Education _____
    Internet _____
    Cable _____
    Other _____
Total Fixed Expenses _____

Variable Expenses
    Utilities _____
    Groceries _____
    Telephone _____
    Tithing/Giving _____
    Taxes _____
    Other (take from nonmonthly list) _____
Total Variable Expenses _____

Installments
    Credit cards _____
    Credit line _____
    Other _____
Total Installments _____

Occasional Expenses
    Clothing _____
    Recreation _____
    Other _____
Total Occasional Expenses _____
TOTAL EXPENSES _____
TOTAL INCOME MINUS EXPENSES _____

FIGURE 8.5
SAMPLE YEARLY BUDGET WORKSHEET

Income

Salaries	40,800.00
Wages (if self-employed)	
Commissions	
Dividends	
Rental income	6,000.00
Other	
Total Income	**46,800.00**

Fixed Expenses

Mortgage/Rent/Housing	13,500.00
Savings	3,600.00
Automobile payments	4,200.00
Automobile insurance	1,680.00
Medical and dental care	900.00
Education	
Internet	227.40
Cable	
Other	
Total Fixed Expenses	**24,107.40**

Variable Expenses

Utilities	3,000.00
Groceries	3,600.00
Telephone	900.00
Tithing/Giving	4,800.00
Taxes	
Other (take from nonmonthly list)	3,065.00
Total Variable Expenses	**15,365.00**

Installments

Credit cards	3,060.00
Credit line	
Other	
Total Installments	**3,060.00**

Occasional Expenses

Clothing	1,200.00
Recreation	600.00
Other	
Total Occasional Expenses	**1,800.00**
TOTAL EXPENSES	**44,332.40**
TOTAL INCOME MINUS EXPENSES	**2,467.60**

YEARLY BUDGET WORKSHEET

Income
  Salaries _____
  Wages (if self-employed) _____
  Commissions _____
  Dividends _____
  Rental income _____
  Other _____
Total Income _____

Fixed Expenses
  Mortgage/Rent/Housing _____
  Savings _____
  Automobile payments _____
  Automobile insurance _____
  Medical and dental care _____
  Education _____
  Internet _____
  Cable _____
  Other _____
Total Fixed Expenses _____

Variable Expenses
  Utilities _____
  Groceries _____
  Telephone _____
  Tithing/Giving _____
  Taxes _____
  Other (take from nonmonthly list) _____
Total Variable Expenses _____

Installments
  Credit cards _____
  Credit line _____
  Other _____
Total Installments _____

Occasional Expenses
  Clothing _____
  Recreation _____
  Other _____
Total Occasional Expenses _____
TOTAL EXPENSES _____
TOTAL INCOME MINUS EXPENSES _____

9

Stating Your Case to Creditors

Once you have reviewed your budget and find you are unable to pay all your bills, you have to contact your creditors. Obviously you will be uncomfortable doing this, but reverse the scenario. If you were the creditor, wouldn't you prefer a client called you first to work something out rather than your making the initial call?

Wayne and Marilyn's Story

Wayne and Marilyn had always had a steady income and paid their bills on time. Marilyn had to quit her job to stay at home with a child who was ill. The couple's income dropped drastically, and they found themselves getting more and more in debt.

Letters and telephone calls from angry creditors demanding payment came every day. The telephone calls became so frequent and harassing that Wayne and Marilyn began screening them and refused to answer their phone if it was a creditor. The letters they were receiving were left unopened and put into a basket never to be read. Because the couple felt they had taken enough abuse, they chose to do nothing.

With the stress of delinquent bills and an ill child, marital strife was inevitable. Constant arguments arose over who to pay and what to do. Doing nothing is the worst thing you can do because it leaves you powerless to solve your problem.

When Wayne and Marilyn came to see me, I had them bring all their bills and nasty letters. As we went through each bill, I instructed them to make a list of the creditors, payments, delinquent payments, number of months the bills were late, and the balances.

Once we were able to see how bad the situation was, we could enact a plan. It wasn't going to happen overnight, but with a plan they could try to work through each bill and one day get them all paid off.

I had guided Wayne and Marilyn to review their finances to see how much extra money they had after they took care of their essential living expenses. The extra came to a total of $200 a month. We decided to take that $200 and use it to pay off one bill at a time. For example, they would offer a creditor $200 to pay off a bill of $600. If the creditor was agreeable to this offer, the creditor would then send a letter to Wayne and Marilyn stating that their balance would become zero on receipt of the $200.

When the couple came across a creditor who wouldn't work with them, they moved on to the next one who would accept their offer. They knew their credit report was already ruined, so they had nothing more to lose (except a possible lawsuit from a creditor).

With this plan they were able to slowly work themselves out of the disaster they were facing. It took a plan and communication with the creditors to be a success. By taking control of the situation, they were able to resolve their problems and reduce their debt.

Talk to Your Creditors

Communicating with your creditors will help solve your problem faster than avoiding them. Having no communication with creditors, as your payments become delinquent, will only cause you more anguish. Creditors want to know about any problems you may be facing. By failing to communicate with them in any way, creditors may feel that you don't care about paying them and may expedite the collection process, which would only make matters worse for you.

By keeping creditors informed about your situation, you have a much better chance of working out a payment schedule. A creditor would rather work something out with you than turn your account over to a collection agency or, for that matter, see you file for bankruptcy.

In dealing with creditors, you can call or write a letter explaining your situation. Your problems may result from an interruption in your employment, divorce, taxes, illness, or some other reason that may disrupt your meeting your financial obligations.

If you call creditors, make sure that you write down the name of the person you spoke with as well as the date and the gist of the conversation. In fact, keep a log of all conversations. See the Sample Creditor Communication Log in Figure 9.1 and then complete your own worksheet that follows.

FIGURE 9.1
SAMPLE CREDITOR COMMUNICATION LOG

Date	Time	Contact	Company	Conversation
9/2/00	10:20 AM	John Doe	ABC Bank	Creditor will accept a $200 payment instead of $400 payment.

Creditor Communication Log

Date	Time	Contact	Company	Conversation

If you come to an agreement with a creditor to make a payment for a lesser amount than the one required, make sure you get the argument in writing from the creditor before you begin making payment. And be sure the creditor does not report your account as a "rolling late," which means a partial payment is made that results in the account being continuously late and is then reported on your credit report as late.

If you decide to write a letter rather than call, try to send a payment in the amount you are proposing. This will show you are serious about following through to repay the debt, but wait for a response from the creditor in writing before making additional payments. See the Sample Letter to Creditor shown in Figure 9.2.

Make sure whichever creditors you are paying first are from your Category One priority list. The remaining creditors should be paid when you have the extra money.

 FIGURE 9.2
SAMPLE LETTER TO CREDITOR

(Date)

Company Name

Re: Account number

Dear Company Name,

I am a customer of yours and have recently experienced a financial hardship. The company I am working for has cut back my hours. My income has dropped, which is making it difficult to pay all my bills.

I am able to pay $20 per month until my hours increase. I am enclosing a check for $20 to be credited to my account. Please accept this payment and let me know if my proposal for future payments is acceptable to your company.

Please send me your response in writing and make this letter a part of my file.

Sincerely,

Don Smith

[MAIL CERTIFIED WITH A RETURN RECEIPT REQUESTED]

Negotiating Your Debt

If you have found yourself buried under delinquent bills and pressure from creditors to pay, try negotiating. The more behind you are with a bill, the easier it is to negotiate a settlement. If you're not delinquent, a creditor has no motivation to settle. As far as they can see, you seem not to be in any financial distress when your monthly payments are made on time. So negotiating only works and is acceptable by most creditors if you are delinquent.

There is no rule for the amount to offer a creditor for settling debts. Every creditor has its bottom for how low it will go in accepting an amount lower than the full balance. Some creditors will discount 20 percent, whereas others may discount as much as 50 to 80 percent of the balance.

If you feel you can't negotiate with a creditor yourself to settle your account, ask a third party such as a friend or relative to do it for you. You may also consider hiring a credit counseling company to assist you.

Here are some guidelines to follow when negotiating with a creditor:

- Know how much you can offer the creditor before making the offer. Don't make any offers until you have reviewed your budget and finances; if you don't have the money, don't make an offer. If you can, have the money ready to pay when you make the offer.
- If you can't pay the whole balance on an outstanding bill of $500, offer to pay $300 over a six-month period with no additional finance charges. If the creditor accepts your offer, get it in writing before you start making the payments. Make sure the creditor's letter states that once the final payment is received at the end of the six-month period, the account is satisfied and no additional fees are required.
- Find out what the creditor is willing to do to ease the pressure. For example, many creditors allow you to make interest-only payments for a limited time. Others may allow you to defer a payment for one or more months. And some may offer to settle your account by accepting a 60 percent discount from your balance if it's paid by a certain date.
- Because some bill collectors or collection agencies will mislead you, be careful about any information you give them. Never give them your bank account number or employment information.
- If a bill collector or collection agency thinks it can get a higher amount of money from you than you are willing to pay, don't back down. If you know you can only pay $50 per month, for example, and the collection agency is demanding $150, stick with the $50. The agency can take it or leave it even though it may say it can't accept $50 as payment. Mail it anyway, preferably in the form of a cashier's check or money order (keep all copies of checks). It's highly unlikely the agency will return it. Be sure to mail it by certified mail with a

return receipt requested. Don't let the creditor or collection agency bully you or threaten you into paying something you can't afford. Pay only when you have the money.

- Many creditors have a reaging program. If your account has not been charged off or placed in collection, a creditor may allow you to set up a new payment schedule. Once you have made the number of payments required by the creditor, the account will become current. For example, if you were five months late, the creditor would reduce your interest rate and allow you to make three consecutive payments. If the payments were made on time, your account would be brought up to a current status, and all past-due payments would be dropped and your credit report made current.

After making payment arrangements with a creditor, you may find you're unable to keep them. In that case, notify the creditor immediately and make new arrangements. In addition, request and make sure to get a letter from the creditor *before* you send any money confirming your new payment arrangements. If you send money before receiving written confirmation of the arrangements, you risk the creditor's denying any such arrangements were made.

Include in your negotiation that the creditor removes any negative information being reported on your credit report. Some creditors may be unwilling to do this but can if they so choose. If they won't remove negative information, attempt to have them show the account as paid or satisfied or not settled; settled is viewed as negative.

Communication with the Creditor

When a creditor has given up trying to collect a debt from you, many times the account is turned over to a collection agency. As stated earlier, collection agencies have a reputation for being very aggressive and demanding. They know that they have the best chance of collecting a debt within the first 90 days of contacting you. The longer the debt remains unpaid, the less the chance of collecting, which is why collection agencies are so aggressive during the first 90 days.

Initially, a collection agency sends you a letter asking for payment, which is followed by a telephone call. At first, the conversations are pleasant, but the more time that elapses without your paying the bill, the more aggressive and intimidating the collection agency becomes.

When you get the first letter, review it carefully. If there are any discrepancies you have 30 days to dispute the validity of the debt. Send a letter to the collection agency by certified mail with a return receipt request asking for documentation from the creditor regarding the bill. The collection agency must send you verification and cannot continue trying to collect the debt until it has sent you the validation. If the debt is valid, the collection agency will then try to collect.

Don't agree to make any payments until all of your essential bills are paid and you have money to work with. If you have the cash to settle the account for less, make an offer, but do it only if you can follow through immediately. For example, if your debt is $200 and you offer $75, make sure you can send the money immediately once the agency accepts your offer. And get the acceptance by the collection agency in writing before you send any money. I have heard of many people sending payments on the basis of an oral agreement and expecting the debt to be paid off and settled but only later discovering the creditor or collection agency never remembered the agreement. Protect yourself and don't get trapped.

If the collection agency has an account that they haven't purchased from the original creditor, it must get approval of any discount that is offered from the original creditor before acceptance.

Don't be afraid to offer less than the amount you owe. If you offer monthly payments, collection agencies typically won't give you a discount. The best time of the month to make offers on any accounts with creditors or collection agencies is at the end of the month because most companies have quotas to meet. At the end of the month, their goal is to have as many accounts as possible paid off.

It is important that you familiarize yourself with the Fair Debt Collection Practices Act (see Appendix B). This law came into effect because of "evidence of abusive, deceptive, and unfair debt collection practices that have contributed to the number of personal bankruptcies, to marital instability, to the loss of jobs, and to the invasion of individual privacy." You can obtain a copy of this act by writing the Federal Trade Commission or visiting its Web site at <www.FTC.gov>. If you have a complaint, file it with the Federal Trade Commission.

Setting Repayment Schedules

Several different problems that you may need assistance with could arise when negotiating with your creditors. Review the creditors that are on your priority list, as all of them must be paid. (Refer to Chapter 5.) Following are some suggestions to help you determine what is right for your situation. See the Sample Repayment Worksheet in Figure 9.3 on page 145 and then complete the worksheet that follows.

Mortgage payments. Above all other bills, your mortgage payment must always be made and preferably when it's due. By missing your house payments, you risk foreclosure, which can take 6 to 18 months to complete. And foreclosure is the last thing you want to have happen.

If you're in over your head, you might consider selling the house, but sell before you fall behind, if possible. If you have equity in the house, you could use that money to purchase or rent another home. Remember that if the payment has not been delinquent, your credit report will not be affected.

If you have missed one or two payments, the lender usually will accept only the full payment that is past due. For example, suppose you missed one payment and your next payment is due, but the lender will only accept the payment that is due if the missed payment is included. If the delinquent payment is not included, it's not uncommon for a lender to send the whole payment back.

Get in touch with the mortgage company immediately if you foresee a problem making a payment or if you have missed any payments. Stay in communication with the company and try to have a repayment plan set up for you. If notified early enough, some mortgage companies allow you to make an interest-only payment and apply the principal to the balance.

If you have fallen behind, see if the lender will allow you to increase your monthly payment by adding your delinquent payment to the payment due. For example, if you missed one payment of $1,000, you would add an additional $100 to your payment, for a total of $1,100 for ten months. At the end of the ten months, your payment would be current.

If you have tried to work with the creditor but nothing seems to be working and the house has fallen into foreclosure, offer the lender a quit-claim deed. A quitclaim deed is a deed that gives your property back to the lender in exchange for, or cancellation of, the debt. The lender would then stop all foreclosure proceedings (which saves it money), and you'll avoid a negative entry on your credit report.

A good resource to contact if you are having problems is Homesavers U.S.A. at 800-750-8956.

Rent payments. Renters should make sure payments stay on time. If you think you are going to be late, communicate with the landlord to explain the problem. Remember that the landlord is probably making payments to a lender on the home you're renting and is counting on your money to pay his lender.

If you're going to be only a couple of weeks late, the landlord will usually work with you. If you've been a longtime tenant, the landlord may allow you to make partial payments, such as a payment every other week until you catch up.

It's easier to keep you as a tenant than to evict you. The landlord usually loses money trying to rerent after a prolonged vacancy. If the landlord agrees to work with you in paying the rent, mail a certified letter stating the approved arrangement with a return receipt request. Be sure to follow through with your promise.

If you're unable to keep the arrangement, look for a cheaper home or apartment, but do it before you fall behind so you can get a good reference.

Automobile payments. A lender who is financing a car loan can instigate a repossession of your car when he feels threatened in any way. Always contact the lender immediately if you know your payment is going to be late. Most lenders will work with you and even have special programs.

Some lenders allow you to defer a car payment for 1 month or sometimes longer. That means they'll accept the deferred payment and add it on to the remaining balance of the contract. Thus, a 36-month contract would be extended to a 37-month contract.

The lender may allow you to make interest-only payments, with the principal added to the balance and due at the end of your contract.

Refinancing your vehicle may also help you reduce your payments, but refinance only if your monthly payment is reduced. You'll have additional months to pay on the loan, but refinancing can take the pressure off while you're trying to get back on your feet.

If the payments are too high, sell the car and use the money to pay off the loan and apply the difference to a more affordable vehicle.

A repossession on your credit report can hurt your chances of getting another vehicle for several years. A lender will sell the repossessed vehicle, but you will owe the difference if the vehicle is sold for less than your balance. For example, if you owed $12,000 on the vehicle and the lender sold it for $10,000, you would be responsible for the $2,000 balance remaining. This would be noted on your credit report, and the lender would still try to collect this from you.

Secured loan payments. Secured loans are usually for such items as jewelry, electronic equipment, furniture, and the like. They are loans secured by the item that is financed and is used as collateral. If payments were stopped, the pledged items will be lost.

If you have this type of loan, be sure to communicate with the lender and negotiate your payment arrangement to reduce your payments.

Unsecured credit and charge payments. Most credit card companies don't work with you to reduce your payments until you've fallen behind. If you haven't fallen behind, the companies perceive there's no financial distress.

When negotiating with a credit card company, call to let it know your situation. It's better to do this before you fall behind so it can place a note or statement in its files.

If you realize that your finances are spiraling downward and you're not sure how you are going to come out, always keep one credit card current. This one credit card may help you on the road to recovery; and you need one credit card for identification to reserve a hotel or automobile. If you have two credit cards with ABC Company, for example, and one is current and the other delinquent, the company may eventually close both accounts. Therefore, keep a credit card of a company in which you have only one account.

If a credit card company agrees to accept a lower payment, get the agreement in writing. Occasionally, a creditor will allow you to make a payment of 2 or 3 percent of the outstanding balance without a finance charge.

Most credit cards are unsecured, which means the lender can't take anything from you that was charged on your account. Its only recourse for collecting would be to sue you and get a court judgment. Normally, however, credit card companies don't go that far and will either charge off the account or turn it over to a collection agency. Of course, they do report this negative activity on your credit reports.

The older a delinquency, the more leverage you have to negotiate a settlement with a creditor. It is more receptive to a settlement offer after the account is delinquent for four to six months. Usually after six months, the creditor will charge off the account (meaning write it off as a loss) or turn it over to a collection agency.

Most creditors will work with you if you get assistance from a credit counseling company for debt management. This will be discussed in the next chapter.

Student loans. Contact the lender who has your student loan. You may be able to get the student loan deferred if you supply the lender with a letter explaining your financial hardship. If the lender thinks you have a legitimate reason for not paying, it may postpone the payment, although the interest will continue to accrue until you begin making payments. Review your original papers from the time you took out the loan to see what the lender's policies are regarding deferments and delinquent accounts. Above all, stay in touch with the lender. You may be able to refinance your student loan to get a lower interest rate and lower your monthly payment.

Taxes. If you owe back taxes, the Internal Revenue Service or state revenue agency can try to collect by garnishing your wages, attaching (levying) your bank accounts, and placing a lien on your home or other property.

Contact the IRS and state department to arrange repayment or to make an offer in compromise. If accepted, an offer in compromise will reduce the amount you owe. For example, you may owe $15,000 in back taxes; you can contact a tax relief company to help you negotiate with the IRS, or you can do it yourself. Let's suppose you offer $5,000 to settle the back taxes; the IRS will review your financial situation and determine if it will accept your offer or make one of its own. Once the offer is accepted, you can make payments or pay the amount in full.

Whether you make a payment arrangement on your own or through an offer in compromise, stick to it or the result may be severe penalties and the compromise arrangement canceled and the whole balance required to be paid in full.

Insurance. Most states require car owners to carry *automobile insurance.* Otherwise, you risk being cited for not having insurance if you have an accident, possibly resulting in your losing your driver's license or being jailed. If your vehicle is leased or you are purchasing with a loan, the lender will require that you carry insurance. If you don't, the lender will use its own policy, which is much costlier than one you would get, and you are responsible for making the payments. Call your insurance company to find out if you can get a higher deductible or other discount to reduce your monthly payments, and do comparison shopping on rates of other insurance companies.

Most lenders who are financing your home require *homeowners insurance.* If you let your homeowners insurance lapse, the lender will use its own policy, which will cost you more than you need to pay. Contact your insurance company to see what type of policy you can carry that would satisfy your lender's conditions; and shop other insurance companies for a cheaper rate.

Medical insurance is essential. In the event you have a medical problem and your policy has lapsed, you may not be able to get medical insurance because of a preexisting condition. Call your insurance agent to find out if you could raise your deductible to get a lower rate; and do comparison shopping to see if you can find a cheaper policy.

Some companies offer health benefits and discounts that are not insurance policies but are health plans that include physicians, vision, pharmaceutical, and chiropractic coverage (www.financialvictory.com; 714-541-2637).

Doctor, dentist, accountant, and attorney bills. Many doctors, attorneys, and accountants accept partial payments. If you realize you are having a problem paying any bills for these professional services, negotiate a settlement for less than the amount owed. If the professional agrees, have her send you the settlement offer in writing. Then pay it off.

DEBT DESTROYER TIPS

- Contact your creditor immediately if you are having financial problems.

- Get any agreement you make with creditors in writing before you make a payment or settlement.

- Don't negotiate with a creditors unless you know you can make the payments or pay the debt off in full.

- Know your rights under the Fair Debt Collection Practices Act.

FIGURE 9.3
SAMPLE REPAYMENT WORKSHEET

Make a list of each creditor and collection agency to which you owe money. Include the minimum payment, the past-due amount, the balance, and the amount you can pay. Do this monthly until all your accounts are paid off.

SEPTEMBER

Creditor	Minimum Payment	Past-Due Amount	Balance	Amount I Can Pay
ABC Bank	$40	$80	$2,250	$50

Repayment Worksheet

Creditor	Minimum Payment	Past-Due Amount	Balance	Amount I Can Pay

$\boxed{10}$

Tips to Get Out of Debt

Getting out of debt is serious business. It takes discipline and perseverance, but you can do it!

Several different strategies are available to get out of debt. You need to determine which one fits your situation and then use it.

Without looking, do you have any idea how much your present balance, credit limit, minimum payment, and interest rate are on all your credit cards? Complete the following Debt Worksheet. Try it first without looking at your statements. Once you have completed it, do a second Debt Worksheet listing all your credit card accounts and the information from your recent statements. How knowledgeable were you? Compare the two worksheets. Keep Debt Worksheet #2 (with your credit card statement information) close by, because you'll be using it as a reference for getting out of debt.

Were you surprised to see the difference between Debt Worksheet #1 and Debt Worksheet #2? Most individuals know very little about the details of their credit cards because they don't read the credit card statement each month. They look at the payment due and maybe the balances, but that's all. Most people are more aware of what their payment is than what interest rate they are paying. By not paying attention to what interest you are paying, you'll prolong the life of the debt. This is especially true if you are making only the minimum monthly payment.

Tip 1. Consolidate your credit cards. Once you have reviewed your Debt Worksheet #2, you may consider moving your major credit cards that are charging higher interest rates to those with lower interest rates.

DEBT WORKSHEET #1 (from your memory)

Creditor Name	Balance	Credit Limit	Minimum Payment	Interest Rate

DEBT WORKSHEET #2 (from your credit card statements)

Creditor Name	Balance	Credit Limit	Minimum Payment	Interest Rate

FIGURE 10.1
CONSOLIDATING CREDIT CARD DEBT: THREE EXAMPLES

Example A

Credit Limit	Interest Rate	Current Balance	Minimum Payment
$5,000	16%	$1,200	$24
2,000	21	1,800	36
1,000	22	500	15

Example B

Credit Limit	Interest Rate	Current Balance	Minimum Payment
$5,000	16%	$1,200 + $500* = $1,700	$24 + $15* = $39
2,000	21	1,800	36
1,000	22	0	0

Example C

Credit Limit	Interest Rate	Current Balance	Minimum Payment
$5,000	16%	$1,700 + $1,800* = $3,500	$39 + $36* = $75
2,000	21	0	0
1,000	22	0	0

*Notice that by moving the minimum payments and balances from each of the credit cards, you are making one larger payment at a lower interest, which will allow you to pay off the debt faster and save money on interest. Try to pay more than the minimum payment each month.

For example, you have two credit cards (see Figure 10.1). One has a credit limit of $5,000, an interest rate of 16 percent, and a balance of $1,200. Your other credit card has a credit limit of $2,000, an interest rate of 21 percent, and a balance of $1,800. Get a cash advance from your credit card with the 16 percent interest rate and pay off the credit card with the $1,800 balance. You would now owe $3,000 on the credit card with the 16 percent interest rate and have saved 5 percent interest. Add the payment you would be making on the card with the 21 percent interest rate to the payment you would make on the credit card with the 16 percent interest rate, and you'll be able to pay off the debt more rapidly and save money by eliminating the higher interest. The key to making this work is that you *don't charge* anything else to the account with the 21 percent rate. To play it safe, contact the credit card company after you have transferred the 21 percent interest rate card and close the account, helping you to resist using it.

Department store credit cards should be consolidated into one major credit card such as a Visa or MasterCard with a lower interest rate. Interest rates on department store cards are usually higher than most major credit cards, starting from 21 percent and going higher. Close all your department store accounts after you transfer the balances to one major card.

Tip 2. Make extra payments. Most of us never calculate how long it will take to pay off our credit card debt nor how much we will actually pay in interest charges before the debt is paid off.

By adding an extra amount–$5, $10, or more–to your monthly credit card payment, your debt will be paid off more quickly and you'll save a large amount in interest charges.

The average household carries a minimum of five credit cards with balances. Based on a balance of $2,000 with no new charges and paying the minimum amount of 3 percent each month at 21 percent interest, it would take more than 16 years to pay off one credit card. The interest paid would be $2,504.62; this added to the $2,000 balance totals $4,504.62 that you would have paid for using your charge card.

Look at the sample chart in Figure 10.2 to see the difference in savings that are realized by adding additional money to your minimum payment.

Tip 3. Pay off your credit cards. After you have reviewed your Debt Worksheet #2, arrange your credit cards in order from the one with the highest balance to the one with the lowest balance.

For example:

ABC Company	Balance: $2,300
XYZ Company	1,200
ALPHA Credit Card	1,000
Department Store	500
Department Store	275

Experts differ about which cards to pay off first: high-interest ones with high balances or high-interest ones with low balances. The decision is yours, but the quickest way to get out of debt and feel as though you are accomplishing an objective is to pay off the lower balances first.

The payment you would be making to the lowest balance now that it's paid off should be added to the next credit card balance you are trying to pay off. For instance, the balance of $275 required a minimum payment of $15. Once you pay off this card, add the $15 to the minimum payment on the next balance of $500, and continue doing this until that card is also paid off. Then add the two payments you were making on the department store cards to the next balance plus the minimum payment. These extra payments apply to the principal and result in the balances decreasing rapidly. See Figure 10.3 on page 152 before completing your Payoff Strategy Worksheet.

FIGURE 10.2
CREDIT CARD CHART

Balance	Number Years until Paid	Total Interest Paid	$5 Extra Interest Saved	Number Years Saved	$10 Extra Interest Saved	Number Years Saved
$2,000	16.1	$2,504.62	$738.59	5.8	$1,113.70	8.4
1,900	15.8	2,364.62	714.91	5.8	1,073.24	8.3
1,800	15.4	2,224.65	690.21	5.8	1,031.26	8.3
1,700	15.0	2,084.61	664.31	5.6	987.56	8.1
1,600	14.7	1,944.63	637.15	5.6	942.14	8.0
1,500	14.3	1,804.61	608.60	5.5	894.78	7.8
1,400	13.8	1,664.65	578.54	5.4	845.32	7.7
1,300	13.3	1,524.64	546.71	5.3	793.55	7.5
1,200	12.8	1,384.64	512.96	5.2	739.26	7.3
1,100	12.2	1,244.65	477.06	5.0	682.17	7.1
1,000	11.5	1,104.63	438.66	4.8	621.96	6.8

Tip 4. Don't reduce your yearly estimated payments. When you are listing your projected expenses at the beginning of each year (see yearly worksheet) and you've estimated a certain amount to be paid toward credit card debt, divide that amount by 12 (months). That is the monthly amount you will be paying. As your balances decrease, your required minimum payments will also decrease. Use the monthly amount that you originally estimated to continue paying the balances down each month rather than gauging it by the required minimum amount on your statement.

For example, if you have calculated from your yearly worksheet that $6,000 per year will be paid toward credit card debt, you would divide that by 12 months, which equals $500 per month to be paid toward credit card bills. Because the balances are decreasing and the minimum payments reduced, you have to stick with your plan by continuing to budget $500 a month and applying the excess to whatever credit card you want to pay off first. Don't look at excess money as extra until all your debts are paid off.

Tip 5. Consider carefully when to refinance or take on an equity loan.
Refinancing your mortgage is an option only if the amount of the monthly payment is less than you are paying now. Refinancing could be done for a lower interest rate or to consolidate your bills. If it is to consolidate your bills, then your monthly mortgage payment must be lower than the bills

FIGURE 10.3
SAMPLE PAYOFF STRATEGY (based on allocated amount of $500 per month)*

Month	Creditor	Balance	Minimum Payment	Amount Paid
Month #1				
	ABC Company	$2,300	$40	$ 45
	XYZ Company	1,200	19	25
	ALPHA Credit	1,000	20	25
	Dept. Store	500	10	130
	Dept. Store	275	10	275
Month #2				
	ABC Company	2,255	40	45
	XYZ Company	1,175	19	25
	ALPHA Credit	975	20	60
	Dept. Store	370	10	370
	Dept. Store	0	0	0
Month #3				
	ABC Company	2,210	40	45
	XYZ Company	1,150	19	25
	ALPHA Credit	915	15	430
	Dept. Store	0	0	0
	Dept. Store	0	0	0

*This example does not reflect interest, so be sure to add the interest when determining what amount to pay.

PAYOFF STRATEGY WORKSHEET

Month	Creditor	Balance	Minimum Payment	Amount Paid

you are paying off and the mortgage payment together. For example, a mortgage payment of $1,000 per month and credit card bills of $500 per month total $1,500 monthly. If your total payment after a refinance is $1,200, you have saved $300. A lender will evaluate your situation by calculating the ratio of your monthly income to your new payment minus your debts. If the ratio is between 25 and 33 percent, you'll probably qualify for the new refinance loan.

If it seems your bills will be paid off within a three-year period without refinancing the house, then don't do the refinance. Refinancing should be done only if you are going to end up with a lower payment and if you are willing to discipline yourself by breaking the bondage of credit card use.

A refinance can cost thousands of dollars in loan fees and charges plus extending the life of your loan. New mortgages can be for 15, 20, or 30 years.

A *home equity loan* is known as a second mortgage. It can be set up at a fixed rate of interest for 15, 20, or 25 years or as an equity line whereby you are approved for a certain amount of money (equity from your home) and withdraw the money as you need it. For example, you may have an equity line of $50,000 but only need to withdraw $15,000 for home improvements or to pay off credit cards, although you can use the money for anything you want. The equity line works like a credit card, so there is a danger you'll consider it easy money.

An equity line without a fixed interest rate or set number of years is not my first choice; because most of the equity lines don't have a fixed interest rate, and they can be misleading. The interest rate is usually lower for the first three months of the equity line loan and then adjusts to a much higher interest rate that leads to payments higher than most people anticipate and this creates a false sense of security. If you are late in making the payments, you risk losing your home through foreclosure, just as you would with your primary mortgage.

When you refinance your property or try to obtain a second mortgage, you must have some equity in the property. If you want to refinance your entire loan in order to take out cash, most lenders want to see at least a 75 to 80 percent loan-to-value ratio. That means that if your property had an appraisal of $100,000, the lender would loan you up to $75,000 or $80,000 (depending on the lender). Using the $75,000 as an example, you subtract your current balance from $75,000. Thus, if the balance on the mortgage was $50,000 and you could borrow $75,000, you'd net $25,000 cash less the cost of your loan.

Some lenders make 100 percent and 125 percent equity loans, but these types of loans are harder to qualify for. The risk of a 100 or 125 percent loan is overencumbering your property, taking all of the equity out of it and more. These types of loans are also risky because if the value of your property drops, you'll owe more than the property's worth, making it difficult to sell.

FIGURE 10.4
COST SAVINGS CONVERTING TO A BIWEEKLY MORTGAGE (based on 7%, $100,000 loan amount, 30 years)

Year	Loan Balance		Yearly Interest Paid		Yearly Principal Paid		Total Interest	
	Biweekly	Standard	Biweekly	Standard	Biweekly	Standard	Biweekly	Standard
2002	98,564.59	99,158.45	5,882.92	5,811.48	1,435.41	841.55	5,882.92	5,811.48
2003	96,755.02	98,081.81	6,839.36	6,906.98	1,809.57	1,076.65	12,722.28	12,718.46
2004	94,814.42	96,927.33	6,708.33	6,829.15	1,940.60	1,154.48	19,430.61	19,547.62
2005	92,733.30	95,689.40	6,567.82	6,745.70	2,081.11	1,237.93	25,998.43	26,293.31
2006	90,501.50	94,361.98	6,417.13	6,656.21	2,231.80	1,327.42	32,415.56	32,949.52
2007	88,108.10	92,938.59	6,255.53	6,560.25	2,393.40	1,423.38	38,671.09	39,509.77
2008	85,541.40	91,412.31	6,082.23	6,457.35	2,566.70	1,526.28	44,753.32	45,967.12
2009	82,788.85	89,775.70	5,896.39	6,347.02	2,752.55	1,636.61	50,649.71	52,314.13
2010	79,837.00	88,020.77	5,697.08	6,228.70	2,951.85	1,754.93	56,346.79	58,542.84
2011	76,671.42	86,138.98	5,483.34	6,101.84	3,165.59	1,881.79	61,830.13	64,644.68
2012	73,276.62	84,121.16	5,254.13	5,965.81	3,394.80	2,017.82	67,084.27	70,610.48
2013	69,636.01	81,957.47	5,008.32	5,819.94	3,640.61	2,163.69	72,092.59	76,430.42
2014	65,731.79	79,637.36	4,744.72	5,663.52	3,904.21	2,320.11	76,837.31	82,093.95
2015	61,544.89	77,149.53	4,462.02	5,495.80	4,186.91	2,487.83	81,299.34	87,589.75
2016	57,054.82	74,481.86	4,158.86	5,315.96	4,490.07	2,667.67	85,458.20	92,905.71
2017	52,239.63	71,621.34	3,833.75	5,123.11	4,815.18	2,860.52	89,291.95	98,028.82
2018	47,075.79	68,554.04	3,485.09	4,916.32	5,163.84	3,067.31	92,777.04	102,945.14
2019	41,538.05	65,265.00	3,111.19	4,694.59	5,537.74	3,289.04	95,888.23	107,639.73
2020	35,599.34	61,738.19	2,710.22	4,456.82	5,938.71	3,526.81	98,598.46	112,096.56
2021	29,230.63	57,956.43	2,280.22	4,201.87	6,368.72	3,781.76	100,878.67	116,298.43
2022	22,400.77	53,901.29	1,819.07	3,928.49	6,829.86	4,055.14	102,697.74	120,226.91
2023	15,076.38	49,553.00	1,324.54	3,635.34	7,324.39	4,348.29	104,022.29	123,862.26
2024	7,221.65	44,890.37	794.20	3,321.00	7,854.73	4,662.63	104,816.49	127,183.26
2025	0.00	39,890.69	229.77	2,983.94	7,221.65	4,999.69	105,046.26	130,167.20
2026	0.00	34,529.57	0.00	2,622.51	0.00	5,361.12	105,046.26	132,789.71
2027	0.00	28,780.90	0.00	2,234.96	0.00	5,748.67	105,046.26	135,024.67
2028	0.00	22,616.65	0.00	1,819.39	0.00	6,164.24	105,046.26	136,844.05
2029	0.00	16,006.79	0.00	1,373.77	0.00	6,609.86	105,046.26	138,217.83
2030	0.00	8,919.11	0.00	895.94	0.00	7,087.69	105,046.26	139,113.77
2031	0.00	1,319.05	0.00	383.57	0.00	7,600.05	105,046.26	139,497.35
2032	0.00	0.00	0.00	11.55	0.00	1,319.05	105,046.26	139,508.90

Source: <www.mortgage-x.com>.

Tip 6. Reduce the life of your mortgage. You can reduce the life of your typical 30-year mortgage by adding money to your house payment each month. By setting up a biweekly payment schedule, you can reduce years off your loan. The biweekly payment is comparable to one extra payment a year. And that one extra payment or more a year will save you hundreds of thousands of dollars for the life of your loan (see Figure 10.4).

See Appendix A or visit <www.mortgage-x.com> to calculate the savings on your loan by paying it biweekly.

Once your credit cards are paid off, add extra payments to your house payment. If you add extra payments, make sure you write a note to your lender to apply the extra amount to the principal of your loan; you can generally note this on your monthly mortgage payment stub.

Tip 7. Engage a credit counselor. You should consider getting in touch with a credit counseling company to consolidate your debts, whether you are delinquent in your payments, are overextended with your credit cards, or are just tired of paying high interest rates.

Credit counselors are noted for their ability to rebuild your relationship with your creditors, becoming the middle party in communicating with creditors. They help you work out your problems and develop a repayment program that will satisfy both you and your creditors.

Most credit counseling companies offer nonprofit services. A small monthly donation and small percentage (called "fair share") are paid the company by the creditors.

When you contact a credit counselor, have a list of your bills ready with creditors' names, balances owed, and payments due as well as the amount of your income and living expenses. The counselor will examine your income, assets, debts, and expenses to determine what you can afford to pay.

If you have received any late notices, demand notices for payment, collection notices, notices of a legal action against you, court judgments, or anything else that you feel is significant for the counselor to review, have it ready to give the counselor. The counselor needs the whole picture to develop a payment plan that will help you and satisfy your creditors.

Once the counselor receives all the necessary information from you regarding your financial situation, she will contact your creditors to work out a repayment schedule.

Most creditors are anxious to work with a credit counseling service because they know that you are seeking help and not filing for bankruptcy. And they know they will never be able to collect the debt if you file for bankruptcy.

The credit counselor works with a creditor to lower your payment by reducing the interest to as low as zero or as high as 11 percent. Each creditor uses a different formula to lower the rate.

By reducing your interest rate, your payments will be lower than those you are paying now. The payments will apply more toward your principal, which allows you to pay off your debts in three to five years, saving you thousands of dollars in interest and making you debt free. Your late fees and over-the-limit fees will stop accruing when you work with a credit counseling company. If you are late, the account will be reaged and brought current. Reaging an account means the creditor agrees to bring the account current once he receives an agreed number of payments.

The credit counseling company sets your payments so you are paying one monthly payment to the counseling service to cover all your debts; and the counseling service then disburses the payments to your creditors. You'll know every month how much you'll be spending toward your bills, relieved that the balances are going down and seeing the light at the end of the tunnel.

Although there are a number of debt management companies, I recommend the Debt Relief Clearinghouse, which offers debt management programs and referrals to companies such as Cambridge Credit Counseling and others that will fit your needs. It offers valuable incentive programs to its clients and can be reached at 888-4debthelp (888-433-2843) or at its Web site <www.debtreliefonline.org>.

Don't wait until you are too deep in trouble to seek help. It's never too late. If you suspect you are overextended or are anticipating a job layoff, a divorce, a disability, or a reduction of income, get help right away.

Tip 8. Use money in your savings account to pay off debts. A question I hear repeatedly: Should I use my savings account to pay off my debts?

If the money you have in savings is earning 6 percent interest and you are paying 18 percent or more in interest on your debts, you're losing money.

Keep a small amount of money in your savings account for a rainy day, but use the remaining money to pay down some of your debt.

Tip 9. File for bankruptcy only as a last resort. Before ever considering a bankruptcy, make sure you have consulted a credit counseling or debt management company, such as the Debt Relief Clearinghouse noted in Tip 7. It could be your answer to avoiding bankruptcy.

Bankruptcy laws may be changing, so be sure to contact an attorney. Credit counseling may be mandatory when the laws change.

Bankruptcy should always be the last resort. A bankruptcy follows you for ten years on your credit report. If an employer is considering hiring you and runs a credit report listing the bankruptcy, you may not get the job. It will take you several years to rebuild your credit report. If you are in the market for a home, mortgage, credit card, or automobile, you'll be charged high interest rates.

For some people, however, bankruptcy is the right choice. You need to ask yourself: Can I live with the consequences? Don't file for a bankruptcy just because you are tired of hearing from the creditors. And don't let a creditor bully you into a bankruptcy.

There are three types of bankruptcies: A *Chapter 7* pertains to everyone; a *Chapter 13* pertains to individuals; and a *Chapter 11* pertains to business reorganizations as well as to individuals.

An individual can only file for a Chapter 11 if the debt is larger than the maximum allowed in a Chapter 13. A Chapter 11 is usually filed by a business and entails a reorganization of the debts of the business.

Chapter 7. A Chapter 7 bankruptcy is known as a straight bankruptcy. More than two-thirds of all people filing for bankruptcy file a Chapter 7 because it allows most of their debts to disappear without having to be paid.

Some debts, however, you can't discharge through a bankruptcy, including student loans, overdue taxes, alimony, child support, and fraudulent loans. A loan would be considered fraudulent if a creditor could prove you exaggerated your income or other information on your loan application.

Charging many purchases before filing for bankruptcy can also be viewed as fraudulent. A creditor will take note of what purchases are made several months before a bankruptcy filing.

If filing for a bankruptcy, it is advisable to have an attorney represent you; it's too risky to do it yourself. There are things you may omit and not fully understand without the counsel of an attorney.

Once you have filed for bankruptcy, you must go to a meeting with the trustee (the person in charge of your bankruptcy). The trustee must determine what assets you have that can be sold to pay off the creditors. In addition, the trustee determines what debts you have that will be discharged through the bankruptcy. *Dischargeable debts* disappear after the bankruptcy, which means you don't have to pay them. Dischargeable debts include most unsecured debts, such as credit card bills, medical bills, collection accounts, judgments, and rent.

Chapter 13. A Chapter 13 bankruptcy is known as the federal repayment plan, or wage earner's plan. In a Chapter 13, you are allowed to keep all your property, and the court will assign a trustee to determine how much you should pay each month to settle your debts.

In filing for a Chapter 13, you are required to submit a detailed budget of your living expenses and bills. You then propose an amount that you can pay each month to the trustee, who will disburse payments to the creditors. The payment plan is for a three-year to five-year period, during which all interest charges and late fees are stopped.

If the court approves your payment proposal, you begin making payments. At the end of the three-year to five-year program (based on what the court agrees to), any amount still owed on the debt is forgiven by the court, and no more payments are required.

The main difference between a Chapter 7 bankruptcy and a Chapter 13 is that the Chapter 7 wipes out most debts without their being repaid. A Chapter 13, on the other hand, allows you to keep secured items like your cars, home, or furniture by lowering your payments.

To qualify for a Chapter 13, you must be employed and earn enough money to meet your budgeted living expenses plus the payments you agreed to pay with the court trustee. If you are unable to keep your payment arrangements in the Chapter 13, you can then file a Chapter 7 to discharge your debts and eliminate all your payments.

Both a Chapter 7 and Chapter 13 appear on your credit reports for up to ten years. Bankruptcy proceedings are beyond the scope of this book, so I strongly suggest that in addition to consulting with a bankruptcy attorney, you pick up a copy of *The Bankruptcy Kit* (Dearborn Trade) to give you an overview of what to expect.

Tip 10. Avoid borrowing from family or friends. Sometimes a family member or friend will volunteer financial help, but it's not always the best option for you. Many relationships are ruined as a result of borrowing money from a friend or family member. If you do borrow money, sign a promissory note agreeing to pay the person back when you have the funds.

Don't use the money that you borrow from family and friends to pay credit card bills. Use it for survival—mortgage, rent, food, and utilities. If you use the money for other things, you risk falling behind with your rent or mortgage and having your utilities turned off and being unable to feed your family.

Remember that the bill collector yelling the loudest is not the one to pay first. It is the bills to keep a roof over your head and food on the table that must be paid first.

Don't get in the habit of accepting money from family or friends. You must find other remedies to solve your financial problems rather than using family or friends as a crutch.

Jack and Margaret's Story

Jack and Margaret had fallen behind in their payments. Not all their payments were behind, but they knew they were overextended and treading water. If an emergency arose, they would go under. Their interest rates were high on all their credit cards, and they felt as if they would never be able to pay off their debts.

Bankruptcy seemed the only solution. Jack and Margaret came to see me, bringing all their bills with a list of their income and expenses. Their credit card payments alone had reached $600 a month in addition to all their other living expenses.

After reviewing their situation, I recommended that they contact a credit counseling company before filing for a bankruptcy. The couple got in touch with the Debt Relief Clearinghouse, which was able to get them in the right debt management program. Jack and Margaret were able to negotiate with the creditors to reduce their interest rates and payments. Their credit card payments were reduced from $600 to $400 a month and would be paid off within three to five years.

When Jack and Margaret were able to see their payments reduced and that their debts would be paid off within three to five years, they decided against bankruptcy. They knew that in the long run their credit rating would appear better than if they would have the stigma of a bankruptcy following them for the next ten years.

DEBT DESTROYER TIPS

- Add extra money to your minimum payments.

- Determine how much you can pay each month on credit card debt. Continue with that payment until your debt is paid off, and don't lower that amount (even if the minimum payments drop lower).

- Don't refinance or take out equity from your home if the balances on your debt will be paid off within three years.

- Add extra payments to your mortgage.

- Get in touch with a credit counseling or debt management company to find out how your payments can be reduced if you are overextended or have fallen behind making your payments.

11

Debt Free! Now What?

You're down to the last payment and your last creditor will be paid off. Debt free! Free at last! What a relief! It was a long journey, but you finally accomplished your dream.

But there is still more that you have to do! Don't sit back until you have ordered copies of your personal credit reports from all three of the credit reporting agencies: TransUnion, Equifax, and Experian. If you own a business, you can request a copy of your business credit rating from Dun & Bradstreet. It is imperative you make sure that information on your credit reports is being reported accurately.

Richard and Doreen's Story

After being in debt for what seemed an eternity, Richard and Doreen finally paid off their debts. It had taken several years and considerable sacrifice, but they did it. With no debt, Richard and Doreen decided to buy a home, something they had dreamed of doing but were unable to before because of their high debt.

When Richard and Doreen sought prequalification for a loan, a credit report was run. To their surprise, the credit report was returned with several incorrect entries.

Some accounts that had been paid off were still showing a balance. Other accounts that were paid off appeared to be open. And there were accounts that listed late payments, which Richard and Doreen knew weren't correct.

I went over the credit report with the couple and explained that their credit report was good, but some of the entries had to be addressed. Credit scores, known as FICO scores, weren't as high as they had to be to qualify for the best interest rates as a result of the inaccurate entries on the report.

As we reviewed each entry on the report, we discovered that although the accounts were paid off, they had never been closed, and thus it appeared that Richard and Doreen had unused credit, which lowered their score. In addition, the accounts showing late payments and the accounts still reporting balances even though they were paid were also causing a low score.

Before Richard and Doreen could go any further with their qualification for a home, we had to take time out to have the credit report corrected. Richard and Doreen got in touch with each of the creditors that had not reported the accounts paid and requested a letter from each stating that the accounts were paid. They also called and wrote letters to the creditors who were still reporting open accounts, requesting that the accounts be closed.

After receiving the letters from the creditors and waiting at least four weeks from the date they canceled their accounts, Richard and Doreen requested copies of their credit reports from TransUnion, Equifax, and Experian to confirm that the creditors had removed incorrect information and closed the accounts. When the couple received the reports, they found that some of the creditors had corrected their entries but some had not.

Richard and Doreen wrote letters to all three of the credit reporting agencies to dispute the entries they knew were inaccurate. They also attached the letters from the creditors to the letters they wrote to the credit reporting agencies demanding the credit report be updated with the correct information.

The agencies investigated the items that Richard and Doreen were disputing, and an updated credit report was mailed to them with the corrections. Once the credit reports were updated, the couple's FICO scores went up, and they were able to qualify for the best home interest rates.

Had Richard and Doreen done their homework before trying to prequalify for the loan by getting their credit reports from all three of the credit reporting agencies, the problems would have been corrected, and the couple would have avoided a wait.

Credit Reports

If you have been turned down for credit, you are entitled to a free credit report from the credit reporting agency listed on the letter of denial from the creditor to which you had applied. Your request must be made within 60 days of the denial letter. Some states offer free credit reports. Contact each credit reporting agency to find out the fee for your state.

FIGURE 11.1
SAMPLE CREDIT REPORT REQUEST FORMS—Form A

USE IF YOU HAVE BEEN TURNED DOWN FOR CREDIT WITHIN THE PAST 60 DAYS!
SAMPLE ONLY! DO NOT USE!

Dear Credit Agency,

Please send me a free copy of my credit report. I was turned down for credit by
_____ (creditor's name that denied credit).

Full Name _____

Current Address _____

City _____ State _____ Zip _____

Previous Address _____

City _____ State _____ Zip _____

Social Security Number* _____

Date of Birth _____

Sincerely,

(Sign name)

*Also enclose a copy of your driver's license and any bill with your name and address printed on it for identification.

If you haven't been turned down for credit, there a fee is charged, the average being $8.50 for each report, but varying by state. (See Sample Credit Request Forms in Figure 11.1.) A husband and wife have separate credit reports even if they have joint accounts, so if you are married, request separate reports.

Once you have received a copy of your credit report from all three reporting agencies, review each entry. Each of the agencies breaks down its code to help you understand the report. If you find information on the credit report that is inaccurate, you have the right under the Fair Credit Reporting Act to dispute the entry with the credit reporting agency, which must rein-

FIGURE 11.1 (Continued)
SAMPLE CREDIT REPORT REQUEST FORMS—Form B

USE IF YOU HAVE *NOT* BEEN TURNED DOWN FOR CREDIT.
SAMPLE ONLY! DO NOT USE!

Dear Credit Agency,

Please send me a copy of my credit report. I am enclosing the necessary fee.

Full Name _____

Current Address _____

City _____ State _____ Zip _____

Previous Address _____

City _____ State _____ Zip _____

Social Security Number* _____

Date of Birth _____

Sincerely,

(Sign name)

*Also enclose a copy of your driver's license and any bill with your name and address printed on it for identification.

vestigate the entry with the creditor. The investigation must be completed within 30 days of the receipt of your letter of dispute. To review the act, visit <www.ftc.gov/bcp/online/pubs/credit/fcra.htm>.

If the creditor fails to respond within that 30-day period, the reporting agency must remove the entry you are disputing from the credit report. If the creditor does respond and corrects the inaccurate entry, the credit agency will update your report. It is also possible that the creditor may respond and make no changes to the credit report. If you are not satisfied with your updated credit report, you can write a 100-word statement on any of the remaining items on the credit report explaining your side of the story. This consumer statement will then appear on your credit report every time it is run. If you don't want to write this 100-word statement, you can write another dispute letter 120 days from the date of your most recent updated credit report.

Another thing you can do is contact the creditor directly and explain the errors you see it is reporting. Ask the creditor to write you a letter with the correction. Once you receive that letter, write another letter to the credit reporting agency and attach the creditor's letter. The credit reporting agency will then update its files and send you the updated credit report.

It is important that you dispute your inaccurate information with all three credit reporting agencies. An item removed by one credit bureau is not a guarantee of removal by the other two. Each credit reporting agency gets its information from its paid subscribers—that is, the creditors reporting the information. The creditor-subscribers may not subscribe to all of the credit reporting agencies, which explains why some creditors on one report are not on the others.

Disputing Your Credit Report

When engaged in a dispute with credit reporting agencies, you can use their dispute forms or write your own letter. You can also dispute by telephone or online at the credit reporting agencies' Web sites. If you write your own letter, don't be too wordy; just state the facts.

If there are more than four entries that you have to dispute on your credit report, don't dispute all of them in one letter. Break the letters up and space them every 30 days. If you are sending more than one letter with additional disputes listed, you will receive updated credit reports approximately 45 days after you mail each letter. If you haven't received an updated credit report before the time you're ready to mail your second letter, mail the letter anyway.

Once all of your dispute letters are mailed and all the updated credit reports are received, review what items were removed or corrected. If you have to repeat the process for the remaining items, space the next letters 120 days from the most recent letter.

Don't write a fictitious story; don't try to change your identity; and don't dispute information that is 100 percent accurate. (Review the entries such as amount, credit ratings, date, account numbers, and so on. Each entry must be accurate or you can dispute it.) Handwrite your letters or use your letterhead, which adds a personal touch to the letters. (See Sample Dispute Letters in Figure 11.2.)

FIGURE 11.2
SAMPLE DISPUTE LETTERS—Letter A

July 10, 2____

Dear Credit Bureau,

I am responding to a credit report I received from your company. There are errors listed.

I never paid Nelson Co. 30 days late, account number 12340. Please correct this.

My account at ABC Co. was paid off in full and not charged off. Please remove this.

I do not owe this tax lien, docket #2222222.

Com. Collection account # 4444444 is not mine.

My name is Joe L. Smith and I live at 4322 Park Ave., Anytown, CA 77777. My Social Security number is 222-00-0000. My previous address was 8765 Spring Park Way, Anytown, CA 77777. My birthdate is 11/7/65.

Sincerely,

Joe L. Smith

Requesting Your Credit Report

To request copies of your credit report, include your full name, current address, previous address, Social Security number, and date of birth.

Include with your request letter a copy of your driver's license and any bill with your name and address printed on it for identification. If you don't include this additional information, the credit reporting agency will not send you your credit report.

To request your credit reports, call each bureau to find out the fee for your state and the address of the credit reporting agency closest to you. You can also request your credit report online.

FIGURE 11.2 (Continued)
SAMPLE DISPUTE LETTERS—Letter B

(NOTICE DATE: 30 DAYS LATER)

August 10, 2_____

Dear Credit Bureau,

I am responding to a credit report I received from your company. There are errors listed.

This bankruptcy docket #987768 for $125,000 dated 9-21-98 is wrong and should not be on my credit report. Please remove this.

My account at Websters Co. was paid off in full and is not a collection account. Please remove this.

Auto Mart, account number 290596, was paid as agreed and should have a positive rating. Please correct this.

My name is Joe L. Smith and I live at 4322 Park Ave., Anytown, CA 77777. My Social Security number is 222-00-0000. My previous address was 8765 Spring Park Way, Anytown, CA 77777. My birthdate is 11/7/65.

Sincerely,

Joe L. Smith

TransUnion	Equifax	Experian
800-888-4213	800-685-1111	888-397-3742
<www.tuc.com>	<www.equifax.com>	<www.experian.com>

If you own a business and want to get your business rating, contact:
Dun & Bradstreet
908-665-5000
<www.DNB.com>

    As you review your credit report, make sure that all the accounts you paid off are indeed closed. You will have to contact each of the listed creditors by telephone and in writing requesting them to close the accounts. If you don't, it will appear as though you have unused credit that can be used against you when you apply for future credit and it can hurt your debt ratios.

Because FICO scores are being used more frequently, I recommend that you keep two to three lines of credit open and close everything else. If you have no credit activity, your FICO score can be low; but one way to have a desirable FICO score is to charge small purchases. For example, charge $25 a month and pay it off monthly, which indicates a good payment pattern.

Now that you're debt free, don't get carried away and begin running up your debt again. Remember how hard it was to pay off your high debt? If your debt is too high, your FICO scores will be lowered; for example, if you have a credit limit of $2,000 and owe $1,900, your FICO score will be lowered. Don't fall into the same trap again.

ChexSystems

If you have ever had a bank account closed for any reason—insufficient funds or overdrafts, for example—and you never paid the bank money you owed, your name may appear on a reporting system called ChexSystems.

Most banks report accounts that were closed for negative reasons to ChexSystems; and many banks subscribe to this network. If your name is on a ChexSystems report and you try to open a checking or savings account, for example, with a ChexSystems subscriber, your request will probably be denied. In fact, you would have to find a bank that is not a ChexSystems subscriber to open a new account.

ChexSystems is regulated by the Fair Credit Reporting Act, which allows you to dispute an entry by following the same procedures you do when disputing your credit report. Ask the bank that has denied you an account to give you the name of the bank that is reporting you. Also ask for the address of ChexSystems from the bank to receive a copy of your ChexSystems report.

To get more information about ChexSystems, visit <www.Aboutchecking.com>.

Reward Yourself

Unless you reward yourself for the progress you've made by getting out of debt, you'll become discouraged. Take that long-deserved vacation and celebrate. But don't overdo it. Pay cash for the vacation using traveler's checks, a debit card (in place of a Visa or MasterCard), or your credit card (but only if you have the cash in an account to pay all of it when the bill arrives).

Buy that suit or dress that you have waited for. Whatever you want to do to reward yourself (without excessive spending and within your budget), go for it. You deserve it!

DEBT DESTROYER TIPS

- Get a copy of your credit report from all three credit reporting agencies to make sure there are no errors.

- It's a good idea to get your credit report from all three credit reporting agencies at least once a year or before making a major purchase such as a home or automobile.

- Close all unused credit cards with each creditor.

- Dispute any inaccurate credit entry with the credit reporting agency reporting the item.

12

What Card Should You Have?

Now that you're debt free, make sure you can keep your credit under control. In today's society, you must have a good credit history, but you don't have to have debt to go along with it. Credit cards should be used only for convenience, an emergency, and to build a good payment history on your credit report. A credit card used for convenience should be paid off in full at the end of the month. If you need the credit card for an emergency, such as an unexpected automobile repair, pay off the balance as soon as possible. To use a credit card for creating a payment history requires making small purchases charged to your card each month—for example, $25—and paying off the balance in full at the end of each month; doing that will establish a good payment pattern. You must have an acceptable payment history to make a major purchase such as a home or automobile. The past two years of your payment history are weighed heavily in creating your FICO score, which, as noted before, is one of the main factors a lender looks at to determine whether you qualify for a preferred interest rate or whether you'll be denied credit.

There are several different types of credit cards that you can apply for. The trick is to know the differences between them and to shop for the best deal. But before looking for a credit card, know what your goals are. It's also advisable to familiarize yourself with a few phrases used in the credit world that will help you decipher a card's terms and disclosures. Finally, before you apply for any credit card, check your credit report to be certain it's in good shape, and make sure you know your FICO scores.

Types of Credit Cards

Many companies offer credit cards, the most familiar being Visa and MasterCard. Then there are travel and entertainment cards, such as American Express, Diners Club, and Carte Blanche. Department stores also have their own cards, which includes retailers such as Macy's, Bloomingdale's, and Neiman Marcus as well as Target, Sears, JC Penney, and Wal-Mart. Then there are merchant cards; for example, a credit card from a tire shop, a gasoline company, or a local housewares store. And last, but not least, there are "affinity" or incentive cards that a company or institution has cosponsored with a bank; the most familiar example is an airline card that offers frequent-flier miles or discounts on future purchases through regular use of the card.

With so many different types of credit cards out there, it's easy to see how you can have too much credit—and probably too much debt! When considering an application for credit, you have to understand that a credit card is a loan. And it's a loan that comes with a higher interest rate than the rate on a personal loan extended by a bank or a credit union. Many cards also charge an annual fee, although some don't.

In addition, you can be assessed for making a late payment or for exceeding your credit limit. Delinquent payments can cost you $25 or more per incident; and some credit card companies increase interest rates for every late payment. Think of the effect these penalties have on your credit rating. If you find it difficult to pay your bills on time, you'd be better off sticking to a debit card that subtracts money from your bank account so you aren't assessed a late penalty fee or no negative entry is made on your credit report.

Types of Credit

Let's examine how the various available cards function. Essentially, there are five types of plastic credit cards, three of which are specifically used for credit. Understanding the different uses helps to guide you in making a decision once you're ready to apply.

Bank Cards

The well-known Visa and MasterCard are universal charge cards because they're so widely accepted throughout the world. You'll often find the logos for both cards displayed at most business establishments and retail venues.

Banks and other institutions offer both Visa and MasterCard cards. Money is generated whenever you, the cardholder, use the card to make a purchase; and merchants also pay a percentage of the purchase to the card-issuing company. Credit is an extremely lucrative business with annual profits in the trillions.

When looking for either a Visa or MasterCard, I've already advised you to shop around. Both cards tend to be competitive in their interest rates; you may find rates as low as 5.99 percent or some as high as 29 percent. Be sure to compare annual fees along with the percentage charged if you take a cash advance; you'll often be assessed an additional 3 to 4 percent when taking out cash. Remember to always read the fine print associated with any card you apply for. It's also best to obtain a card that has a grace, or float, period, which means that during the 25-day to 30-day billing cycle, you won't be assessed interest or finance charges as long as you pay the balance in full within the grace period.

Gold or platinum cards are premium cards that typically have higher credit limits, usually between $5,000 to $50,000, and they offer additional privileges too. Qualifying for gold or platinum cards is more difficult than for a standard card.

Travel and Entertainment Cards

American Express, Diners Club, and Carte Blanche are considered travel and entertainment cards used frequently by business travelers. These cards generally charge an annual fee and also require full payment of the account balance each month. If you don't make full payment by the due date, you are given a one-month grace period without an interest charge, but failure to pay within this grace period results in finance charges. Should the balance still be owed after three months, the account will most likely be closed, but interest will be charged until the account is paid off.

Travel and entertainment cards have stricter credit requirements and terms than do bank cards because by the end of each billing period, travel and entertainment card holders must pay their balances in full, which is what distinguishes them from bank cards. Companies like American Express make money by charging cardholders and merchants high annual fees. For instance, American Express offers three types of cards: the green card, the gold card, and the platinum card, each with its own credit limit and annual fee. Merchants pay a fee every time the American Express card is used.

Seller Credit Cards

These are cards offered by a business such as a department store, a tire shop, a furniture or jewelry store, or even an appliance shop. Oil and gas company cards fall within this category along with airline and rental car company cards. The companies offer cards to generate more business, which explains why their cards can only be used within their own establishment. They're convenient, but be careful! These cards generally have very high interest rates, even though most don't have annual fees; it's far wiser to use a bank card with a low interest rate than it is to use several seller cards with their typically higher interest rates.

ATM Cards

Banks, savings and loans, and credit unions all offer automated teller machine (ATM) cards, which are available 24 hours a day and thus give customers greater flexibility in using banking services. You can use your ATM card to withdraw money from your account, make a deposit, transfer money, check your account balance, and make a loan payment; a few machines even let you purchase postage stamps. So long as you use your own bank's or an affiliated branch's ATM, you won't be charged a fee. If you use another bank's machine, however, you will probably be charged a service fee; and these fees can add up quickly, so take that into consideration. ATM transactions and fees are not included in your credit report.

Debit Cards

Banks issue debit cards, which are basically ATM cards that also work as a check when you make a purchase. Typically, debit cards display a Visa or MasterCard logo, but unlike a credit card, the purchase amount is immediately subtracted from your checking account. The processing time of a debit transaction can take a few minutes or a few days. You can also use the debit card to get cash from your bank's ATM. Just be sure that you track all of your purchases and withdrawals as you would with ATM withdrawals from your checking account and other ATM transactions. No credit is associated with a debit card, so if you make a mistake and overdraw your account, you'll be charged overdraft fees and be required to pay for any debts you incur.

Distinctions between a Credit Card and a Debit Card

- A credit card offers a float period because you are not required to pay the transaction amount immediately. A debit card registers a transaction deduction immediately.
- If a dispute should arise, you have more leverage with a credit card because it creates a bill rather than paying a bill as a debit card does.
- If you lose your credit card or if it is stolen, your liability is less than it is with a debit card.

CREDIT CARD ORGANIZER WORKSHEET

Exercise: To better organize your credit records, list the cards that you presently have. Include the creditor's name and address and your account number.

Major Credit Cards (Discover, Visa, MasterCard)

_____   _____
_____   _____
_____   _____
_____   _____

Charge Cards (oil & gas company and department, furniture, jewelry, and tire stores)

_____   _____
_____   _____
_____   _____
_____   _____

Travel and Entertainment Cards (American Express, Carte Blanche, Diners Club)

_____   _____
_____   _____
_____   _____
_____   _____

ATM and Debit Cards

_____   _____
_____   _____
_____   _____
_____   _____

- Interest is generally charged for credit card transactions that are not paid off by the billing date. Debit cards charge no interest; they only deduct the amount of the purchase from your account.
- A credit card has no connection to your *bank account*, but it is the bank where you have an open account that issues an ATM or debit card.
- Your credit card payment history is reported on your credit report. Debit card transactions are not reported to a credit reporting agency.

Shopping for Credit

To assist you with your credit card research, you can visit <www.card trak.com> for listings of various credit cards as well as a list of different banks and relevant institutions. You can look for specific types of cards, such as gold cards carrying a higher limit and higher interest rates or low-interest-rate cards or cards with no annual fee. The Web site also includes a list of secured credit cards for individuals who have had past credit problems or a bankruptcy.

Questions You Want to Ask a Card Issuer

- How much is the annual fee?
- What is the interest rate?
- Is there a grace period? (Most banks have a 20-day to 25-day grace period for paying off your new current balance to avoid your paying interest.)
- What will your credit limit be?
- What are the interest or finance charges for credit card transactions?
- How much is your over-the-limit fee?
- How much is your late fee?

Secured Credit Cards: Caution!

A number of banks offer secured credit cards to individuals who have had past credit problems or a bankruptcy. A secured credit card can be helpful in reestablishing credit, but you must understand how a secured credit card works.

Basically, a secured credit card is one with a bank that requires you to deposit a certain amount of money into a savings account and then issues you a Visa or MasterCard with a credit limit of the amount of your deposit. For example, if you deposited $400 into an account, you would have a $400 credit limit. Secured credit cards charge higher interest rates and annual fees; however, they also pay interest on the deposit you make in your account.

Many banks that offer secured credit cards may be located outside your state, so contact the Better Business Bureau to check out the bank. When submitting your application and deposit, mail it via registered mail and request a return receipt. Most important: *Be absolutely sure the company you're sending money to is a legitimate bank and not a phony business or a scam!* Check with your bank to see if it offers a secured credit card program.

Card Approval and Usage

Secured cards are not marked as such, so most people can't tell a secured card from a regular one. A large number of people who apply for a secured card are approved because the bank has a deposit that secures any transactions on which cardholders may default. If you are turned down for a secured card, chances are your application was incomplete. A letter explaining why you were turned down will be sent to your return address and should explain why your application was denied.

Be sure to make all of your payments on time as your payment patterns will be reported to one of the three credit reporting agencies (Equifax, Experian, TransUnion). If you've never had credit, a solid payment history with a secured card will help you establish credit. If you've previously had problem credit or no credit at all, a secured card can help you rebuild your credit rating.

You can close your account at any time as long as your charges have all been paid off. Once you establish a good payment history, apply for a preferred card with lower interest rates. Once approved for a preferred card, you may wish to cancel your secured card. Just continue making steady payments and limit the number of cards you apply for. Don't lose track of your initial credit goals.

Banks That Offer Secured Credit Cards

Again, make sure that the bank or company you're dealing with is legitimate. You may want to try your own bank first to see if it offers a secured credit card. If you do apply for a secured credit card from an advertisement, call the number listed on the application and also see if it has a customer assistance program. Finally, contact your better business bureau to see if the bank or institution has had any complaints against it. Remember: You cannot be too cautious when dealing with your money and credit.

To help you find a secured credit card, visit <www.cardtrak.com> for the banks that provide these cards. You should also complete the following worksheet: Tracking Your Secured Credit Cards.

Teaser Rate Credit Cards

Teaser rate credit cards offer low interest rates initially—but only for a short period. Should you apply for a teaser card, you need to know how long the low interest rate period will be. Next, you'll need to know what the increase will be once that period is up. Banks and companies offer teaser rates to generate business; many people respond but fail to read the fine print and may end up with higher interest rates than they would if they'd applied for another card. It's up to you to exercise caution when applying for credit. If a deal looks too good to be true, it probably is.

TRACKING YOUR SECURED CREDIT CARDS WORKSHEET

When applying for secured credit cards, you'll want to keep track of the following information, especially the amount you put down as a deposit along with the interest the bank has to pay you for that deposit.

Name of bank or company _____
Visa or MasterCard _____
Minimum deposit _____
Annual fee _____
Interest rate _____
Interest paid by bank _____

Name of bank or company _____
Visa or MasterCard _____
Minimum deposit _____
Annual fee _____
Interest rate _____
Interest paid by bank _____

Name of bank or company _____
Visa or MasterCard _____
Minimum deposit _____
Annual fee _____
Interest rate _____
Interest paid by bank _____

If you decide to transfer your balances to a low-interest-rate credit card, make sure that you close the accounts that you are transferring. This will look better on your credit report.

Lana's Story

When Lana received an offer for a low-interest-rate card, she applied and was approved. When she received her credit card, Lana moved all her high-interest-rate credit cards to the lower-rate card.

After several months in which Lana's payments were made on time, one of the payments arrived one day after the due date to the creditor. Lana's interest rate shot up higher than the interest rates of the credit cards she had transferred, and her payments sky-rocketed.

When Lana called and told me the situation, I asked if she had read the fine print on the disclosure that accompanied the initial application. The disclosure indicated that if a payment was one day late, the interest rate would increase. By not reading the fine print, Lana learned the hard way. She eventually refinanced her house and was able to pay off the credit card.

Preapproved and Unsolicited Credit Cards

As I've already mentioned, the credit business generates huge profits each year. Frequently, to generate even more business, companies will mail out preapproved credit card applications. If you receive one of these preapproved applications, don't believe the hype. Read the fine print. Normally, the form will be fairly simple and straightforward, but it will require your signature. When you sign one of these applications, you are giving the creditor permission to run a credit check on you. The credit card company can also report any activity that you've had with it.

The catch: Should your credit history fail to meet the creditor's standards, you won't receive a credit card, or the credit limits offered might be low as protection for the company against potential problems. Should you be granted a low credit limit, however, chances are you can increase it by establishing a good payment pattern.

Review Your Application

Be sure to look for the following information on your preapproved credit card application:

- Fixed or variable interest
- Account balance ranges
- Monthly finance charges
- Yearly interest rates or annual percentage rate (APR)
- Yearly fee
- The number of days you're allowed to pay off the full balance without incurring an interest charge (the grace or float period)
- Whether interest is charged once a purchase is made must be stated on the application
- Cash advance fees, late charges, over-the-limit fees, and/or returned check fees

On receipt of the credit card, all account activity begins.

Preapproved Cards in the Mail

If you receive a preapproved credit card in the mail and decide that you don't want it, *do not throw it away!* First, by throwing it away you risk someone else using it. Second, you haven't informed the company issuing the card that you're not interested; and failure to do so will result in an open

FIGURE 12.1
SAMPLE PREAPPROVED CREDIT CARD REJECTION LETTER

Month/Date/2____

Big Deal Credit Company
16875 Main Street
Luckytown, State, Zip

Sent via Certified Mail

Re: Account Number 0123456789

Dear Customer Service Department,

I received a Big Deal preapproved credit card in the mail. I have no interest in your card services at this time. I've cut the card up and am returning it with this letter. Kindly cancel my account immediately.

Yours truly,

Jane Byers

account. If the company charges an annual fee (which of course, you don't pay), a negative entry could be made on your credit report. Also, when potential creditors see your open account, they may deny any future credit applications from you because you have too much current credit.

To avoid these scenarios, cut up the credit card and return it to the issuer. Include a letter telling the company that you are not interested in using the card or having an open account with the company (see Figure 12.1). Make sure to send this letter certified mail and request a return receipt; this will help you avoid a credit entry on your report. Follow this same process for any card you don't want or don't want to renew. Wait three weeks and then request a copy of your credit report. Review it, checking to see that no entry was reported.

Allison's Story

Allison received a preapproved credit card in the mail. She didn't want the card, so she just threw it in the trash. As time went by, she began receiving credit card statements in the mail. She threw these in the trash, never opening them thinking the card was canceled. Some time later, she needed to request a copy of her credit report. To her surprise, she found negative entries on it made by the company whose card she'd thrown in the trash. Her report stated that she'd failed to make payment.

When Allison contacted the company about the entry, she was told that she'd failed to make the annual fee payment. She responded that she'd thrown the card in the trash. Because she failed to inform the company directly, they refused to waive the fee.

The Importance of Limiting Your Credit

You've just read about the different types of credit cards and their functions. You've familiarized yourself with standard credit phrases and terminology, and you've learned to read the fine print on any credit application you sign and submit. Now it's important that you consider how much credit you can handle. For most people, two to three cards are enough. I suggest using only one card and reserving the other two for emergencies. You may want to carry one card and put the other two in a safe place.

In general, most people can only manage a 10 percent debt ratio. Never charge items under $25 dollars unless you are trying to build a credit history; use cash instead. Plan credit purchases to avoid impulse buys, and strive to pay off your credit card balance each month. If you find yourself tempted to purchase something you can't afford, don't buy it. Wait a few days. Given some time to reconsider, most of us can withstand the temptation to buy on a whim. Remember that you want to avoid overextending yourself and falling back into the debt trap.

D E B T   D E S T R O Y E R   T I P S

- Use your credit cards only for convenience (pay back your accounts in full at the end of the month), an emergency, or to build a good payment history.

- Get rid of your high-interest department store cards and use a low-interest Visa or MasterCard.

- Keep open only two or three credit card accounts.

- Close all credit card accounts that you transfer to a low-interest credit card account.

- Close all unused credit card accounts.

13

Breaking the Habits of Debt

With your newfound freedom from debt, it's never too late to set new financial goals. Your first goal was to be debt free, and you have accomplished that.

Your new goals should be building wealth. Think of the years you've lost in savings just by being in debt. The most important thing you can do to build wealth is break the habits of debt. If your old habits of spending aren't broken, it won't be long until the urge to use your credit cards reappears.

You'll have days when you feel the urge to go out and spend. That's normal. But don't do it! You will save yourself from starting the debt cycle all over again.

If you refinanced your home or took out an equity loan on your home to pay off your debts, don't start using your credit cards again. If you do, you risk running up more debt followed by your debt ratios becoming too high and possibly going into bankruptcy or losing your home in a foreclosure. These are all results of not being able to pay your bills.

Plan ahead on a weekly, monthly, and yearly basis what you will spend. Have family meetings so both you and your spouse agree on all the expenditures.

If you own your own business, calculate every week what you need to spend money on. And always be ahead of what you need.

You can begin saving once you have broken the habits of debt. By getting in the habit of applying extra money from your paid-off debt to reducing the remaining debt, you can begin saving. All of the money you were using to pay off your debts can begin to work for you instead of against you. You can begin to make money.

Goals to Aim For

1. Don't use credit cards for purchases unless you have the money to pay the bill in full when it arrives at the end of the month. Refer to your budget. Pay by check or debit card and register each purchase. Open an interest-paying checking account. Keep your spending journal with you to show how your cash was spent and what you charged. This will remind you not to make frivolous purchases.

2. Start saving your money; aim for saving at least 10 percent of your take-home pay. Contact a financial planner to help you invest your money to make it grow.

3. Have an emergency fund built up that will equal at least four months of living expenses.

4. Open a separate account to deposit money for your nonmonthly expenses such as property taxes, insurance, auto maintenance, repairs, and the like. Deposit cash monthly into this account based on your yearly budget.

5. Buy insurance to protect your family. Shop around and buy only what you need.

6. Set up a retirement account because Social Security won't be enough for you to live on. Open an IRA or 401(k) at your place of business. Chances are your employer will match part of what you contribute, which will make your investment worth even more. Consult a financial planner to determine how much you need to save each month to apply toward retirement.

7. Give to your local charity, church, or religious organization, or any needy cause. When you are able to give to a worthy cause, you'll feel great knowing you have helped others—and you'll receive a tax deduction. Your donations don't necessarily have to be cash either; American Vets and many other charitable groups, for example, accept clothing and small household items, and will provide you with a receipt.

8. Purchase a home. The ability to purchase a home provides you the security of an investment that will increase in value. It will also allow you to write off your interest and property taxes.

9. Consider what you need for college funds. If you were able to set money aside toward your child's educational fund, then neither you nor your child will require student loans. The earlier you start saving, the more you'll have. A financial planner can help you calculate

the approximate cost of college and how much you should be saving on a monthly basis.

10. Invest in your business by having ready cash to put back into your business, and your profits should increase. Dreams of starting a business are more of a reality if your finances are in order.

Now that you can take a breath of fresh air, make a list of dreams that you can turn into reality by being debt free—and go for it! Complete the following Debt-Free Dream List Worksheet.

DEBT DESTROYER TIPS

- If you feel the urge to charge, go home and sleep on it.

- Don't run up new charges after you have refinanced your home to pay off your bills. Not even if it's "just this one time."

- Start making your dreams come true.

DEBT-FREE DREAM LIST WORKSHEET

Make a list of all the things you can now do as a result of being debt free.

Examples:

1. Start a college fund
2. Start a business
3. Go on a vacation
4. Save for a dream house
5. Invest more money for retirement
6. _____
7. _____
8. _____
9. _____
10. _____
11. _____
12. _____
13. _____
14. _____
15. _____
16. _____
17. _____
18. _____
19. _____
20. _____

MAKE A PLEDGE TO YOURSELF

1. I know that I have a weakness when it comes to credit cards.

2. If I am tempted to use my credit cards, I will walk away from the situation and reassess the purchase.

3. I will pay off my credit card balances every month.

4. I will keep a daily journal of all my expenses, credit card charges, and cash expenditures.

5. I will put 10 percent of my income into a savings plan.

6. I will have monthly meetings with my spouse to review our budget.

7. I will set financial goals.

8. I will make sure the mortgage, rent, utilities, and food bills are paid first.

9. I will seek professional help from a credit counselor if my debt ratio is above 20 percent or if I'm having trouble paying my bills.

10. I will seek the assistance of a financial planner to set up a plan for retirement and investments.

Signature _____ Date _____

Spouse's Signature _____ Date _____

$$\boxed{\text{A}}$$

Cost Savings Converting to a Biweekly Mortgage

Based on 12%, $100,000 loan amount, 30 years

Year	Loan Balance		Yearly Interest Paid		Yearly Principal Paid		Total Interest	
	Biweekly	Standard	Biweekly	Standard	Biweekly	Standard	Biweekly	Standard
2002	98,781.08	99,700.65	10,095.82	9,986.77	1,218.92	299.35	210,095.82	129,986.77
2003	97,171.93	99,299.80	11,762.82	11,942.51	1,609.15	400.84	21,858.64	21,929.28
2004	95,358.13	98,848.12	11,558.16	11,891.67	1,813.81	451.68	33,416.79	33,820.95
2005	93,313.63	98,339.16	11,327.47	11,834.38	2,044.50	508.97	44,744.26	45,655.34
2006	91,009.10	97,765.64	11,067.44	11,769.84	2,304.53	573.52	55,811.70	57,425.17
2007	88,411.47	97,119.39	10,774.33	11,697.10	2,597.63	646.25	66,586.03	69,122.27
2008	85,483.46	96,391.18	10,443.95	11,615.14	2,928.01	728.21	77,029.98	80,737.41
2009	82,183.05	95,570.61	10,071.55	11,522.78	3,300.41	820.57	87,101.53	92,260.19
2010	78,462.87	94,645.97	9,651.79	11,418.71	3,720.18	924.64	96,753.32	103,678.90
2011	74,269.54	93,604.07	9,178.63	11,301.45	4,193.33	1,041.90	105,931.95	114,980.35
2012	69,542.88	92,430.02	8,645.30	11,169.31	4,726.66	1,174.04	114,577.26	126,149.66
2013	64,215.05	91,107.08	8,044.14	11,020.41	5,327.83	1,322.94	122,621.39	137,170.07
2014	58,209.61	89,616.35	7,366.52	10,852.63	6,005.45	1,490.72	129,987.91	148,022.69
2015	51,440.35	87,936.57	6,602.71	10,663.57	6,769.25	1,679.79	136,590.62	158,686.26
2016	43,810.15	86,043.75	5,741.76	10,450.53	7,630.21	1,892.82	142,332.38	169,136.79
2017	35,209.49	83,910.86	4,771.30	10,210.47	8,600.66	2,132.88	147,103.68	179,347.26
2018	25,514.95	81,507.48	3,677.42	9,939.97	9,694.54	2,403.38	150,781.11	189,287.22
2019	14,587.40	78,799.28	2,444.42	9,635.16	10,927.54	2,708.19	153,225.53	198,922.38
2020	2,270.03	75,747.62	1,054.59	9,291.69	12,317.37	3,051.66	154,280.12	208,214.07
2021	0.00	72,308.94	29.02	8,904.66	2,270.03	3,438.69	154,309.14	217,118.73
2022	0.00	68,434.14	0.00	8,468.55	0.00	3,874.80	154,309.14	225,587.29
2023	0.00	64,067.92	0.00	7,977.13	0.00	4,366.22	154,309.14	233,564.42
2024	0.00	59,147.95	0.00	7,423.38	0.00	4,919.97	154,309.14	240,987.80
2025	0.00	53,604.01	0.00	6,799.41	0.00	5,543.94	154,309.14	247,787.21
2026	0.00	47,356.96	0.00	6,096.30	0.00	6,247.05	154,309.14	253,883.51
2027	0.00	40,317.62	0.00	5,304.02	0.00	7,039.34	154,309.14	259,187.53
2028	0.00	32,385.52	0.00	4,411.25	0.00	7,932.10	154,309.14	263,598.78
2029	0.00	23,447.43	0.00	3,405.26	0.00	8,938.09	154,309.14	267,004.04
2030	0.00	13,375.77	0.00	2,271.69	0.00	10,071.66	154,309.14	269,275.73
2031	0.00	2,026.77	0.00	994.35	0.00	11,349.00	154,309.14	270,270.08
2032	0.00	0.00	0.00	30.45	0.00	2,026.77	154,309.14	270,300.53

Source: <www.mortgage-x.com>.

Based on 11.75%, $100,000 loan amount, 30 years

Year	Loan Balance		Yearly Interest Paid		Yearly Principal Paid		Total Interest	
	Biweekly	Standard	Biweekly	Standard	Biweekly	Standard	Biweekly	Standard
2002	98,782.00	99,683.89	9,885.51	9,777.99	1,218.00	316.11	9,885.51	9,777.99
2003	97,177.78	99,261.57	11,518.10	11,690.59	1,604.23	422.32	21,403.61	21,468.58
2004	95,374.01	98,786.86	11,318.56	11,638.21	1,803.77	474.71	32,722.17	33,106.79
2005	93,345.89	98,253.27	11,094.20	11,579.33	2,028.13	533.59	43,816.37	44,686.11
2006	91,065.49	97,653.49	10,841.93	11,513.14	2,280.39	599.78	54,658.31	56,199.26
2007	88,501.46	96,979.32	10,558.29	11,438.74	2,564.04	674.17	65,216.60	67,638.00
2008	85,618.50	96,221.52	10,239.37	11,355.12	2,882.96	757.80	75,455.96	78,993.12
2009	82,376.94	95,369.73	9,880.77	11,261.12	3,241.56	851.79	85,336.73	90,254.24
2010	78,732.19	94,412.28	9,477.57	11,155.47	3,644.75	957.45	94,814.31	101,409.71
2011	74,634.09	93,336.07	9,024.23	11,036.71	4,098.10	1,076.21	103,838.53	112,446.42
2012	70,026.25	92,126.37	8,514.49	10,903.22	4,607.84	1,209.70	112,353.02	123,349.64
2013	64,845.27	90,766.62	7,941.35	10,753.17	5,180.98	1,359.75	120,294.36	134,102.80
2014	59,019.85	89,238.21	7,296.91	10,584.50	5,825.41	1,528.41	127,591.28	144,687.31
2015	52,469.85	87,520.21	6,572.33	10,394.92	6,550.00	1,718.00	134,163.61	155,082.23
2016	45,105.14	85,589.12	5,757.61	10,181.82	7,364.71	1,931.09	139,921.22	165,264.05
2017	36,824.37	83,418.49	4,841.56	9,942.29	8,280.77	2,170.63	144,762.78	175,206.34
2018	27,513.61	80,978.63	3,811.57	9,673.05	9,310.76	2,439.87	148,574.34	184,879.39
2019	17,044.74	78,236.12	2,653.46	9,370.41	10,468.87	2,742.51	151,227.80	194,249.80
2020	5,273.71	75,153.44	1,351.30	9,030.23	11,771.03	3,082.68	152,579.10	203,280.04
2021	0.00	71,688.38	141.00	8,647.86	5,273.71	3,465.06	152,720.10	211,927.90
2022	0.00	67,793.52	0.00	8,218.06	0.00	3,894.86	152,720.10	220,145.96
2023	0.00	63,415.55	0.00	7,734.94	0.00	4,377.97	152,720.10	227,880.90
2024	0.00	58,494.53	0.00	7,191.90	0.00	4,921.01	152,720.10	235,072.80
2025	0.00	52,963.12	0.00	6,581.51	0.00	5,531.41	152,720.10	241,654.31
2026	0.00	46,745.60	0.00	5,895.40	0.00	6,217.52	152,720.10	247,549.70
2027	0.00	39,756.87	0.00	5,124.18	0.00	6,988.74	152,720.10	252,673.88
2028	0.00	31,901.25	0.00	4,257.30	0.00	7,855.61	152,720.10	256,931.19
2029	0.00	23,071.24	0.00	3,282.90	0.00	8,830.02	152,720.10	260,214.09
2030	0.00	13,145.95	0.00	2,187.63	0.00	9,925.28	152,720.10	262,401.72
2031	0.00	1,989.55	0.00	956.51	0.00	11,156.40	152,720.10	263,358.24
2032	0.00	0.00	0.00	29.27	0.00	1,989.55	152,720.10	263,387.50

Source: <www.mortgage-x.com>.

Based on 11.5%, $100,000 loan amount, 30 years

Year	Loan Balance		Yearly Interest Paid		Yearly Principal Paid		Total Interest	
	Biweekly	Standard	Biweekly	Standard	Biweekly	Standard	Biweekly	Standard
2002	98,781.95	99,666.28	9,675.16	9,569.19	1,218.05	333.72	9,675.16	9,569.19
2003	97,181.35	99,221.44	11,273.19	11,438.66	1,600.60	444.84	20,948.34	21,007.85
2004	95,386.13	98,722.66	11,078.57	11,384.72	1,795.22	498.78	32,026.91	32,392.57
2005	93,372.64	98,163.40	10,860.29	11,324.24	2,013.50	559.26	42,887.21	43,716.81
2006	91,114.32	97,536.33	10,615.47	11,256.42	2,258.32	627.07	53,502.68	54,973.23
2007	88,581.42	96,833.22	10,340.89	11,180.38	2,532.90	703.11	63,843.57	66,153.62
2008	85,740.54	96,044.84	10,032.91	11,095.12	2,840.87	788.37	73,876.48	77,248.74
2009	82,554.25	95,160.87	9,687.50	10,999.53	3,186.29	883.97	83,563.98	88,248.27
2010	78,980.54	94,169.71	9,300.08	10,892.34	3,573.71	991.16	92,864.05	99,140.60
2011	74,972.30	93,058.37	8,865.55	10,772.15	4,008.24	1,111.35	101,729.61	109,912.75
2012	70,476.71	91,812.26	8,378.20	10,637.39	4,495.59	1,246.11	110,107.80	120,550.14
2013	65,434.50	90,415.05	7,831.58	10,486.39	5,042.21	1,397.21	117,939.38	131,036.43
2014	59,779.22	88,848.41	7,218.50	10,316.86	5,655.28	1,566.64	125,157.89	141,353.29
2015	53,436.32	87,091.81	6,530.88	10,126.89	6,342.90	1,756.60	131,688.77	151,480.18
2016	46,322.18	85,122.20	5,759.66	9,913.89	7,114.13	1,969.61	137,448.43	161,394.07
2017	38,343.05	82,913.75	4,894.66	9,675.05	7,979.13	2,208.44	142,343.09	171,069.13
2018	29,393.74	80,437.52	3,924.48	9,407.26	8,949.31	2,476.24	146,267.57	180,476.39
2019	19,356.30	77,661.01	2,836.34	9,106.99	10,037.44	2,776.50	149,103.91	189,583.38
2020	8,098.41	74,547.83	1,615.90	8,770.32	11,257.89	3,113.18	150,719.81	198,353.69
2021	0.00	71,057.15	326.46	8,392.81	8,098.41	3,490.68	151,046.28	206,746.51
2022	0.00	67,143.19	0.00	7,969.54	0.00	3,913.96	151,046.28	214,716.04
2023	0.00	62,754.62	0.00	7,494.93	0.00	4,388.57	151,046.28	222,210.97
2024	0.00	57,833.90	0.00	6,962.78	0.00	4,920.72	151,046.28	229,173.75
2025	0.00	52,316.50	0.00	6,366.09	0.00	5,517.40	151,046.28	235,539.85
2026	0.00	46,130.05	0.00	5,697.06	0.00	6,186.44	151,046.28	241,236.90
2027	0.00	39,193.45	0.00	4,946.89	0.00	6,936.60	151,046.28	246,183.80
2028	0.00	31,415.72	0.00	4,105.77	0.00	7,777.73	151,046.28	250,289.56
2029	0.00	22,694.86	0.00	3,162.64	0.00	8,720.85	151,046.28	253,452.20
2030	0.00	12,916.53	0.00	2,105.16	0.00	9,778.34	151,046.28	255,557.36
2031	0.00	1,952.47	0.00	919.44	0.00	10,964.05	151,046.28	256,476.80
2032	0.00	0.00	0.00	28.11	0.00	1,952.47	151,046.28	256,504.92

Source: <www.mortgage-x.com>.

Based on 11.25%, $100,000 loan amount, 30 years

Year	Loan Balance		Yearly Interest Paid		Yearly Principal Paid		Total Interest	
	Biweekly	Standard	Biweekly	Standard	Biweekly	Standard	Biweekly	Standard
2002	98,780.88	99,647.78	9,464.76	9,360.39	1,219.12	352.22	9,464.76	9,360.39
2003	97,182.57	99,179.35	11,028.08	11,186.71	1,598.32	468.43	20,492.84	20,547.11
2004	95,394.37	98,655.43	10,838.20	11,131.21	1,788.20	523.93	31,331.04	31,678.31
2005	93,393.73	98,069.42	10,625.76	11,069.13	2,000.64	586.01	41,956.80	42,747.44
2006	91,155.42	97,413.98	10,388.08	10,999.70	2,238.31	655.44	52,344.89	53,747.14
2007	88,651.19	96,680.88	10,122.17	10,922.04	2,504.23	733.10	62,467.06	64,669.18
2008	85,849.46	95,860.92	9,824.67	10,835.17	2,801.73	819.96	72,291.72	75,504.35
2009	82,714.88	94,943.80	9,491.82	10,738.02	3,134.58	917.12	81,783.54	86,242.37
2010	79,207.91	93,918.02	9,119.43	10,629.35	3,506.97	1,025.78	90,902.97	96,871.73
2011	75,284.31	92,770.70	8,702.80	10,507.81	3,923.60	1,147.32	99,605.77	107,379.54
2012	70,894.59	91,487.43	8,236.67	10,371.87	4,389.73	1,283.26	107,842.44	117,751.41
2013	65,983.36	90,052.12	7,715.17	10,219.82	4,911.23	1,435.31	115,557.61	127,971.24
2014	60,488.67	88,446.74	7,131.71	10,049.76	5,494.69	1,605.38	122,689.32	138,021.00
2015	54,341.21	86,651.15	6,478.94	9,859.54	6,147.46	1,795.59	129,168.26	147,880.54
2016	47,463.43	84,642.81	5,748.62	9,646.79	6,877.78	2,008.34	134,916.88	157,527.33
2017	39,768.57	82,396.50	4,931.53	9,408.83	7,694.87	2,246.30	139,848.41	166,936.17
2018	31,159.54	79,884.04	4,017.38	9,142.68	8,609.02	2,512.46	143,865.79	176,078.84
2019	21,527.77	77,073.89	2,994.62	8,844.99	9,631.78	2,810.15	146,860.41	184,923.83
2020	10,751.72	73,930.78	1,850.36	8,512.02	10,776.04	3,143.11	148,710.76	193,435.85
2021	0.00	70,415.25	575.10	8,139.61	10,751.72	3,515.53	149,285.87	201,575.46
2022	0.00	66,483.18	0.00	7,723.07	0.00	3,932.07	149,285.87	209,298.52
2023	0.00	62,085.21	0.00	7,257.17	0.00	4,397.97	149,285.87	216,555.70
2024	0.00	57,166.15	0.00	6,736.07	0.00	4,919.06	149,285.87	223,291.77
2025	0.00	51,664.25	0.00	6,153.23	0.00	5,501.90	149,285.87	229,445.00
2026	0.00	45,510.45	0.00	5,501.34	0.00	6,153.80	149,285.87	234,946.34
2027	0.00	38,627.51	0.00	4,772.20	0.00	6,882.94	149,285.87	239,718.54
2028	0.00	30,929.04	0.00	3,956.67	0.00	7,698.47	149,285.87	243,675.20
2029	0.00	22,318.41	0.00	3,044.51	0.00	8,610.63	149,285.87	246,719.71
2030	0.00	12,687.54	0.00	2,024.27	0.00	9,630.87	149,285.87	248,743.98
2031	0.00	1,915.54	0.00	883.14	0.00	10,771.99	149,285.87	249,627.12
2032	0.00	0.00	0.00	26.98	0.00	1,915.54	149,285.87	249,654.10

Source: <www.mortgage-x.com>.

Based on 11%, $100,000 loan amount, 30 years

Year	Loan Balance		Yearly Interest Paid		Yearly Principal Paid		Total Interest	
	Biweekly	Standard	Biweekly	Standard	Biweekly	Standard	Biweekly	Standard
2002	98,778.76	99,628.36	9,254.32	9,151.59	1,221.24	371.64	9,254.32	9,151.59
2003	97,181.35	99,135.23	10,782.79	10,934.75	1,597.41	493.13	20,037.11	20,086.34
2004	95,398.60	98,585.03	10,597.46	10,877.68	1,782.74	550.20	30,634.57	30,964.03
2005	93,409.02	97,971.17	10,390.63	10,814.02	1,989.58	613.86	41,025.19	41,778.04
2006	91,188.62	97,286.27	10,159.80	10,742.98	2,220.41	684.90	51,184.99	52,521.02
2007	88,710.60	96,522.11	9,902.19	10,663.72	2,478.02	764.16	61,087.18	63,184.75
2008	85,945.09	95,669.53	9,614.69	10,575.30	2,765.51	852.58	70,701.87	73,760.04
2009	82,858.72	94,718.28	9,293.84	10,476.64	3,086.37	951.24	79,995.71	84,236.68
2010	79,414.28	93,656.96	8,935.76	10,366.56	3,444.44	1,061.32	88,931.47	94,603.24
2011	75,570.22	92,472.83	8,536.14	10,243.75	3,844.06	1,184.13	97,467.61	104,846.99
2012	71,280.17	91,151.67	8,090.16	10,106.72	4,290.05	1,321.16	105,557.77	114,953.71
2013	66,492.40	89,677.62	7,592.43	9,953.84	4,787.78	1,474.04	113,150.20	124,907.54
2014	61,149.15	88,033.00	7,036.96	9,783.26	5,343.25	1,644.62	120,187.15	134,690.80
2015	55,185.98	86,198.07	6,417.04	9,592.95	5,963.17	1,834.93	126,604.19	144,283.75
2016	48,530.97	84,150.80	5,725.20	9,380.61	6,655.01	2,047.27	132,329.38	153,664.36
2017	41,103.85	81,866.62	4,953.09	9,143.70	7,427.12	2,284.18	137,282.47	162,808.07
2018	32,815.05	79,318.12	4,091.40	8,879.38	8,288.80	2,548.50	141,373.87	171,687.45
2019	23,564.58	76,474.71	3,129.74	8,584.47	9,250.46	2,843.41	144,503.61	180,271.92
2020	13,240.89	73,302.27	2,056.51	8,255.44	10,323.69	3,172.44	146,560.12	188,527.35
2021	1,719.45	69,762.71	858.76	7,888.32	11,521.44	3,539.56	147,418.89	196,415.68
2022	0.00	65,813.56	17.16	7,478.73	1,719.45	3,949.15	147,436.05	203,894.41
2023	0.00	61,407.42	0.00	7,021.74	0.00	4,406.14	147,436.05	210,916.15
2024	0.00	56,491.41	0.00	6,511.87	0.00	4,916.01	147,436.05	217,428.02
2025	0.00	51,006.52	0.00	5,942.99	0.00	5,484.89	147,436.05	223,371.01
2026	0.00	44,886.92	0.00	5,308.29	0.00	6,119.60	147,436.05	228,679.29
2027	0.00	38,059.17	0.00	4,600.13	0.00	6,827.75	147,436.05	233,279.43
2028	0.00	30,441.33	0.00	3,810.03	0.00	7,617.85	147,436.05	237,089.46
2029	0.00	21,941.95	0.00	2,928.51	0.00	8,499.37	147,436.05	240,017.97
2030	0.00	12,459.04	0.00	1,944.97	0.00	9,482.91	147,436.05	241,962.93
2031	0.00	1,878.77	0.00	847.62	0.00	10,580.26	147,436.05	242,810.55
2032	0.00	0.00	0.00	25.87	0.00	1,878.77	147,436.05	242,836.42

Source: <www.mortgage-x.com>.

Based on 10.75%, $100,000 loan amount, 30 years

Year	Loan Balance		Yearly Interest Paid		Yearly Principal Paid		Total Interest	
	Biweekly	Standard	Biweekly	Standard	Biweekly	Standard	Biweekly	Standard
2002	98,775.54	99,607.97	9,043.84	8,942.79	1,224.46	392.03	9,043.84	8,942.79
2003	97,177.60	99,088.98	10,537.32	10,682.78	1,597.94	519.00	19,581.15	19,625.57
2004	95,398.70	98,511.36	10,356.36	10,624.16	1,778.90	577.62	29,937.52	30,249.72
2005	93,418.36	97,868.49	10,154.91	10,558.91	1,980.35	642.87	40,092.43	40,808.63
2006	91,213.75	97,153.00	9,930.65	10,486.29	2,204.61	715.49	50,023.07	51,294.92
2007	88,759.48	96,356.70	9,680.99	10,405.47	2,454.27	796.31	59,704.06	61,700.39
2008	86,027.28	95,470.44	9,403.06	10,315.52	2,732.20	886.25	69,107.12	72,015.92
2009	82,985.68	94,484.08	9,093.65	10,215.41	3,041.61	986.36	78,200.78	82,231.33
2010	79,599.63	93,386.30	8,749.21	10,104.00	3,386.05	1,097.78	86,949.98	92,335.32
2011	75,830.13	92,164.51	8,365.76	9,979.99	3,769.50	1,221.78	95,315.74	102,315.32
2012	71,633.76	90,804.72	7,938.89	9,841.98	4,196.37	1,359.79	103,254.63	112,157.30
2013	66,962.17	89,291.32	7,463.67	9,688.38	4,671.59	1,513.39	110,718.30	121,845.68
2014	61,761.55	87,606.98	6,934.64	9,517.43	5,200.62	1,684.34	117,652.94	131,363.11
2015	55,972.00	85,732.38	6,345.70	9,327.17	5,789.56	1,874.60	123,998.64	140,690.28
2016	49,526.81	83,646.02	5,690.07	9,115.42	6,445.19	2,086.36	129,688.71	149,805.70
2017	42,351.74	81,323.99	4,960.19	8,879.75	7,175.07	2,322.03	134,648.90	158,685.45
2018	34,364.13	78,739.67	4,147.65	8,617.46	7,987.60	2,584.32	138,796.55	167,302.91
2019	25,471.98	75,863.43	3,243.11	8,325.54	8,892.15	2,876.24	142,039.66	175,628.45
2020	15,572.85	72,662.30	2,236.12	8,000.64	9,899.14	3,201.13	144,275.78	183,629.09
2021	4,552.69	69,099.58	1,115.10	7,639.05	11,020.16	3,562.73	145,390.88	191,268.14
2022	0.00	65,134.41	103.97	7,236.61	4,552.69	3,965.16	145,494.85	198,504.75
2023	0.00	60,721.35	0.00	6,788.71	0.00	4,413.06	145,494.85	205,293.47
2024	0.00	55,809.80	0.00	6,290.22	0.00	4,911.55	145,494.85	211,583.69
2025	0.00	50,343.45	0.00	5,735.42	0.00	5,466.35	145,494.85	217,319.12
2026	0.00	44,259.63	0.00	5,117.96	0.00	6,083.82	145,494.85	222,437.07
2027	0.00	37,488.59	0.00	4,430.74	0.00	6,771.04	145,494.85	226,867.81
2028	0.00	29,952.71	0.00	3,665.90	0.00	7,535.88	145,494.85	230,533.71
2029	0.00	21,565.60	0.00	2,814.66	0.00	8,387.12	145,494.85	233,348.37
2030	0.00	12,231.09	0.00	1,867.27	0.00	9,334.51	145,494.85	235,215.64
2031	0.00	1,842.17	0.00	812.86	0.00	10,388.92	145,494.85	236,028.50
2032	0.00	0.00	0.00	24.79	0.00	1,842.17	145,494.85	236,053.29

Source: <www.mortgage-x.com>.

Based on 10.5%, $100,000 loan amount, 30 years

Year	Loan Balance		Yearly Interest Paid		Yearly Principal Paid		Total Interest	
	Biweekly	Standard	Biweekly	Standard	Biweekly	Standard	Biweekly	Standard
2002	98,771.18	99,586.59	8,833.31	8,733.98	1,228.82	413.41	8,833.31	8,733.98
2003	97,171.24	99,040.53	10,291.67	10,430.81	1,599.94	546.06	19,124.99	19,164.79
2004	95,394.55	98,434.28	10,114.92	10,370.63	1,776.69	606.24	29,239.90	29,535.42
2005	93,421.58	97,761.23	9,918.64	10,303.82	1,972.97	673.05	39,158.54	39,839.24
2006	91,230.64	97,014.01	9,700.67	10,229.65	2,190.94	747.22	48,859.21	50,068.89
2007	88,797.65	96,184.44	9,458.62	10,147.30	2,432.99	829.57	58,317.84	60,216.19
2008	86,095.88	95,263.45	9,189.84	10,055.88	2,701.77	920.99	67,507.68	70,272.07
2009	83,095.63	94,240.96	8,891.36	9,954.38	3,000.25	1,022.49	76,399.03	80,226.45
2010	79,763.92	93,105.79	8,559.90	9,841.70	3,331.71	1,135.17	84,958.94	90,068.16
2011	76,064.14	91,845.52	8,191.83	9,716.60	3,699.78	1,260.27	93,150.77	99,784.76
2012	71,955.62	90,446.37	7,783.09	9,577.72	4,108.52	1,399.16	100,933.86	109,362.48
2013	67,393.21	88,893.02	7,329.20	9,423.52	4,562.41	1,553.35	108,263.06	118,786.00
2014	62,326.77	87,168.49	6,825.17	9,252.34	5,066.44	1,724.53	115,088.23	128,038.34
2015	56,700.61	85,253.91	6,265.45	9,062.29	5,626.16	1,914.58	121,353.68	137,100.63
2016	50,452.89	83,128.33	5,643.89	8,851.30	6,247.72	2,125.57	126,997.57	145,951.93
2017	43,514.95	80,768.51	4,953.67	8,617.05	6,937.94	2,359.82	131,951.24	154,568.98
2018	35,810.54	78,148.63	4,187.20	8,356.99	7,704.41	2,619.88	136,138.44	162,925.97
2019	27,254.97	75,240.04	3,336.05	8,068.27	8,555.56	2,908.60	139,474.49	170,994.24
2020	17,754.22	72,010.90	2,390.86	7,747.73	9,500.75	3,229.14	141,865.35	178,741.98
2021	7,203.87	68,425.90	1,341.26	7,391.82	10,550.35	3,585.00	143,206.61	186,133.85
2022	0.00	64,445.82	254.53	6,996.79	7,203.87	3,980.08	143,461.15	193,130.64
2023	0.00	60,027.12	0.00	6,558.17	0.00	4,418.70	143,461.15	199,688.82
2024	0.00	55,121.47	0.00	6,071.22	0.00	4,905.65	143,461.15	205,760.04
2025	0.00	49,675.20	0.00	5,530.60	0.00	5,446.27	143,461.15	211,290.64
2026	0.00	43,628.73	0.00	4,930.40	0.00	6,046.47	143,461.15	216,221.04
2027	0.00	36,915.91	0.00	4,264.06	0.00	6,712.81	143,461.15	220,485.10
2028	0.00	29,463.33	0.00	3,524.28	0.00	7,452.59	143,461.15	224,009.38
2029	0.00	21,189.44	0.00	2,702.98	0.00	8,273.89	143,461.15	226,712.36
2030	0.00	12,003.74	0.00	1,791.17	0.00	9,185.70	143,461.15	228,503.53
2031	0.00	1,805.74	0.00	778.88	0.00	10,198.00	143,461.15	229,282.41
2032	0.00	0.00	0.00	23.73	0.00	1,805.74	143,461.15	229,306.15

Source: <www.mortgage-x.com>.

Based on 10.25%, $100,000 loan amount, 30 years

Year	Loan Balance		Yearly Interest Paid		Yearly Principal Paid		Total Interest	
	Biweekly	Standard	Biweekly	Standard	Biweekly	Standard	Biweekly	Standard
2002	98,765.64	99,564.16	8,622.75	8,525.18	1,234.36	435.84	8,622.75	8,525.18
2003	97,162.18	98,989.79	10,045.86	10,178.84	1,603.46	574.38	18,668.61	18,704.02
2004	95,386.01	98,353.69	9,873.15	10,117.12	1,776.17	636.09	28,541.76	28,821.14
2005	93,418.52	97,649.25	9,681.83	10,048.77	1,967.49	704.45	38,223.58	38,869.90
2006	91,239.10	96,869.10	9,469.90	9,973.00	2,179.42	780.14	47,693.48	48,842.98
2007	88,824.93	96,005.13	9,235.15	9,889.24	2,414.17	863.97	56,928.63	58,732.22
2008	86,150.72	95,048.32	8,975.11	9,796.40	2,674.21	956.81	65,903.74	68,528.62
2009	83,188.46	93,988.69	8,687.06	9,693.59	2,962.26	1,059.63	74,590.79	78,222.21
2010	79,907.12	92,815.20	8,367.98	9,579.73	3,281.34	1,173.49	82,958.77	87,801.94
2011	76,272.34	91,515.62	8,014.53	9,453.63	3,634.78	1,299.59	90,973.31	97,255.57
2012	72,246.04	90,076.38	7,623.02	9,313.98	4,026.30	1,439.23	98,596.32	106,569.55
2013	67,786.05	88,482.50	7,189.33	9,159.33	4,459.99	1,593.89	105,785.65	115,728.88
2014	62,845.65	86,717.34	6,708.92	8,988.06	4,940.39	1,765.16	112,494.57	124,716.94
2015	57,373.11	84,762.51	6,176.77	8,798.38	5,472.54	1,954.83	118,671.34	133,515.32
2016	51,311.10	82,597.62	5,587.30	8,588.33	6,062.01	2,164.89	124,258.65	142,103.65
2017	44,596.12	80,200.10	4,934.34	8,355.70	6,714.98	2,397.52	129,192.99	150,459.35
2018	37,157.84	77,544.96	4,211.04	8,098.07	7,438.28	2,655.14	133,404.03	158,557.42
2019	28,918.36	74,604.50	3,409.83	7,812.76	8,239.48	2,940.45	136,813.86	166,370.18
2020	19,791.37	71,348.09	2,522.33	7,496.80	9,126.99	3,256.42	139,336.19	173,866.98
2021	9,681.28	67,741.75	1,539.22	7,146.88	10,110.10	3,606.34	140,875.41	181,013.86
2022	0.00	63,747.89	457.50	6,759.36	9,681.28	3,993.86	141,332.91	187,773.21
2023	0.00	59,324.87	0.00	6,330.20	0.00	4,423.02	141,332.91	194,103.41
2024	0.00	54,426.58	0.00	5,854.92	0.00	4,898.29	141,332.91	199,958.33
2025	0.00	49,001.94	0.00	5,328.57	0.00	5,424.64	141,332.91	205,286.91
2026	0.00	42,994.39	0.00	4,745.67	0.00	6,007.55	141,332.91	210,032.58
2027	0.00	36,341.30	0.00	4,100.13	0.00	6,653.09	141,332.91	214,132.70
2028	0.00	28,973.31	0.00	3,385.22	0.00	7,368.00	141,332.91	217,517.92
2029	0.00	20,813.58	0.00	2,593.49	0.00	8,159.73	141,332.91	220,111.41
2030	0.00	11,777.05	0.00	1,716.69	0.00	9,036.53	141,332.91	221,828.10
2031	0.00	1,769.50	0.00	745.66	0.00	10,007.55	141,332.91	222,573.76
2032	0.00	0.00	0.00	22.70	0.00	1,769.50	141,332.91	222,596.47

Source: <www.mortgage-x.com>.

Based on 10%, $100,000 loan amount, 30 years

Year	Loan Balance		Yearly Interest Paid		Yearly Principal Paid		Total Interest	
	Biweekly	Standard	Biweekly	Standard	Biweekly	Standard	Biweekly	Standard
2002	98,758.87	99,540.65	8,412.15	8,316.37	1,241.13	459.35	8,412.15	8,316.37
2003	97,150.32	98,936.68	9,799.89	9,926.88	1,608.54	603.98	18,212.04	18,243.25
2004	95,372.95	98,269.45	9,631.06	9,863.64	1,777.37	667.22	27,843.10	28,106.89
2005	93,409.03	97,532.36	9,444.51	9,793.77	1,963.92	737.09	37,287.61	37,900.66
2006	91,238.97	96,718.09	9,238.38	9,716.59	2,170.06	814.27	46,525.98	47,617.24
2007	88,841.15	95,818.55	9,010.61	9,631.32	2,397.82	899.54	55,536.59	57,248.56
2008	86,191.66	94,824.82	8,758.94	9,537.13	2,649.49	993.73	64,295.52	66,785.69
2009	83,264.07	93,727.04	8,480.85	9,433.07	2,927.58	1,097.79	72,776.37	76,218.76
2010	80,029.21	92,514.30	8,173.57	9,318.12	3,234.86	1,212.74	80,949.94	85,536.88
2011	76,454.83	91,174.57	7,834.04	9,191.13	3,574.39	1,339.73	88,783.99	94,728.01
2012	72,505.28	89,694.55	7,458.88	9,050.84	3,949.55	1,480.02	96,242.87	103,778.86
2013	68,141.18	88,059.56	7,044.34	8,895.87	4,364.09	1,634.99	103,287.21	112,674.72
2014	63,319.04	86,253.36	6,586.29	8,724.66	4,822.14	1,806.20	109,873.50	121,399.38
2015	57,990.77	84,258.03	6,080.16	8,535.53	5,328.27	1,995.33	115,953.66	129,934.91
2016	52,103.26	82,053.76	5,520.91	8,326.59	5,887.52	2,204.27	121,474.57	138,261.50
2017	45,597.79	79,618.67	4,902.96	8,095.77	6,505.47	2,435.08	126,377.53	146,357.27
2018	38,409.52	76,928.60	4,220.16	7,840.79	7,188.27	2,690.07	130,597.69	154,198.06
2019	30,466.77	73,956.85	3,465.68	7,559.10	7,942.75	2,971.76	134,063.38	161,757.16
2020	21,690.36	70,673.91	2,632.02	7,247.92	8,776.41	3,282.94	136,695.40	169,005.09
2021	11,992.79	67,047.21	1,710.86	6,904.16	9,697.57	3,626.70	138,406.26	175,909.24
2022	1,277.38	63,040.74	693.01	6,524.39	10,715.42	4,006.47	139,099.27	182,433.63
2023	0.00	58,614.75	9.73	6,104.86	1,277.38	4,426.00	139,109.00	188,538.50
2024	0.00	53,725.29	0.00	5,641.40	0.00	4,889.46	139,109.00	194,179.90
2025	0.00	48,323.85	0.00	5,129.41	0.00	5,401.45	139,109.00	199,309.31
2026	0.00	42,356.80	0.00	4,563.81	0.00	5,967.05	139,109.00	203,873.13
2027	0.00	35,764.92	0.00	3,938.98	0.00	6,591.88	139,109.00	207,812.11
2028	0.00	28,482.79	0.00	3,248.73	0.00	7,282.13	139,109.00	211,060.84
2029	0.00	20,438.13	0.00	2,486.19	0.00	8,044.66	139,109.00	213,547.03
2030	0.00	11,551.08	0.00	1,643.81	0.00	8,887.05	139,109.00	215,190.84
2031	0.00	1,733.45	0.00	713.22	0.00	9,817.64	139,109.00	215,904.07
2032	0.00	0.00	0.00	21.70	0.00	1,733.45	139,109.00	215,925.77

Source: <www.mortgage-x.com>.

Based on 9.75%, $100,000 loan amount, 30 years

Year	Loan Balance		Yearly Interest Paid		Yearly Principal Paid		Total Interest	
	Biweekly	Standard	Biweekly	Standard	Biweekly	Standard	Biweekly	Standard
2002	98,750.82	99,516.02	8,201.52	8,107.57	1,249.18	483.98	8,201.52	8,107.57
2003	97,135.58	98,881.11	9,553.77	9,674.94	1,615.24	634.92	17,755.28	17,782.50
2004	95,355.24	98,181.44	9,388.67	9,610.19	1,780.34	699.66	27,143.96	27,392.69
2005	93,392.94	97,410.43	9,206.70	9,538.84	1,962.31	771.01	36,350.66	36,931.53
2006	91,230.06	96,560.79	9,006.13	9,460.21	2,162.87	849.64	45,356.79	46,391.75
2007	88,846.12	95,624.51	8,785.07	9,373.57	2,383.94	936.28	54,141.86	55,765.32
2008	86,218.52	94,592.75	8,541.40	9,278.09	2,627.61	1,031.76	62,683.26	65,043.41
2009	83,322.34	93,455.77	8,272.83	9,172.87	2,896.17	1,136.98	70,956.09	74,216.28
2010	80,130.15	92,202.85	7,976.81	9,056.93	3,192.19	1,252.92	78,932.91	83,273.21
2011	76,611.68	90,822.15	7,650.54	8,929.16	3,518.47	1,380.69	86,583.45	92,202.37
2012	72,733.59	89,300.66	7,290.91	8,788.36	3,878.09	1,521.49	93,874.36	100,990.73
2013	68,459.12	87,624.01	6,894.53	8,633.20	4,274.47	1,676.65	100,768.90	109,623.94
2014	63,747.75	85,776.38	6,457.64	8,462.22	4,711.37	1,847.63	107,226.53	118,086.16
2015	58,554.83	83,740.33	5,976.09	8,273.81	5,192.92	2,036.05	113,202.62	126,359.96
2016	52,831.13	81,496.65	5,445.32	8,066.18	5,723.69	2,243.68	118,647.94	134,426.14
2017	46,522.42	79,024.17	4,860.29	7,837.37	6,308.71	2,472.48	123,508.23	142,263.51
2018	39,568.89	76,299.56	4,215.48	7,585.23	6,953.53	2,724.62	127,723.71	149,848.75
2019	31,904.64	73,297.09	3,504.76	7,307.39	7,664.25	3,002.47	131,228.46	157,156.13
2020	23,457.02	69,988.44	2,721.39	7,001.20	8,447.62	3,308.65	133,949.85	164,157.34
2021	14,145.97	66,342.38	1,857.95	6,663.80	9,311.05	3,646.06	135,807.81	170,821.13
2022	3,883.23	62,324.51	906.27	6,291.98	10,262.74	4,017.87	136,714.08	177,113.11
2023	0.00	57,896.91	74.88	5,882.25	3,883.23	4,427.60	136,788.96	182,995.36
2024	0.00	53,017.79	0.00	5,430.73	0.00	4,879.12	136,788.96	188,426.10
2025	0.00	47,641.11	0.00	4,933.18	0.00	5,376.68	136,788.96	193,359.27
2026	0.00	41,716.14	0.00	4,384.88	0.00	5,924.98	136,788.96	197,744.15
2027	0.00	35,186.95	0.00	3,780.67	0.00	6,529.19	136,788.96	201,524.82
2028	0.00	27,991.93	0.00	3,114.84	0.00	7,195.02	136,788.96	204,639.65
2029	0.00	20,063.19	0.00	2,381.11	0.00	7,928.74	136,788.96	207,020.76
2030	0.00	11,325.89	0.00	1,572.56	0.00	8,737.30	136,788.96	208,593.32
2031	0.00	1,697.59	0.00	681.55	0.00	9,628.30	136,788.96	209,274.87
2032	0.00	0.00	0.00	20.72	0.00	1,697.59	136,788.96	209,295.59

Source: <www.mortgage-x.com>.

Based on 9.5%, $100,000 loan amount, 30 years

Year	Loan Balance		Yearly Interest Paid		Yearly Principal Paid		Total Interest	
	Biweekly	Standard	Biweekly	Standard	Biweekly	Standard	Biweekly	Standard
2002	98,741.46	99,490.23	7,990.85	7,898.77	1,258.54	509.77	7,990.85	7,898.77
2003	97,117.85	98,822.99	9,307.50	9,423.02	1,623.60	667.24	17,298.35	17,321.78
2004	95,332.75	98,089.53	9,146.00	9,356.79	1,785.10	733.46	26,444.35	26,678.58
2005	93,370.09	97,283.28	8,968.44	9,284.00	1,962.66	806.25	35,412.80	35,962.58
2006	91,212.20	96,397.02	8,773.22	9,203.98	2,157.89	886.27	44,186.01	45,166.56
2007	88,839.67	95,422.79	8,558.58	9,116.02	2,372.53	974.23	52,744.59	54,282.58
2008	86,231.15	94,351.87	8,322.58	9,019.33	2,608.52	1,070.92	61,067.18	63,301.91
2009	83,363.17	93,174.66	8,063.12	8,913.05	2,867.99	1,177.20	69,130.29	72,214.96
2010	80,209.91	91,880.62	7,777.84	8,796.21	3,153.26	1,294.04	76,908.14	81,011.17
2011	76,743.00	90,458.15	7,464.20	8,667.78	3,466.91	1,422.47	84,372.33	89,678.95
2012	72,931.24	88,894.51	7,119.35	8,526.60	3,811.76	1,563.65	91,491.68	98,205.55
2013	68,740.33	87,175.67	6,740.20	8,371.42	4,190.91	1,718.83	98,231.88	106,576.97
2014	64,132.56	85,286.25	6,323.33	8,200.83	4,607.77	1,889.43	104,555.21	114,777.79
2015	59,066.46	83,209.30	5,865.01	8,013.30	5,066.10	2,076.95	110,420.22	122,791.10
2016	53,496.44	80,926.22	5,361.09	7,807.17	5,570.02	2,283.08	115,781.31	130,598.27
2017	47,372.39	78,416.55	4,807.05	7,580.58	6,124.06	2,509.67	120,588.35	138,178.85
2018	40,639.18	75,657.81	4,197.90	7,331.50	6,733.21	2,758.75	124,786.25	145,510.36
2019	33,236.23	72,625.26	3,528.16	7,057.71	7,402.95	3,032.55	128,314.41	152,568.06
2020	25,096.92	69,291.75	2,791.79	6,756.73	8,139.31	3,333.52	131,106.20	159,324.80
2021	16,148.01	65,627.38	1,982.19	6,425.89	8,948.91	3,664.36	133,088.39	165,750.68
2022	6,308.96	61,599.34	1,092.06	6,062.21	9,839.05	4,028.04	134,180.45	171,812.89
2023	0.00	57,171.53	191.59	5,662.44	6,308.96	4,427.81	134,372.04	177,475.33
2024	0.00	52,304.27	0.00	5,222.99	0.00	4,867.26	134,372.04	182,698.32
2025	0.00	46,953.94	0.00	4,739.92	0.00	5,350.33	134,372.04	187,438.24
2026	0.00	41,072.60	0.00	4,208.92	0.00	5,881.33	134,372.04	191,647.16
2027	0.00	34,607.56	0.00	3,625.21	0.00	6,465.04	134,372.04	195,272.36
2028	0.00	27,500.88	0.00	2,983.57	0.00	7,106.68	134,372.04	198,255.93
2029	0.00	19,688.87	0.00	2,278.25	0.00	7,812.00	134,372.04	200,534.18
2030	0.00	11,101.55	0.00	1,502.92	0.00	8,587.33	134,372.04	202,037.10
2031	0.00	1,661.95	0.00	650.65	0.00	9,439.60	134,372.04	202,687.75
2032	0.00	0.00	0.00	19.76	0.00	1,661.95	134,372.04	202,707.51

Source: <www.mortgage-x.com>.

Based on 9.25%, $100,000 loan amount, 30 years

Year	Loan Balance		Yearly Interest Paid		Yearly Principal Paid		Total Interest	
	Biweekly	Standard	Biweekly	Standard	Biweekly	Standard	Biweekly	Standard
2002	98,730.72	99,463.22	7,780.15	7,689.98	1,269.28	536.78	7,780.15	7,689.98
2003	97,097.04	98,762.24	9,061.10	9,171.12	1,633.68	700.98	16,841.25	16,861.10
2004	95,305.33	97,993.60	8,903.07	9,103.46	1,791.71	768.64	25,744.33	25,964.56
2005	93,340.31	97,150.76	8,729.75	9,029.27	1,965.03	842.84	34,474.08	34,993.83
2006	91,185.20	96,226.57	8,539.67	8,947.92	2,155.11	924.19	43,013.75	43,941.75
2007	88,821.61	95,213.18	8,331.20	8,858.71	2,363.58	1,013.40	51,344.95	52,800.46
2008	86,229.40	94,101.96	8,102.56	8,760.89	2,592.22	1,111.21	59,447.51	61,561.35
2009	83,386.42	92,883.49	7,851.81	8,653.63	2,842.97	1,218.47	67,299.32	70,214.98
2010	80,268.44	91,547.41	7,576.80	8,536.02	3,117.98	1,336.08	74,876.12	78,751.00
2011	76,848.85	90,082.36	7,275.19	8,407.06	3,419.59	1,465.05	82,151.31	87,158.06
2012	73,098.47	88,475.89	6,944.40	8,265.64	3,750.38	1,606.46	89,095.71	95,423.70
2013	68,985.30	86,714.37	6,581.61	8,110.58	4,113.17	1,761.52	95,677.32	103,534.28
2014	64,474.26	84,782.82	6,183.73	7,940.55	4,511.05	1,931.55	101,861.05	111,474.83
2015	59,526.85	82,664.82	5,747.37	7,754.11	4,947.41	2,117.99	107,608.42	119,228.94
2016	54,100.85	80,342.39	5,268.79	7,549.67	5,425.99	2,322.43	112,877.21	126,778.62
2017	48,149.99	77,795.79	4,743.92	7,325.50	5,950.86	2,546.60	117,621.13	134,104.12
2018	41,623.48	75,003.37	4,168.27	7,079.69	6,526.51	2,792.41	121,789.40	141,183.81
2019	34,465.64	71,941.43	3,536.94	6,810.16	7,157.84	3,061.95	125,326.34	147,993.97
2020	26,615.40	68,583.93	2,844.54	6,514.61	7,850.24	3,357.50	128,170.88	154,508.57
2021	18,005.78	64,902.35	2,085.16	6,190.53	8,609.62	3,681.58	130,256.04	160,699.10
2022	8,563.33	60,865.41	1,252.33	5,835.16	9,442.45	4,036.94	131,508.37	166,534.27
2023	0.00	56,438.81	349.68	5,445.50	8,563.33	4,426.60	131,858.05	171,979.77
2024	0.00	51,584.93	0.00	5,018.23	0.00	4,853.88	131,858.05	176,998.00
2025	0.00	46,262.54	0.00	4,549.71	0.00	5,322.39	131,858.05	181,547.71
2026	0.00	40,426.41	0.00	4,035.97	0.00	5,836.13	131,858.05	185,583.68
2027	0.00	34,026.95	0.00	3,472.65	0.00	6,399.46	131,858.05	189,056.33
2028	0.00	27,009.78	0.00	2,854.94	0.00	7,017.16	131,858.05	191,911.27
2029	0.00	19,315.30	0.00	2,177.62	0.00	7,694.49	131,858.05	194,088.89
2030	0.00	10,878.10	0.00	1,434.91	0.00	8,437.19	131,858.05	195,523.80
2031	0.00	1,626.52	0.00	620.52	0.00	9,251.58	131,858.05	196,144.32
2032	0.00	0.00	0.00	18.83	0.00	1,626.52	131,858.05	196,163.15

Source: <www.mortgage-x.com>.

Based on 9%, $100,000 loan amount, 30 years

Year	Loan Balance		Yearly Interest Paid		Yearly Principal Paid		Total Interest	
	Biweekly	Standard	Biweekly	Standard	Biweekly	Standard	Biweekly	Standard
2002	98,718.58	99,434.97	7,569.43	7,481.19	1,281.42	565.03	7,569.43	7,481.19
2003	97,073.06	98,698.76	8,814.58	8,919.27	1,645.52	736.20	16,384.01	16,400.46
2004	95,272.86	97,893.50	8,659.89	8,850.21	1,800.20	805.26	25,043.90	25,250.67
2005	93,303.44	97,012.70	8,490.67	8,774.67	1,969.43	880.80	33,534.57	34,025.34
2006	91,148.87	96,049.27	8,305.53	8,692.05	2,154.56	963.43	41,840.10	42,717.39
2007	88,791.77	94,995.47	8,102.99	8,601.67	2,357.10	1,053.80	49,943.09	51,319.06
2008	86,213.10	93,842.82	7,881.42	8,502.82	2,578.68	1,152.66	57,824.51	59,821.87
2009	83,392.01	92,582.03	7,639.01	8,394.69	2,821.08	1,260.78	65,463.52	68,216.56
2010	80,305.74	91,202.98	7,373.82	8,276.42	3,086.28	1,379.05	72,837.34	76,492.98
2011	76,929.34	89,694.56	7,083.69	8,147.05	3,376.40	1,508.42	79,921.03	84,640.03
2012	73,235.54	88,044.64	6,766.30	8,005.55	3,693.80	1,649.92	86,687.33	92,645.58
2013	69,194.51	86,239.95	6,419.06	7,850.78	4,041.03	1,804.69	93,106.39	100,496.36
2014	64,773.61	84,265.96	6,039.19	7,681.49	4,420.90	1,973.98	99,145.58	108,177.85
2015	59,937.12	82,106.81	5,623.61	7,496.31	4,836.49	2,159.16	104,769.19	115,674.16
2016	54,645.98	79,745.10	5,168.96	7,293.77	5,291.14	2,361.70	109,938.15	122,967.93
2017	48,857.46	77,161.86	4,671.57	7,072.23	5,788.53	2,583.25	114,609.72	130,040.16
2018	42,524.78	74,336.29	4,127.42	6,829.90	6,332.67	2,825.57	118,737.14	136,870.05
2019	35,596.81	71,245.66	3,532.12	6,564.84	6,927.97	3,090.63	122,269.26	143,434.90
2020	28,017.58	67,865.10	2,880.86	6,274.92	7,579.23	3,380.55	125,150.13	149,709.81
2021	19,725.87	64,167.43	2,168.38	5,957.80	8,291.71	3,697.67	127,318.51	155,667.61
2022	10,654.71	60,122.89	1,388.93	5,610.93	9,071.17	4,044.54	128,707.44	161,278.55
2023	730.82	55,698.95	536.20	5,231.53	9,923.89	4,423.94	129,243.64	166,510.07
2024	0.00	50,860.00	3.68	4,816.53	730.82	4,838.94	129,247.32	171,326.60
2025	0.00	45,567.14	0.00	4,362.60	0.00	5,292.87	129,247.32	175,689.21
2026	0.00	39,777.76	0.00	3,866.10	0.00	5,789.38	129,247.32	179,555.30
2027	0.00	33,445.30	0.00	3,323.01	0.00	6,332.46	129,247.32	182,878.31
2028	0.00	26,518.82	0.00	2,728.98	0.00	6,926.49	129,247.32	185,607.30
2029	0.00	18,942.58	0.00	2,079.23	0.00	7,576.24	129,247.32	187,686.53
2030	0.00	10,655.64	0.00	1,368.53	0.00	8,286.94	129,247.32	189,055.06
2031	0.00	1,591.32	0.00	591.16	0.00	9,064.31	129,247.32	189,646.22
2032	0.00	0.00	0.00	17.92	0.00	1,591.32	129,247.32	189,664.14

Source: <www.mortgage-x.com>.

Based on 8.75%, $100,000 loan amount, 30 years

Year	Loan Balance		Yearly Interest Paid		Yearly Principal Paid		Total Interest	
	Biweekly	Standard	Biweekly	Standard	Biweekly	Standard	Biweekly	Standard
2002	98,704.97	99,405.41	7,358.67	7,272.42	1,295.03	594.59	7,358.67	7,272.42
2003	97,045.81	98,632.47	8,567.94	8,667.46	1,659.16	772.94	15,926.62	15,939.88
2004	95,235.19	97,789.12	8,416.49	8,597.05	1,810.61	843.35	24,343.11	24,536.93
2005	93,259.30	96,868.94	8,251.22	8,520.23	1,975.89	920.18	32,594.32	33,057.16
2006	91,103.05	95,864.93	8,070.85	8,436.40	2,156.25	1,004.00	40,665.18	41,493.56
2007	88,749.97	94,769.47	7,874.03	8,344.94	2,353.08	1,095.46	48,539.20	49,838.50
2008	86,182.10	93,574.21	7,659.23	8,245.15	2,567.87	1,195.26	56,198.43	58,083.65
2009	83,379.83	92,270.07	7,424.83	8,136.27	2,802.27	1,304.14	63,623.27	66,219.91
2010	80,321.75	90,847.13	7,169.03	8,017.46	3,058.07	1,422.94	70,792.30	74,237.38
2011	76,984.54	89,294.57	6,889.89	7,887.84	3,337.22	1,552.57	77,682.19	82,125.22
2012	73,342.69	87,600.57	6,585.26	7,746.41	3,641.84	1,694.00	84,267.45	89,871.62
2013	69,368.41	85,752.26	6,252.83	7,592.09	3,974.28	1,848.31	90,520.27	97,463.72
2014	65,031.35	83,735.57	5,890.05	7,423.72	4,337.06	2,016.69	96,410.32	104,887.43
2015	60,298.40	81,535.17	5,494.15	7,240.01	4,732.95	2,200.40	101,904.47	112,127.44
2016	55,133.41	79,134.33	5,062.12	7,039.56	5,164.99	2,400.85	106,966.59	119,167.00
2017	49,496.95	76,514.77	4,590.65	6,820.85	5,636.46	2,619.55	111,557.24	125,987.85
2018	43,345.99	73,656.59	4,076.14	6,582.22	6,150.96	2,858.18	115,633.38	132,570.07
2019	36,633.55	70,538.04	3,514.67	6,321.85	6,712.44	3,118.55	119,148.04	138,891.93
2020	29,308.39	67,135.40	2,901.94	6,037.77	7,325.16	3,402.64	122,049.99	144,929.69
2021	21,314.57	63,422.80	2,233.29	5,727.80	7,993.82	3,712.60	124,283.28	150,657.49
2022	12,591.07	59,371.99	1,503.60	5,389.60	8,723.51	4,050.81	125,786.88	156,047.09
2023	3,071.26	54,952.17	707.30	5,020.59	9,519.81	4,419.82	126,494.18	161,067.68
2024	0.00	50,129.72	46.35	4,617.96	3,071.26	4,822.45	126,540.53	165,685.63
2025	0.00	44,867.97	0.00	4,178.65	0.00	5,261.75	126,540.53	169,864.29
2026	0.00	39,126.90	0.00	3,699.33	0.00	5,741.07	126,540.53	173,563.62
2027	0.00	32,862.83	0.00	3,176.34	0.00	6,264.06	126,540.53	176,739.96
2028	0.00	26,028.14	0.00	2,605.71	0.00	6,834.69	126,540.53	179,345.67
2029	0.00	18,570.84	0.00	1,983.10	0.00	7,457.30	126,540.53	181,328.77
2030	0.00	10,434.20	0.00	1,303.77	0.00	8,136.63	126,540.53	182,632.54
2031	0.00	1,556.36	0.00	562.56	0.00	8,877.85	126,540.53	183,195.10
2032	0.00	0.00	0.00	17.04	0.00	1,556.36	126,540.53	183,212.15

Source: <www.mortgage-x.com>.

Based on 8.5%, $100,000 loan amount, 30 years

Year	Loan Balance		Yearly Interest Paid		Yearly Principal Paid		Total Interest	
	Biweekly	Standard	Biweekly	Standard	Biweekly	Standard	Biweekly	Standard
2002	98,689.85	99,374.52	7,147.90	7,063.65	1,310.15	625.48	7,147.90	7,063.65
2003	97,015.18	98,563.27	8,321.21	8,415.71	1,674.67	811.25	15,469.10	15,479.37
2004	95,192.19	97,680.31	8,172.89	8,344.01	1,822.99	882.96	23,641.99	23,823.37
2005	93,207.75	96,719.31	8,011.43	8,265.96	1,984.44	961.00	31,653.42	32,089.33
2006	91,047.55	95,673.31	7,835.68	8,181.02	2,160.20	1,045.95	39,489.10	40,270.35
2007	88,696.03	94,534.97	7,644.36	8,088.56	2,351.52	1,138.40	47,133.46	48,358.91
2008	86,136.25	93,295.95	7,436.09	7,987.94	2,559.78	1,239.02	54,569.55	56,346.85
2009	83,349.76	91,947.41	7,209.38	7,878.42	2,786.49	1,348.54	61,778.93	64,225.27
2010	80,316.48	90,479.67	6,962.59	7,759.22	3,033.28	1,467.74	68,741.53	71,984.50
2011	77,014.55	88,882.20	6,693.95	7,629.49	3,301.93	1,597.47	75,435.47	79,613.99
2012	73,420.18	87,143.52	6,401.51	7,488.29	3,594.37	1,738.68	81,836.98	87,102.27
2013	69,507.47	85,251.16	6,083.17	7,334.60	3,912.71	1,892.36	87,920.15	94,436.88
2014	65,248.24	83,191.54	5,736.64	7,167.34	4,259.24	2,059.63	93,656.79	101,604.21
2015	60,611.77	80,949.86	5,359.41	6,985.28	4,636.46	2,241.68	99,016.20	108,589.50
2016	55,564.67	78,510.04	4,948.78	6,787.14	5,047.10	2,439.82	103,964.98	115,376.64
2017	50,070.58	75,854.56	4,501.78	6,571.48	5,494.10	2,655.48	108,466.75	121,948.12
2018	44,089.88	72,964.36	4,015.18	6,336.76	5,980.69	2,890.20	112,481.94	128,284.88
2019	37,579.51	69,818.69	3,485.50	6,081.29	6,510.38	3,145.67	115,967.44	134,366.18
2020	30,492.53	66,394.97	2,908.90	5,803.25	7,086.98	3,423.72	118,876.34	140,169.42
2021	22,777.89	62,668.63	2,281.23	5,500.62	7,714.64	3,726.34	121,157.57	145,670.04
2022	14,379.99	58,612.92	1,597.98	5,171.25	8,397.90	4,055.72	122,755.55	150,841.29
2023	5,238.32	54,198.71	854.21	4,812.76	9,141.67	4,414.20	123,609.75	155,654.05
2024	0.00	49,394.33	129.03	4,422.58	5,238.32	4,804.38	123,738.78	160,076.63
2025	0.00	44,165.29	0.00	3,997.92	0.00	5,229.04	123,738.78	164,074.55
2026	0.00	38,474.05	0.00	3,535.72	0.00	5,691.24	123,738.78	167,610.26
2027	0.00	32,279.75	0.00	3,032.66	0.00	6,194.30	123,738.78	170,642.93
2028	0.00	25,537.93	0.00	2,485.15	0.00	6,741.82	123,738.78	173,128.07
2029	0.00	18,200.20	0.00	1,889.23	0.00	7,337.73	123,738.78	175,017.30
2030	0.00	10,213.88	0.00	1,240.64	0.00	7,986.32	123,738.78	176,257.94
2031	0.00	1,521.64	0.00	534.72	0.00	8,692.24	123,738.78	176,792.67
2032	0.00	0.00	0.00	16.19	0.00	1,521.64	123,738.78	176,808.85

Source: <www.mortgage-x.com>.

Based on 8.25%, $100,000 loan amount, 30 years

Year	Loan Balance		Yearly Interest Paid		Yearly Principal Paid		Total Interest	
	Biweekly	Standard	Biweekly	Standard	Biweekly	Standard	Biweekly	Standard
2002	98,673.17	99,342.24	6,937.10	6,854.91	1,326.83	657.76	6,937.10	6,854.91
2003	96,981.08	98,491.07	8,074.38	8,164.03	1,692.09	851.17	15,011.48	15,018.93
2004	95,143.72	97,566.96	7,929.10	8,091.09	1,837.36	924.11	22,940.58	23,110.02
2005	93,148.60	96,563.66	7,771.35	8,011.90	1,995.11	1,003.30	30,711.93	31,121.92
2006	90,982.19	95,474.38	7,600.06	7,925.93	2,166.41	1,089.27	38,311.99	39,047.85
2007	88,629.78	94,291.77	7,414.06	7,832.58	2,352.41	1,182.62	45,726.05	46,880.43
2008	86,075.40	93,007.81	7,212.09	7,731.24	2,554.38	1,283.96	52,938.13	54,611.67
2009	83,301.71	91,613.83	6,992.77	7,621.22	2,773.69	1,393.98	59,930.91	62,232.89
2010	80,289.88	90,100.39	6,754.63	7,501.76	3,011.83	1,513.44	66,685.54	69,734.65
2011	77,019.46	88,457.27	6,496.05	7,372.07	3,270.42	1,643.13	73,181.59	77,106.73
2012	73,468.26	86,673.34	6,215.26	7,231.27	3,551.21	1,783.93	79,396.85	84,338.00
2013	69,612.16	84,736.54	5,910.37	7,078.40	3,856.10	1,936.80	85,307.21	91,416.40
2014	65,424.98	82,633.78	5,579.29	6,912.43	4,187.17	2,102.77	90,886.51	98,328.83
2015	60,878.31	80,350.82	5,219.80	6,732.24	4,546.67	2,282.96	96,106.30	105,061.08
2016	55,941.28	77,872.23	4,829.43	6,536.61	4,937.03	2,478.59	100,935.73	111,597.69
2017	50,580.37	75,181.25	4,405.55	6,324.22	5,360.91	2,690.98	105,341.29	117,921.91
2018	44,759.18	72,259.67	3,945.28	6,093.62	5,821.18	2,921.58	109,286.57	124,015.53
2019	38,438.21	69,087.74	3,445.49	5,843.26	6,320.97	3,171.93	112,732.07	129,858.79
2020	31,574.54	65,643.99	2,902.80	5,571.45	6,863.67	3,443.74	115,634.86	135,430.25
2021	24,121.58	61,905.15	2,313.50	5,276.35	7,452.96	3,738.85	117,948.37	140,706.60
2022	16,028.73	57,845.91	1,673.62	4,955.96	8,092.85	4,059.24	119,621.98	145,662.56
2023	7,241.05	53,438.83	978.79	4,608.12	8,787.68	4,407.08	120,600.77	150,270.68
2024	0.00	48,654.10	242.81	4,230.47	7,241.05	4,784.73	120,843.58	154,501.15
2025	0.00	43,459.35	0.00	3,820.45	0.00	5,194.75	120,843.58	158,321.60
2026	0.00	37,819.46	0.00	3,375.30	0.00	5,639.90	120,843.58	161,696.90
2027	0.00	31,696.26	0.00	2,892.01	0.00	6,123.19	120,843.58	164,588.91
2028	0.00	25,048.36	0.00	2,367.30	0.00	6,647.90	120,843.58	166,956.21
2029	0.00	17,830.79	0.00	1,797.63	0.00	7,217.57	120,843.58	168,753.84
2030	0.00	9,994.73	0.00	1,179.14	0.00	7,836.06	120,843.58	169,932.98
2031	0.00	1,487.18	0.00	507.65	0.00	8,507.55	120,843.58	170,440.62
2032	0.00	0.00	0.00	15.35	0.00	1,487.18	120,843.58	170,455.98

Source: <www.mortgage-x.com>.

Based on 8%, $100,000 loan amount, 30 years

Year	Loan Balance		Yearly Interest Paid		Yearly Principal Paid		Total Interest	
	Biweekly	Standard	Biweekly	Standard	Biweekly	Standard	Biweekly	Standard
2002	98,654.87	99,308.53	6,726.28	6,646.18	1,345.13	691.47	6,726.28	6,646.18
2003	96,943.41	98,415.77	7,827.47	7,912.42	1,711.47	892.76	14,553.76	14,558.59
2004	95,089.63	97,448.92	7,685.16	7,838.32	1,853.78	966.85	22,238.92	22,396.92
2005	93,081.70	96,401.82	7,531.01	7,758.07	2,007.93	1,047.10	29,769.93	30,154.99
2006	90,906.80	95,267.81	7,364.04	7,671.16	2,174.90	1,134.01	37,133.97	37,826.15
2007	88,551.05	94,039.67	7,183.19	7,577.04	2,355.75	1,228.13	44,317.16	45,403.19
2008	85,999.41	92,709.60	6,987.30	7,475.11	2,551.64	1,330.07	51,304.46	52,878.30
2009	83,235.60	91,269.14	6,775.12	7,364.71	2,763.82	1,440.46	58,079.58	60,243.01
2010	80,241.96	89,709.12	6,545.30	7,245.15	2,993.64	1,560.02	64,624.88	67,488.16
2011	76,999.38	88,019.62	6,296.37	7,115.67	3,242.57	1,689.50	70,921.25	74,603.84
2012	73,487.18	86,189.89	6,026.73	6,975.45	3,512.21	1,829.73	76,947.98	81,579.28
2013	69,682.92	84,208.29	5,734.68	6,823.58	3,804.26	1,981.60	82,682.66	88,402.86
2014	65,562.32	82,062.22	5,418.34	6,659.11	4,120.60	2,146.07	88,101.00	95,061.97
2015	61,099.07	79,738.03	5,075.70	6,480.98	4,463.24	2,324.19	93,176.70	101,542.95
2016	56,264.69	77,220.94	4,704.56	6,288.08	4,834.38	2,517.10	97,881.26	107,831.03
2017	51,028.31	74,494.92	4,302.56	6,079.16	5,236.38	2,726.02	102,183.82	113,910.19
2018	45,356.51	71,542.65	3,867.13	5,852.90	5,671.81	2,952.27	106,050.95	119,763.09
2019	39,213.07	68,345.34	3,395.50	5,607.86	6,143.44	3,197.31	109,446.45	125,370.96
2020	32,558.78	64,882.65	2,884.65	5,342.49	6,654.29	3,462.69	112,331.10	130,713.45
2021	25,351.16	61,132.57	2,331.32	5,055.09	7,207.62	3,750.09	114,662.42	135,768.53
2022	17,544.19	57,071.22	1,731.98	4,743.83	7,806.96	4,061.34	116,394.39	140,512.37
2023	9,088.05	52,672.79	1,082.80	4,406.74	8,456.14	4,398.43	117,477.19	144,919.11
2024	0.00	47,909.29	379.63	4,041.68	9,088.05	4,763.50	117,856.82	148,960.79
2025	0.00	42,750.43	0.00	3,646.31	0.00	5,158.87	117,856.82	152,607.10
2026	0.00	37,163.38	0.00	3,218.12	0.00	5,587.05	117,856.82	155,825.22
2027	0.00	31,112.60	0.00	2,754.40	0.00	6,050.77	117,856.82	158,579.62
2028	0.00	24,559.62	0.00	2,252.19	0.00	6,552.98	117,856.82	160,831.81
2029	0.00	17,462.74	0.00	1,708.30	0.00	7,096.88	117,856.82	162,540.11
2030	0.00	9,776.83	0.00	1,119.26	0.00	7,685.92	117,856.82	163,659.37
2031	0.00	1,452.98	0.00	481.33	0.00	8,323.84	117,856.82	164,140.70
2032	0.00	0.00	0.00	14.55	0.00	1,452.98	117,856.82	164,155.25

Source: <www.mortgage-x.com>.

Based on 7.75%, $100,000 loan amount, 30 years

Year	Loan Balance		Yearly Interest Paid		Yearly Principal Paid		Total Interest	
	Biweekly	Standard	Biweekly	Standard	Biweekly	Standard	Biweekly	Standard
2002	98,634.92	99,273.34	6,515.46	6,437.46	1,365.08	726.66	6,515.46	6,437.46
2003	96,902.07	98,337.29	7,580.51	7,660.90	1,732.85	936.05	14,095.96	14,098.36
2004	95,029.79	97,326.07	7,441.08	7,585.72	1,872.28	1,011.23	21,537.05	21,684.08
2005	93,006.88	96,233.63	7,290.45	7,504.51	2,022.91	1,092.44	28,827.49	29,188.59
2006	90,821.21	95,053.45	7,127.69	7,416.77	2,185.67	1,180.18	35,955.18	36,605.36
2007	88,459.68	93,778.49	6,951.83	7,321.99	2,361.53	1,274.96	42,907.01	43,927.35
2008	85,908.15	92,401.13	6,761.83	7,219.59	2,551.53	1,377.36	49,668.84	51,146.94
2009	83,151.33	90,913.16	6,556.54	7,108.97	2,756.82	1,487.98	56,225.38	58,255.91
2010	80,172.70	89,305.68	6,334.73	6,989.47	2,978.63	1,607.48	62,560.11	65,245.38
2011	76,954.42	87,569.10	6,095.08	6,860.37	3,218.28	1,736.58	68,655.19	72,105.74
2012	73,477.20	85,693.04	5,836.14	6,720.90	3,477.22	1,876.05	74,491.33	78,826.64
2013	69,720.22	83,666.32	5,556.37	6,570.22	3,756.99	2,026.72	80,047.70	85,396.86
2014	65,660.96	81,476.83	5,254.10	6,407.45	4,059.26	2,189.49	85,301.80	91,804.31
2015	61,275.09	79,111.49	4,927.50	6,231.61	4,385.86	2,365.34	90,229.30	98,035.92
2016	56,536.35	76,556.18	4,574.62	6,041.64	4,738.74	2,555.31	94,803.92	104,077.56
2017	51,416.35	73,795.65	4,193.35	5,836.42	5,120.01	2,760.53	98,997.27	109,913.97
2018	45,884.40	70,813.41	3,781.41	5,614.71	5,531.95	2,982.24	102,778.68	115,528.68
2019	39,907.36	67,591.66	3,336.32	5,375.20	5,977.04	3,221.75	106,115.00	120,903.88
2020	33,449.42	64,111.16	2,855.42	5,116.45	6,457.94	3,480.50	108,970.42	126,020.33
2021	26,471.90	60,351.13	2,335.83	4,836.92	6,977.53	3,760.03	111,306.26	130,857.24
2022	18,932.97	56,289.12	1,774.44	4,534.94	7,538.92	4,062.01	113,080.69	135,392.18
2023	10,787.49	51,900.88	1,167.87	4,208.71	8,145.49	4,388.24	114,248.56	139,600.89
2024	1,986.63	47,160.21	512.51	3,856.27	8,800.85	4,740.67	114,761.07	143,457.17
2025	0.00	42,038.80	19.72	3,475.54	1,986.63	5,121.41	114,780.79	146,932.70
2026	0.00	36,506.07	0.00	3,064.22	0.00	5,532.73	114,780.79	149,996.92
2027	0.00	30,529.00	0.00	2,619.87	0.00	5,977.08	114,780.79	152,616.79
2028	0.00	24,071.88	0.00	2,139.83	0.00	6,457.11	114,780.79	154,756.63
2029	0.00	17,096.18	0.00	1,621.24	0.00	6,975.70	114,780.79	156,377.87
2030	0.00	9,560.24	0.00	1,061.00	0.00	7,535.94	114,780.79	157,438.88
2031	0.00	1,419.06	0.00	455.77	0.00	8,141.18	114,780.79	157,894.65
2032	0.00	0.00	0.00	13.76	0.00	1,419.06	114,780.79	157,908.41

Source: <www.mortgage-x.com>.

Based on 7.5%, $100,000 loan amount, 30 years

Year	Loan Balance		Yearly Interest Paid		Yearly Principal Paid		Total Interest	
	Biweekly	Standard	Biweekly	Standard	Biweekly	Standard	Biweekly	Standard
2002	98,613.26	99,236.63	6,304.62	6,228.78	1,386.74	763.37	6,304.62	6,228.78
2003	96,856.95	98,255.53	7,333.49	7,409.48	1,756.30	981.10	13,638.10	13,638.25
2004	94,964.07	97,198.27	7,196.90	7,333.31	1,892.89	1,057.26	20,835.01	20,971.56
2005	92,923.98	96,058.93	7,049.70	7,251.23	2,040.09	1,139.34	27,884.70	28,222.80
2006	90,725.23	94,831.14	6,891.04	7,162.78	2,198.74	1,227.79	34,775.75	35,385.58
2007	88,355.50	93,508.04	6,720.05	7,067.47	2,369.74	1,323.11	41,495.80	42,453.05
2008	85,801.47	92,082.21	6,535.76	6,964.75	2,554.02	1,425.82	48,031.56	49,417.80
2009	83,048.83	90,545.70	6,337.14	6,854.06	2,752.65	1,536.51	54,368.71	56,271.86
2010	80,082.11	88,889.90	6,123.08	6,734.78	2,966.71	1,655.80	60,491.78	63,006.64
2011	76,884.69	87,105.56	5,892.36	6,606.23	3,197.43	1,784.34	66,384.14	69,612.88
2012	73,438.60	85,182.70	5,643.70	6,467.71	3,446.08	1,922.86	72,027.85	76,080.59
2013	69,724.52	83,110.56	5,375.71	6,318.43	3,714.08	2,072.14	77,403.56	82,399.02
2014	65,721.61	80,877.56	5,086.87	6,157.57	4,002.91	2,233.01	82,490.43	88,556.59
2015	61,407.39	78,471.20	4,775.58	5,984.21	4,314.21	2,406.36	87,266.01	94,540.80
2016	56,757.68	75,878.02	4,440.07	5,797.40	4,649.72	2,593.17	91,706.08	100,338.21
2017	51,746.36	73,083.54	4,078.47	5,596.09	5,011.32	2,794.49	95,784.55	105,934.30
2018	46,345.32	70,072.11	3,688.75	5,379.14	5,401.04	3,011.43	99,473.30	111,313.44
2019	40,524.26	66,826.90	3,268.73	5,145.36	5,821.06	3,245.21	102,742.02	116,458.80
2020	34,250.50	63,329.75	2,816.03	4,893.43	6,273.75	3,497.15	105,558.06	121,352.23
2021	27,488.85	59,561.11	2,328.14	4,621.93	6,761.65	3,768.64	107,886.20	125,974.16
2022	20,201.36	55,499.89	1,802.30	4,329.36	7,287.49	4,061.21	109,688.50	130,303.52
2023	12,347.14	51,123.40	1,235.57	4,014.08	7,854.22	4,376.49	110,924.06	134,317.60
2024	3,882.12	46,407.15	624.76	3,674.32	8,465.03	4,716.25	111,548.83	137,991.92
2025	0.00	41,324.76	69.33	3,308.19	3,882.12	5,082.39	111,618.16	141,300.11
2026	0.00	35,847.82	0.00	2,913.63	0.00	5,476.95	111,618.16	144,213.74
2027	0.00	29,945.68	0.00	2,488.44	0.00	5,902.14	111,618.16	146,702.18
2028	0.00	23,585.35	0.00	2,030.24	0.00	6,360.33	111,618.16	148,732.42
2029	0.00	16,731.25	0.00	1,536.47	0.00	6,854.10	111,618.16	150,268.89
2030	0.00	9,345.04	0.00	1,004.37	0.00	7,386.20	111,618.16	151,273.26
2031	0.00	1,385.43	0.00	430.96	0.00	7,959.61	111,618.16	151,704.22
2032	0.00	0.00	0.00	13.00	0.00	1,385.43	111,618.16	151,717.22

Source: <www.mortgage-x.com>.

Based on 7.25%, $100,000 loan amount, 30 years

Year	Loan Balance		Yearly Interest Paid		Yearly Principal Paid		Total Interest	
	Biweekly	Standard	Biweekly	Standard	Biweekly	Standard	Biweekly	Standard
2002	98,589.83	99,198.35	6,093.77	6,020.11	1,410.17	801.65	6,093.77	6,020.11
2003	96,807.97	98,170.40	7,086.43	7,158.17	1,781.86	1,027.95	13,180.20	13,178.28
2004	94,892.32	97,065.40	6,952.64	7,081.12	1,915.65	1,105.00	20,132.84	20,259.40
2005	92,832.84	95,877.57	6,808.81	6,998.29	2,059.48	1,187.83	26,941.65	27,257.68
2006	90,618.72	94,600.71	6,654.17	6,909.25	2,214.12	1,276.87	33,595.82	34,166.93
2007	88,238.35	93,228.13	6,487.93	6,813.54	2,380.36	1,372.58	40,083.75	40,980.47
2008	85,679.26	91,752.66	6,309.20	6,710.65	2,559.09	1,475.46	46,392.95	47,691.12
2009	82,928.02	90,166.60	6,117.05	6,600.05	2,751.24	1,586.06	52,510.00	54,291.17
2010	79,970.21	88,461.65	5,910.48	6,481.16	2,957.82	1,704.95	58,420.48	60,772.33
2011	76,790.31	86,628.90	5,688.39	6,353.36	3,179.90	1,832.75	64,108.87	67,125.70
2012	73,371.64	84,658.76	5,449.63	6,215.98	3,418.66	1,970.13	69,558.50	73,341.68
2013	69,696.29	82,540.95	5,192.94	6,068.31	3,675.35	2,117.81	74,751.44	79,409.99
2014	65,744.98	80,264.40	4,916.98	5,909.56	3,951.31	2,276.56	79,668.42	85,319.54
2015	61,496.99	77,817.19	4,620.30	5,738.91	4,247.99	2,447.20	84,288.72	91,058.46
2016	56,930.04	75,186.55	4,301.34	5,555.47	4,566.95	2,630.64	88,590.06	96,613.93
2017	52,020.19	72,358.72	3,958.44	5,358.28	4,909.86	2,827.83	92,548.50	101,972.21
2018	46,741.68	69,318.92	3,589.78	5,146.32	5,278.51	3,039.80	96,138.28	107,118.53
2019	41,066.83	66,051.26	3,193.45	4,918.46	5,674.84	3,267.66	99,331.73	112,036.99
2020	34,965.90	62,538.67	2,767.36	4,673.52	6,100.93	3,512.60	102,099.09	116,710.51
2021	28,406.88	58,762.77	2,309.27	4,410.22	6,559.02	3,775.89	104,408.36	121,120.73
2022	21,355.38	54,703.84	1,816.79	4,127.19	7,051.50	4,058.93	106,225.15	125,247.91
2023	13,774.43	50,340.66	1,287.34	3,822.94	7,580.96	4,363.18	107,512.49	129,070.85
2024	5,624.26	45,650.43	718.12	3,495.88	8,150.17	4,690.24	108,230.61	132,566.73
2025	0.00	40,608.62	141.47	3,144.31	5,624.26	5,041.81	108,372.08	135,711.04
2026	0.00	35,188.89	0.00	2,766.38	0.00	5,419.73	108,372.08	138,477.42
2027	0.00	29,362.90	0.00	2,360.13	0.00	5,825.99	108,372.08	140,837.55
2028	0.00	23,100.20	0.00	1,923.42	0.00	6,262.69	108,372.08	142,760.97
2029	0.00	16,368.07	0.00	1,453.98	0.00	6,732.13	108,372.08	144,214.95
2030	0.00	9,131.31	0.00	949.35	0.00	7,236.76	108,372.08	145,164.30
2031	0.00	1,352.09	0.00	406.90	0.00	7,779.22	108,372.08	145,571.20
2032	0.00	0.00	0.00	12.27	0.00	1,352.09	108,372.08	145,583.46

Source: <www.mortgage-x.com>.

Based on 7%, $100,000 loan amount, 30 years

Year	Loan Balance		Yearly Interest Paid		Yearly Principal Paid		Total Interest	
	Biweekly	Standard	Biweekly	Standard	Biweekly	Standard	Biweekly	Standard
2002	98,564.59	99,158.45	5,882.92	5,811.48	1,435.41	841.55	5,882.92	5,811.48
2003	96,755.02	98,081.81	6,839.36	6,906.98	1,809.57	1,076.65	12,722.28	12,718.46
2004	94,814.42	96,927.33	6,708.33	6,829.15	1,940.60	1,154.48	19,430.61	19,547.62
2005	92,733.30	95,689.40	6,567.82	6,745.70	2,081.11	1,237.93	25,998.43	26,293.31
2006	90,501.50	94,361.98	6,417.13	6,656.21	2,231.80	1,327.42	32,415.56	32,949.52
2007	88,108.10	92,938.59	6,255.53	6,560.25	2,393.40	1,423.38	38,671.09	39,509.77
2008	85,541.40	91,412.31	6,082.23	6,457.35	2,566.70	1,526.28	44,753.32	45,967.12
2009	82,788.85	89,775.70	5,896.39	6,347.02	2,752.55	1,636.61	50,649.71	52,314.13
2010	79,837.00	88,020.77	5,697.08	6,228.70	2,951.85	1,754.93	56,346.79	58,542.84
2011	76,671.42	86,138.98	5,483.34	6,101.84	3,165.59	1,881.79	61,830.13	64,644.68
2012	73,276.62	84,121.16	5,254.13	5,965.81	3,394.80	2,017.82	67,084.27	70,610.48
2013	69,636.01	81,957.47	5,008.32	5,819.94	3,640.61	2,163.69	72,092.59	76,430.42
2014	65,731.79	79,637.36	4,744.72	5,663.52	3,904.21	2,320.11	76,837.31	82,093.95
2015	61,544.89	77,149.53	4,462.02	5,495.80	4,186.91	2,487.83	81,299.34	87,589.75
2016	57,054.82	74,481.86	4,158.86	5,315.96	4,490.07	2,667.67	85,458.20	92,905.71
2017	52,239.63	71,621.34	3,833.75	5,123.11	4,815.18	2,860.52	89,291.95	98,028.82
2018	47,075.79	68,554.04	3,485.09	4,916.32	5,163.84	3,067.31	92,777.04	102,945.14
2019	41,538.05	65,265.00	3,111.19	4,694.59	5,537.74	3,289.04	95,888.23	107,639.73
2020	35,599.34	61,738.19	2,710.22	4,456.82	5,938.71	3,526.81	98,598.46	112,096.56
2021	29,230.63	57,956.43	2,280.22	4,201.87	6,368.72	3,781.76	100,878.67	116,298.43
2022	22,400.77	53,901.29	1,819.07	3,928.49	6,829.86	4,055.14	102,697.74	120,226.91
2023	15,076.38	49,553.00	1,324.54	3,635.34	7,324.39	4,348.29	104,022.29	123,862.26
2024	7,221.65	44,890.37	794.20	3,321.00	7,854.73	4,662.63	104,816.49	127,183.26
2025	0.00	39,890.69	229.77	2,983.94	7,221.65	4,999.69	105,046.26	130,167.20
2026	0.00	34,529.57	0.00	2,622.51	0.00	5,361.12	105,046.26	132,789.71
2027	0.00	28,780.90	0.00	2,234.96	0.00	5,748.67	105,046.26	135,024.67
2028	0.00	22,616.65	0.00	1,819.39	0.00	6,164.24	105,046.26	136,844.05
2029	0.00	16,006.79	0.00	1,373.77	0.00	6,609.86	105,046.26	138,217.83
2030	0.00	8,919.11	0.00	895.94	0.00	7,087.69	105,046.26	139,113.77
2031	0.00	1,319.05	0.00	383.57	0.00	7,600.05	105,046.26	139,497.35
2032	0.00	0.00	0.00	11.55	0.00	1,319.05	105,046.26	139,508.90

Source: <www.mortgage-x.com>.

Based on 6.75%, $100,000 loan amount, 30 years

Year	Loan Balance		Yearly Interest Paid		Yearly Principal Paid		Total Interest	
	Biweekly	Standard	Biweekly	Standard	Biweekly	Standard	Biweekly	Standard
2002	98,537.49	99,116.90	5,672.07	5,602.88	1,462.51	883.10	5,672.07	5,602.88
2003	96,697.99	97,989.66	6,592.28	6,655.94	1,839.49	1,127.24	12,264.35	12,258.82
2004	94,730.22	96,783.93	6,464.00	6,577.45	1,967.77	1,205.72	18,728.35	18,836.27
2005	92,625.22	95,494.26	6,326.78	6,493.50	2,105.00	1,289.68	25,055.13	25,329.77
2006	90,373.43	94,114.78	6,179.98	6,403.70	2,251.80	1,379.47	31,235.11	31,733.47
2007	87,964.60	92,639.26	6,022.95	6,307.65	2,408.83	1,475.52	37,258.05	38,041.13
2008	85,387.79	91,061.00	5,854.96	6,204.92	2,576.81	1,578.26	43,113.02	44,246.04
2009	82,631.28	89,372.85	5,675.27	6,095.03	2,756.51	1,688.15	48,788.28	50,341.07
2010	79,682.54	87,567.15	5,483.04	5,977.48	2,948.74	1,805.69	54,271.32	56,318.55
2011	76,528.16	85,635.73	5,277.40	5,851.76	3,154.38	1,931.42	59,548.72	62,170.31
2012	73,153.81	83,569.83	5,057.42	5,717.27	3,374.35	2,065.90	64,606.14	67,887.58
2013	69,544.14	81,360.08	4,822.11	5,573.43	3,609.67	2,209.75	69,428.25	73,461.01
2014	65,682.75	78,996.48	4,570.38	5,419.57	3,861.39	2,363.61	73,998.63	78,880.58
2015	61,552.07	76,468.30	4,301.10	5,255.00	4,130.67	2,528.18	78,299.73	84,135.58
2016	57,133.34	73,764.08	4,013.04	5,078.97	4,418.73	2,704.21	82,312.77	89,214.54
2017	52,406.46	70,871.58	3,704.89	4,890.68	4,726.88	2,892.50	86,017.67	94,105.22
2018	47,349.94	67,777.68	3,375.26	4,689.28	5,056.52	3,093.90	89,392.92	98,794.50
2019	41,940.80	64,468.36	3,022.63	4,473.86	5,409.14	3,309.32	92,415.56	103,268.35
2020	36,154.44	60,928.62	2,645.42	4,243.43	5,786.36	3,539.74	95,060.97	107,511.79
2021	29,964.56	57,142.41	2,241.89	3,996.97	6,189.88	3,786.21	97,302.87	111,508.76
2022	23,343.02	53,092.58	1,810.23	3,733.34	6,621.54	4,049.83	99,113.10	115,242.10
2023	16,259.71	48,760.76	1,348.47	3,451.36	7,083.31	4,331.82	100,461.57	118,693.46
2024	8,682.44	44,127.33	854.50	3,149.75	7,577.27	4,633.43	101,316.07	121,843.21
2025	576.75	39,171.29	326.09	2,827.13	8,105.69	4,956.05	101,642.16	124,670.34
2026	0.00	33,870.16	2.16	2,482.05	576.75	5,301.13	101,644.32	127,152.39
2027	0.00	28,199.93	0.00	2,112.94	0.00	5,670.23	101,644.32	129,265.34
2028	0.00	22,134.89	0.00	1,718.14	0.00	6,065.04	101,644.32	130,983.48
2029	0.00	15,647.55	0.00	1,295.84	0.00	6,487.34	101,644.32	132,279.32
2030	0.00	8,708.52	0.00	844.14	0.00	6,939.03	101,644.32	133,123.46
2031	0.00	1,286.33	0.00	360.99	0.00	7,422.19	101,644.32	133,484.45
2032	0.00	0.00	0.00	10.86	0.00	1,286.33	101,644.32	133,495.31

Source: <www.mortgage-x.com>.

Based on 6.5%, $100,000 loan amount, 30 years

Year	Loan Balance		Yearly Interest Paid		Yearly Principal Paid		Total Interest	
	Biweekly	Standard	Biweekly	Standard	Biweekly	Standard	Biweekly	Standard
2002	98,508.47	99,073.63	5,461.22	5,394.31	1,491.53	926.37	5,461.22	5,394.31
2003	96,636.81	97,893.86	6,345.22	6,405.05	1,871.67	1,179.77	11,806.44	11,799.36
2004	94,639.60	96,635.09	6,219.68	6,326.04	1,997.20	1,258.78	18,026.12	18,125.40
2005	92,508.44	95,292.01	6,085.72	6,241.74	2,131.16	1,343.08	24,111.85	24,367.14
2006	90,234.34	93,858.98	5,942.78	6,151.79	2,274.10	1,433.03	30,054.63	30,518.92
2007	87,807.71	92,329.98	5,790.25	6,055.82	2,426.63	1,529.00	35,844.88	36,574.74
2008	85,218.32	90,698.58	5,627.49	5,953.42	2,589.39	1,631.40	41,472.37	42,528.15
2009	82,455.25	88,957.92	5,453.81	5,844.16	2,763.07	1,740.66	46,926.19	48,372.31
2010	79,506.85	87,100.68	5,268.49	5,727.58	2,948.40	1,857.23	52,194.67	54,099.89
2011	76,360.70	85,119.07	5,070.73	5,603.20	3,146.15	1,981.62	57,265.41	59,703.09
2012	73,003.53	83,004.74	4,859.71	5,470.49	3,357.17	2,114.33	62,125.12	65,173.58
2013	69,421.18	80,748.81	4,634.54	5,328.89	3,582.35	2,255.93	66,759.66	70,502.47
2014	65,598.56	78,341.79	4,394.26	5,177.80	3,822.62	2,407.01	71,153.92	75,680.27
2015	61,519.55	75,773.58	4,137.87	5,016.60	4,079.01	2,568.22	75,291.79	80,696.87
2016	57,166.94	73,033.36	3,864.28	4,844.60	4,352.60	2,740.21	79,156.07	85,541.47
2017	52,522.40	70,109.63	3,572.34	4,661.09	4,644.54	2,923.73	82,728.41	90,202.56
2018	47,566.33	66,990.09	3,260.82	4,465.28	4,956.07	3,119.54	85,989.23	94,667.83
2019	42,277.85	63,661.63	2,928.40	4,256.36	5,288.48	3,328.46	88,917.63	98,924.19
2020	36,634.66	60,110.26	2,573.69	4,033.44	5,643.19	3,551.37	91,491.32	102,957.63
2021	30,612.96	56,321.05	2,195.19	3,795.60	6,021.70	3,789.22	93,686.51	106,753.23
2022	24,187.38	52,278.06	1,791.30	3,541.83	6,425.59	4,042.99	95,477.81	110,295.07
2023	17,330.81	47,964.31	1,360.32	3,271.06	6,856.57	4,313.75	96,838.13	113,566.13
2024	10,014.36	43,361.65	900.43	2,982.16	7,316.45	4,602.65	97,738.56	116,548.29
2025	2,207.18	38,450.75	409.70	2,673.92	7,807.18	4,910.90	98,148.26	119,222.21
2026	0.00	33,210.96	22.30	2,345.02	2,207.18	5,239.79	98,170.56	121,567.23
2027	0.00	27,620.25	0.00	1,994.11	0.00	5,590.71	98,170.56	123,561.34
2028	0.00	21,655.12	0.00	1,619.68	0.00	5,965.13	98,170.56	125,181.02
2029	0.00	15,290.49	0.00	1,220.19	0.00	6,364.63	98,170.56	126,401.21
2030	0.00	8,499.61	0.00	793.94	0.00	6,790.88	98,170.56	127,195.15
2031	0.00	1,253.94	0.00	339.14	0.00	7,245.68	98,170.56	127,534.29
2032	0.00	0.00	0.00	10.20	0.00	1,253.94	98,170.56	127,544.49

Source: <www.mortgage-x.com>.

Based on 6.25%, $100,000 loan amount, 30 years

Year	Loan Balance		Yearly Interest Paid		Yearly Principal Paid		Total Interest	
	Biweekly	Standard	Biweekly	Standard	Biweekly	Standard	Biweekly	Standard
2002	98,477.50	99,028.61	5,250.39	5,185.78	1,522.50	971.39	5,250.39	5,185.78
2003	96,571.36	97,794.33	6,098.19	6,154.33	1,906.14	1,234.28	11,348.57	11,340.11
2004	94,542.44	96,480.67	5,975.40	6,074.94	2,028.92	1,313.67	17,323.98	17,415.05
2005	92,382.83	95,082.50	5,844.71	5,990.44	2,159.61	1,398.17	23,168.69	23,405.49
2006	90,084.11	93,594.40	5,705.60	5,900.51	2,298.72	1,488.10	28,874.29	29,306.00
2007	87,637.31	92,010.59	5,557.53	5,804.79	2,446.79	1,583.82	34,431.82	35,110.79
2008	85,032.91	90,324.90	5,399.92	5,702.92	2,604.40	1,685.69	39,831.74	40,813.71
2009	82,260.74	88,530.78	5,232.16	5,594.49	2,772.17	1,794.12	45,063.90	46,408.20
2010	79,310.01	86,621.27	5,053.59	5,479.09	2,950.73	1,909.52	50,117.49	51,887.29
2011	76,169.21	84,588.92	4,863.52	5,356.27	3,140.80	2,032.34	54,981.01	57,243.55
2012	72,826.09	82,425.86	4,661.21	5,225.54	3,343.12	2,163.06	59,642.21	62,469.10
2013	69,267.63	80,123.66	4,445.86	5,086.41	3,558.46	2,302.20	64,088.07	67,555.51
2014	65,479.95	77,673.39	4,216.64	4,938.33	3,787.68	2,450.28	68,304.72	72,493.84
2015	61,448.28	75,065.50	3,972.66	4,780.72	4,031.66	2,607.88	72,277.38	77,274.56
2016	57,156.92	72,289.88	3,712.96	4,612.98	4,291.36	2,775.63	75,990.34	81,887.54
2017	52,589.14	69,335.71	3,436.54	4,434.45	4,567.79	2,954.16	79,426.88	86,321.98
2018	47,727.12	66,191.54	3,142.31	4,244.43	4,862.02	3,144.18	82,569.19	90,566.41
2019	42,551.92	62,845.12	2,829.12	4,042.19	5,175.20	3,346.42	85,398.31	94,608.60
2020	37,043.35	59,283.45	2,495.76	3,826.94	5,508.56	3,561.67	87,894.07	98,435.54
2021	31,179.96	55,492.70	2,140.93	3,597.85	5,863.39	3,790.76	90,035.00	102,033.39
2022	24,938.88	51,458.11	1,763.24	3,354.02	6,241.08	4,034.59	91,798.24	105,387.41
2023	18,295.78	47,164.01	1,361.22	3,094.51	6,643.10	4,294.10	93,159.46	108,481.92
2024	11,224.76	42,593.71	933.31	2,818.30	7,071.01	4,570.30	94,092.77	111,300.22
2025	3,698.28	37,729.44	477.83	2,524.33	7,526.49	4,864.27	94,570.61	113,824.56
2026	0.00	32,552.28	59.02	2,211.46	3,698.28	5,177.15	94,629.63	116,036.01
2027	0.00	27,042.13	0.00	1,878.45	0.00	5,510.16	94,629.63	117,914.46
2028	0.00	21,177.55	0.00	1,524.03	0.00	5,864.58	94,629.63	119,438.49
2029	0.00	14,935.75	0.00	1,146.81	0.00	6,241.80	94,629.63	120,585.30
2030	0.00	8,292.47	0.00	745.32	0.00	6,643.28	94,629.63	121,330.62
2031	0.00	1,221.88	0.00	318.02	0.00	7,070.59	94,629.63	121,648.64
2032	0.00	0.00	0.00	9.55	0.00	1,221.88	94,629.63	121,658.19

Source: <www.mortgage-x.com>.

Based on 6%, $100,000 loan amount, 30 years

Year	Loan Balance		Yearly Interest Paid		Yearly Principal Paid		Total Interest	
	Biweekly	Standard	Biweekly	Standard	Biweekly	Standard	Biweekly	Standard
2002	98,444.51	98,981.79	5,039.57	4,977.30	1,555.49	1,018.21	5,039.57	4,977.30
2003	96,501.56	97,690.98	5,851.21	5,903.79	1,942.95	1,290.81	10,890.77	10,881.09
2004	94,438.60	96,320.56	5,731.20	5,824.18	2,062.95	1,370.43	16,621.97	16,705.27
2005	92,248.23	94,865.60	5,603.79	5,739.65	2,190.37	1,454.95	22,225.76	22,444.93
2006	89,922.58	93,320.91	5,468.50	5,649.92	2,325.65	1,544.69	27,694.26	28,094.84
2007	87,453.29	91,680.95	5,324.86	5,554.64	2,469.29	1,639.96	33,019.13	33,649.49
2008	84,831.48	89,939.84	5,172.35	5,453.49	2,621.80	1,741.11	38,191.48	39,102.98
2009	82,047.75	88,091.34	5,010.42	5,346.11	2,783.73	1,848.50	43,201.90	44,449.09
2010	79,092.08	86,128.83	4,838.49	5,232.09	2,955.67	1,962.51	48,040.39	49,681.18
2011	75,953.86	84,045.27	4,655.94	5,111.05	3,138.22	2,083.56	52,696.33	54,792.23
2012	72,621.82	81,833.21	4,462.11	4,982.54	3,332.04	2,212.06	57,158.44	59,774.77
2013	69,083.98	79,484.71	4,256.31	4,846.11	3,537.84	2,348.50	61,414.76	64,620.88
2014	65,327.63	76,991.36	4,037.81	4,701.26	3,756.35	2,493.35	65,452.56	69,322.14
2015	61,339.27	74,344.22	3,805.80	4,547.47	3,988.35	2,647.13	69,258.37	73,869.61
2016	57,104.58	71,533.82	3,559.47	4,384.20	4,234.69	2,810.40	72,817.84	78,253.81
2017	52,608.35	68,550.07	3,297.92	4,210.86	4,496.24	2,983.74	76,115.76	82,464.67
2018	47,834.41	65,382.30	3,020.22	4,026.83	4,773.94	3,167.77	79,135.98	86,491.50
2019	42,765.62	62,019.14	2,725.37	3,831.45	5,068.79	3,363.16	81,861.34	90,322.96
2020	37,383.76	58,448.56	2,412.30	3,624.02	5,381.86	3,570.59	84,273.64	93,946.97
2021	31,669.51	54,657.74	2,079.90	3,403.79	5,714.26	3,790.81	86,353.54	97,350.77
2022	25,602.32	50,633.12	1,726.97	3,169.98	6,067.19	4,024.62	88,080.52	100,520.75
2023	19,160.41	46,360.27	1,352.24	2,921.75	6,441.91	4,272.85	89,432.76	103,442.50
2024	12,320.62	41,823.87	954.37	2,658.21	6,839.79	4,536.39	90,387.13	106,100.72
2025	5,058.39	37,007.68	531.92	2,378.42	7,262.23	4,816.19	90,919.05	108,479.13
2026	0.00	31,894.44	107.13	2,081.37	5,058.39	5,113.24	91,026.18	110,560.50
2027	0.00	26,465.83	0.00	1,765.99	0.00	5,428.61	91,026.18	112,326.49
2028	0.00	20,702.39	0.00	1,431.17	0.00	5,763.44	91,026.18	113,757.66
2029	0.00	14,583.48	0.00	1,075.69	0.00	6,118.91	91,026.18	114,833.35
2030	0.00	8,087.16	0.00	698.29	0.00	6,496.32	91,026.18	115,531.64
2031	0.00	1,190.17	0.00	297.61	0.00	6,896.99	91,026.18	115,829.26
2032	0.00	0.00	0.00	8.93	0.00	1,190.17	91,026.18	115,838.19

Source: <www.mortgage-x.com>.

The Fair Debt Collection Practices Act

As amended by Public Law 104-208, 110 Stat. 3009 (Sept. 30, 1996)

To amend the Consumer Credit Protection Act to prohibit abusive practices by debt collectors.

Be it enacted by the Senate and House of Representatives of the United States of America in Congress assembled, That the Consumer Credit Protection Act (15 U.S.C. 1601 et seq.) is amended by adding at the end thereof the following new title:

TITLE VIII—DEBT COLLECTION PRACTICES [Fair Debt Collection Practices Act]

Sec.
801. Short Title
802. Congressional findings and declaration of purpose
803. Definitions
804. Acquisition of location information
805. Communication in connection with debt collection
806. Harassment or abuse
807. False or misleading representations
808. Unfair practice
809. Validation of debts
810. Multiple debts
811. Legal actions by debt collectors
812. Furnishing certain deceptive forms
813. Civil liability
814. Administrative enforcement
815. Reports to Congress by the Commission
816. Relation to State laws
817. Exemption for State regulation
818. Effective date

§ 801. Short Title [15 USC 1601 note]

This title may be cited as the "Fair Debt Collection Practices Act."

§ 802. Congressional findings and declarations of purpose [15 USC 1692]

(a) There is abundant evidence of the use of abusive, deceptive, and unfair debt collection practices by many debt collectors. Abusive debt collection practices contribute to the number of personal bankruptcies, to marital instability, to the loss of jobs, and to invasions of individual privacy.

(b) Existing laws and procedures for redressing these injuries are inadequate to protect consumers.

(c) Means other than misrepresentation or other abusive debt collection practices are available for the effective collection of debts.

(d) Abusive debt collection practices are carried on to a substantial extent in interstate commerce and through means and instrumentalities of such commerce. Even where abusive debt collection practices are purely intrastate in character, they nevertheless directly affect interstate commerce.

(e) It is the purpose of this title to eliminate abusive debt collection practices by debt collectors, to insure that those debt collectors who refrain from using abusive debt collection practices are not competitively disadvantaged, and to promote consistent State action to protect consumers against debt collection abuses.

§ 803. Definitions [15 USC 1692a]

As used in this title—

(1) The term "Commission" means the Federal Trade Commission.

(2) The term "communication" means the conveying of information regarding a debt directly or indirectly to any person through any medium.

(3) The term "consumer" means any natural person obligated or allegedly obligated to pay any debt.

(4) The term "creditor" means any person who offers or extends credit creating a debt or to whom a debt is owed, but such term does not include any person to the extent that he receives an assignment or transfer of a debt in default solely for the purpose of facilitating collection of such debt for another.

(5) The term "debt" means any obligation or alleged obligation of a consumer to pay money arising out of a transaction in which the money, property, insurance or services which are the subject of the transaction are primarily for personal, family, or household purposes, whether or not such obligation has been reduced to judgment.

(6) The term "debt collector" means any person who uses any instrumentality of interstate commerce or the mails in any business the principal purpose of which is the collection of any debts, or who regularly collects or attempts to collect, directly or indirectly, debts owed or due or asserted to be owed or due another. Notwithstanding the exclusion provided by clause (F) of the last sentence of this paragraph, the term includes any creditor who, in the process of collecting his own debts, uses any name other than his own which would indicate that a third person is collecting or attempting to collect such debts. For the purpose of section 808(6), such term also includes any person who uses any instrumentality of interstate commerce or the mails in any business the principal purpose of which is the enforcement of security interests. The term does not include—

(A) any officer or employee of a creditor while, in the name of the creditor, collecting debts for such creditor;

(B) any person while acting as a debt collector for another person, both of whom are related by common ownership or affiliated by corporate control, if the person acting as a debt collector does so only for persons to whom it is so related or affiliated and if the principal business of such person is not the collection of debts;

(C) any officer or employee of the United States or any State to the extent that collecting or attempting to collect any debt is in the performance of his official duties;

(D) any person while serving or attempting to serve legal process on any other person in connection with the judicial enforcement of any debt;

(E) any nonprofit organization which, at the request of consumers, performs bona fide consumer credit counseling and assists consumers in the liquidation of their debts by receiving payments from such consumers and distributing such amounts to creditors; and

(F) any person collecting or attempting to collect any debt owed or due or asserted to be owed or due another to the extent such activity (i) is incidental to a bona fide fiduciary obligation or a bona fide escrow arrangement; (ii) concerns a debt which was originated by such person; (iii) concerns a debt which was not in default at the time it was obtained by such person; or (iv) concerns a debt obtained by such person as a secured party in a commercial credit transaction involving the creditor.

(7) The term "location information" means a consumer's place of abode and his telephone number at such place, or his place of employment.

(8) The term "State" means any State, territory, or possession of the United States, the District of Columbia, the Commonwealth of Puerto Rico, or any political subdivision of any of the foregoing.

§ 804. Acquisition of location information [15 USC 1692b]

Any debt collector communicating with any person other than the consumer for the purpose of acquiring location information about the consumer shall—

(1) identify himself, state that he is confirming or correcting location information concerning the consumer, and, only if expressly requested, identify his employer;

(2) not state that such consumer owes any debt;

(3) not communicate with any such person more than once unless requested to do so by such person or unless the debt collector reasonably believes that the earlier response of such person is erroneous or incomplete and that such person now has correct or complete location information;

(4) not communicate by post card;

(5) not use any language or symbol on any envelope or in the contents of any communication effected by the mails or telegram that indicates that the debt collector is in the debt collection business or that the communication relates to the collection of a debt; and

(6) after the debt collector knows the consumer is represented by an attorney with regard to the subject debt and has knowledge of, or can readily ascertain, such attorney's name and address, not communicate with any person other than that attorney, unless the attorney fails to respond within a reasonable period of time to the communication from the debt collector.

§ 805. Communication in connection with debt collection [15 USC 1692c]

(a) COMMUNICATION WITH THE CONSUMER GENERALLY. Without the prior consent of the consumer given directly to the debt collector or the express permission of a court of competent jurisdiction, a debt collector may not communicate with a consumer in connection with the collection of any debt—

(1) at any unusual time or place or a time or place known or which should be known to be inconvenient to the consumer. In the absence of knowledge of circumstances to the contrary, a debt collector shall assume that the convenient time for communicating with a consumer is after 8 o'clock antimeridian and before 9 o'clock postmeridian, local time at the consumer's location;

(2) if the debt collector knows the consumer is represented by an attorney with respect to such debt and has knowledge of, or can readily ascertain, such attorney's name and address, unless the attorney fails to respond within a reasonable period of time to a communication from the debt collector or unless the attorney consents to direct communication with the consumer; or

(3) at the consumer's place of employment if the debt collector knows or has reason to know that the consumer's employer prohibits the consumer from receiving such communication.

(b) COMMUNICATION WITH THIRD PARTIES. Except as provided in section 804, without the prior consent of the consumer given directly to the debt collector, or the express permission of a court of competent jurisdiction, or as reasonably necessary to effectuate a postjudgment judicial remedy, a debt collector may not communicate, in connection with the collection of any debt, with any person other than a consumer, his attorney, a consumer reporting agency if otherwise permitted by law, the creditor, the attorney of the creditor, or the attorney of the debt collector.

(c) CEASING COMMUNICATION. If a consumer notifies a debt collector in writing that the consumer refuses to pay a debt or that the consumer wishes the debt collector to cease further communication with the consumer, the debt collector shall not communicate further with the consumer with respect to such debt, except—

(1) to advise the consumer that the debt collector's further efforts are being terminated;

(2) to notify the consumer that the debt collector or creditor may invoke specified remedies which are ordinarily invoked by such debt collector or creditor; or

(3) where applicable, to notify the consumer that the debt collector or creditor intends to invoke a specified remedy. If such notice from the consumer is made by mail, notification shall be complete upon receipt.

(d) For the purpose of this section, the term "consumer" includes the consumer's spouse, parent (if the consumer is a minor), guardian, executor, or administrator.

§ 806. Harassment or abuse [15 USC 1692d]

A debt collector may not engage in any conduct the natural consequence of which is to harass, oppress, or abuse any person in connection with the collection of a debt. Without limiting the general application of the foregoing, the following conduct is a violation of this section:

(1) The use or threat of use of violence or other criminal means to harm the physical person, reputation, or property of any person.

(2) The use of obscene or profane language or language the natural consequence of which is to abuse the hearer or reader.

(3) The publication of a list of consumers who allegedly refuse to pay debts, except to a consumer reporting agency or to persons meeting the requirements of section 603(f) or 604(3)1 of this Act.

(4) The advertisement for sale of any debt to coerce payment of the debt.

(5) Causing a telephone to ring or engaging any person in telephone conversation repeatedly or continuously with intent to annoy, abuse, or harass any person at the called number.

(6) Except as provided in section 804, the placement of telephone calls without meaningful disclosure of the caller's identity.

§ 807. False or misleading representations [15 USC 1962e]

A debt collector may not use any false, deceptive, or misleading representation or means in connection with the collection of any debt. Without limiting the general application of the foregoing, the following conduct is a violation of this section:

(1) The false representation or implication that the debt collector is vouched for, bonded by, or affiliated with the United States or any State, including the use of any badge, uniform, or facsimile thereof.

(2) The false representation of—

(A) the character, amount, or legal status of any debt; or

(B) any services rendered or compensation which may be lawfully received by any debt collector for the collection of a debt.

(3) The false representation or implication that any individual is an attorney or that any communication is from an attorney.

(4) The representation or implication that nonpayment of any debt will result in the arrest or imprisonment of any person or the seizure, garnishment, attachment, or sale of any property or wages of any person unless such action is lawful and the debt collector or creditor intends to take such action.

(5) The threat to take any action that cannot legally be taken or that is not intended to be taken.

(6) The false representation or implication that a sale, referral, or other transfer of any interest in a debt shall cause the consumer to—

(A) lose any claim or defense to payment of the debt; or

(B) become subject to any practice prohibited by this title.

(7) The false representation or implication that the consumer committed any crime or other conduct in order to disgrace the consumer.

(8) Communicating or threatening to communicate to any person credit information which is known or which should be known to be false, including the failure to communicate that a disputed debt is disputed.

(9) The use or distribution of any written communication which simulates or is falsely represented to be a document authorized, issued, or approved by any court, official, or agency of the United States or any State, or which creates a false impression as to its source, authorization, or approval.

(10) The use of any false representation or deceptive means to collect or attempt to collect any debt or to obtain information concerning a consumer.

(11) The failure to disclose in the initial written communication with the consumer and, in addition, if the initial communication with the consumer is oral, in that initial oral communication, that the debt collector is attempting to collect a debt and that any information obtained will be used for that purpose, and the failure to disclose in subsequent communications that the communication is from a debt collector, except that this paragraph shall not apply to a formal pleading made in connection with a legal action.

(12) The false representation or implication that accounts have been turned over to innocent purchasers for value.

(13) The false representation or implication that documents are legal process.

(14) The use of any business, company, or organization name other than the true name of the debt collector's business, company, or organization.

(15) The false representation or implication that documents are not legal process forms or do not require action by the consumer.

(16) The false representation or implication that a debt collector operates or is employed by a consumer reporting agency as defined by section 603(f) of this Act.

§ 808. Unfair practices [15 USC 1692f]

A debt collector may not use unfair or unconscionable means to collect or attempt to collect any debt. Without limiting the general application of the foregoing, the following conduct is a violation of this section:

(1) The collection of any amount (including any interest, fee, charge, or expense incidental to the principal obligation) unless such amount is expressly authorized by the agreement creating the debt or permitted by law.

(2) The acceptance by a debt collector from any person of a check or other payment instrument postdated by more than five days unless such person is notified in writing of the debt collector's intent to deposit such check or instrument not more than ten nor less than three business days prior to such deposit.

(3) The solicitation by a debt collector of any postdated check or other postdated payment instrument for the purpose of threatening or instituting criminal prosecution.

(4) Depositing or threatening to deposit any postdated check or other postdated payment instrument prior to the date on such check or instrument.

(5) Causing charges to be made to any person for communications by concealment of the true propose of the communication. Such charges include, but are not limited to, collect telephone calls and telegram fees.

(6) Taking or threatening to take any nonjudicial action to effect dispossession or disablement of property if—

> (A) there is no present right to possession of the property claimed as collateral through an enforceable security interest;

> (B) there is no present intention to take possession of the property; or

> (C) the property is exempt by law from such dispossession or disablement.

(7) Communicating with a consumer regarding a debt by post card.

(8) Using any language or symbol, other than the debt collector's address, on any envelope when communicating with a consumer by use of the mails or by telegram, except that a debt collector may use his business name if such name does not indicate that he is in the debt collection business.

§ 809. Validation of debts [15 USC 1692g]

(a) Within five days after the initial communication with a consumer in connection with the collection of any debt, a debt collector shall, unless the following information is contained in the initial communication or the consumer has paid the debt, send the consumer a written notice containing—

(1) the amount of the debt;

(2) the name of the creditor to whom the debt is owed;

(3) a statement that unless the consumer, within thirty days after receipt of the notice, disputes the validity of the debt, or any portion thereof, the debt will be assumed to be valid by the debt collector;

(4) a statement that if the consumer notifies the debt collector in writing within the thirty-day period that the debt, or any portion thereof, is disputed, the debt collector will obtain verification of the debt or a copy of a judgment against the consumer and a copy of such verification or judgment will be mailed to the consumer by the debt collector; and

(5) a statement that, upon the consumer's written request within the thirty-day period, the debt collector will provide the consumer with the name and address of the original creditor, if different from the current creditor.

(b) If the consumer notifies the debt collector in writing within the thirty-day period described in subsection (a) that the debt, or any portion thereof, is disputed, or that the consumer requests the name and address of the original creditor, the debt collector shall cease collection of the debt, or any disputed portion thereof, until the debt collector obtains verification of the debt or any copy of a judgment, or the name and address of the original creditor, and a copy of such verification or judgment, or name and address of the original creditor, is mailed to the consumer by the debt collector.

(c) The failure of a consumer to dispute the validity of a debt under this section may not be construed by any court as an admission of liability by the consumer.

§ 810. Multiple debts [15 USC 1692h]

If any consumer owes multiple debts and makes any single payment to any debt collector with respect to such debts, such debt collector may not apply such payment to any debt which is disputed by the consumer and, where applicable, shall apply such payment in accordance with the consumer's directions.

§ 811. Legal actions by debt collectors [15 USC 1692i]

(a) Any debt collector who brings any legal action on a debt against any consumer shall—

(1) in the case of an action to enforce an interest in real property securing the consumer's obligation, bring such action only in a judicial district or similar legal entity in which such real property is located; or

(2) in the case of an action not described in paragraph (1), bring such action only in the judicial district or similar legal entity—

(A) in which such consumer signed the contract sued upon; or

(B) in which such consumer resides at the commencement of the action.

(b) Nothing in this title shall be construed to authorize the bringing of legal actions by debt collectors.

§ 812. Furnishing certain deceptive forms [15 USC 1692j]

(a) It is unlawful to design, compile, and furnish any form knowing that such form would be used to create the false belief in a consumer that a person other than the creditor of such consumer is participating in the collection of or in an attempt to collect a debt such consumer allegedly owes such creditor, when in fact such person is not so participating.

(b) Any person who violates this section shall be liable to the same extent and in the same manner as a debt collector is liable under section 813 for failure to comply with a provision of this title.

§ 813. Civil liability [15 USC 1692k]

(a) Except as otherwise provided by this section, any debt collector who fails to comply with any provision of this title with respect to any person is liable to such person in an amount equal to the sum of—

(1) any actual damage sustained by such person as a result of such failure;

(2) (A) in the case of any action by an individual, such additional damages as the court may allow, but not exceeding $1,000; or

(B) in the case of a class action, (i) such amount for each named plaintiff as could be recovered under subparagraph (A), and (ii) such amount as the court may allow for all other class members, without regard to a minimum individual recovery, not to exceed the lesser of $500,000 or 1 per centum of the net worth of the debt collector; and

(3) in the case of any successful action to enforce the foregoing liability, the costs of the action, together with a reasonable attorney's fee as determined by the court. On a finding by the court that an action under this section was brought in bad faith and for the purpose of harassment, the court may award to the defendant attorney's fees reasonable in relation to the work expended and costs.

(b) In determining the amount of liability in any action under subsection (a), the court shall consider, among other relevant factors—

(1) in any individual action under subsection (a)(2)(A), the frequency and persistence of noncompliance by the debt collector, the nature of such noncompliance, and the extent to which such noncompliance was intentional; or

(2) in any class action under subsection (a)(2)(B), the frequency and persistence of noncompliance by the debt collector, the nature of such noncompliance, the resources of the debt collector, the number of persons adversely affected, and the extent to which the debt collector's noncompliance was intentional.

(c) A debt collector may not be held liable in any action brought under this title if the debt collector shows by a preponderance of evidence that the violation was not intentional and resulted from a bona fide error notwithstanding the maintenance of procedures reasonably adapted to avoid any such error.

(d) An action to enforce any liability created by this title may be brought in any appropriate United States district court without regard to the amount in controversy, or in any other court of competent jurisdiction, within one year from the date on which the violation occurs.

(e) No provision of this section imposing any liability shall apply to any act done or omitted in good faith in conformity with any advisory opinion of the Commission, notwithstanding that after such act or omission has occurred, such opinion is amended, rescinded, or determined by judicial or other authority to be invalid for any reason.

§ 814. Administrative enforcement [15 USC 1692l]

(a) Compliance with this title shall be enforced by the Commission, except to the extend that enforcement of the requirements imposed under this title is specifically committed to another agency under subsection (b). For purpose of the exercise by the Commission of its functions and powers under the Federal Trade Commission Act, a violation of this title shall be deemed an unfair or deceptive act or practice in violation of that Act. All of the functions and powers of the Commission under the Federal Trade Commission Act are available to the Commission to enforce compliance by any person with this title, irrespective of whether that person is engaged in commerce or meets any other jurisdictional tests in the Federal Trade Commission Act, including the power to enforce the provisions of this title in the same manner as if the violation had been a violation of a Federal Trade Commission trade regulation rule.

(b) Compliance with any requirements imposed under this title shall be enforced under—

(1) section 8 of the Federal Deposit Insurance Act, in the case of—

(A) national banks, by the Comptroller of the Currency;

(B) member banks of the Federal Reserve System (other than national banks), by the Federal Reserve Board; and

(C) banks the deposits or accounts of which are insured by the Federal Deposit Insurance Corporation (other than members of the Federal Reserve System), by the Board of Directors of the Federal Deposit Insurance Corporation;

(2) section 5(d) of the Home Owners Loan Act of 1933, section 407 of the National Housing Act, and sections 6(i) and 17 of the Federal Home Loan Bank Act, by the Federal Home Loan Bank Board (acting directing or through the Federal Savings and Loan Insurance Corporation), in the case of any institution subject to any of those provisions;

(3) the Federal Credit Union Act, by the Administrator of the National Credit Union Administration with respect to any Federal credit union;

(4) subtitle IV of Title 49, by the Interstate Commerce Commission with respect to any common carrier subject to such subtitle;

(5) the Federal Aviation Act of 1958, by the Secretary of Transportation with respect to any air carrier or any foreign air carrier subject to that Act; and

(6) the Packers and Stockyards Act, 1921 (except as provided in section 406 of that Act), by the Secretary of Agriculture with respect to any activities subject to that Act.

(c) For the purpose of the exercise by any agency referred to in subsection (b) of its powers under any Act referred to in that subsection, a violation of any requirement imposed under this title shall be deemed to be a violation of a requirement imposed under that Act. In addition to its powers under any provision of law specifically referred to in subsection (b), each of the agencies referred to in that subsection may exercise, for the purpose of enforcing compliance with any requirement imposed under this title any other authority conferred on it by law, except as provided in subsection (d).

(d) Neither the Commission nor any other agency referred to in subsection (b) may promulgate trade regulation rules or other regulations with respect to the collection of debts by debt collectors as defined in this title.

§ 815. Reports to Congress by the Commission [15 USC 1692m]

(a) Not later than one year after the effective date of this title and at one-year intervals thereafter, the Commission shall make reports to the Congress concerning the administration of its functions under this title, including such recommendations as the Commission deems necessary or appropriate. In addition, each report of the Commission shall include its assessment of the extent to which compliance with this title is being achieved and a summary of the enforcement actions taken by the Commission under section 814 of this title.

(b) In the exercise of its functions under this title, the Commission may obtain upon request the views of any other Federal agency which exercises enforcement functions under section 814 of this title.

§ 816. Relation to State laws [15 USC 1692n]

This title does not annul, alter, or affect, or exempt any person subject to the provisions of this title from complying with the laws of any State with respect to debt collection practices, except to the extent that those laws are inconsistent with any provision of this title, and then only to the extent of the inconsistency. For purposes of this section, a State law is not inconsistent with this title if the protection such law affords any consumer is greater than the protection provided by this title.

§ 817. Exemption for State regulation [15 USC 1692o]

The Commission shall by regulation exempt from the requirements of this title any class of debt collection practices within any State if the Commission determines that under the law of that State that class of debt collection practices is subject to requirements substantially similar to those imposed by this title, and that there is adequate provision for enforcement.

§ 818. Effective date [15 USC 1692 note]

This title takes effect upon the expiration of six months after the date of its enactment, but section 809 shall apply only with respect to debts for which the initial attempt to collect occurs after such effective date.

Approved September 20, 1977

ENDNOTES

1. So in original; however, should read "604(a)(3)."

LEGISLATIVE HISTORY:

Public Law 95-109 [H.R. 5294]

HOUSE REPORT No. 95-131 (Comm. on Banking, Finance, and Urban Affairs).

SENATE REPORT No. 95-382 (Comm. on Banking, Housing, and Urban Affairs).

CONGRESSIONAL RECORD, Vol. 123 (1977):

    Apr. 4, considered and passed House.

    Aug. 5, considered and passed Senate, amended.

    Sept. 8, House agreed to Senate amendment.

WEEKLY COMPILATION OF PRESIDENTIAL DOCUMENTS, Vol. 13, No. 39:

    Sept. 20, Presidential statement.

AMENDMENTS:

SECTION 621, SUBSECTIONS (b)(3), (b)(4) and (b)(5) were amended to transfer certain administrative enforcement responsibilities, pursuant to Pub. L. 95-473, § 3(b), Oct. 17, 1978. 92 Stat. 166; Pub. L. 95-630, Title V. § 501, November 10, 1978, 92 Stat. 3680; Pub. L. 98-443, § 9(h), Oct. 4, 1984, 98 Stat. 708.

SECTION 803, SUBSECTION (6), defining "debt collector," was amended to repeal the attorney at law exemption at former Section (6)(F) and to redesignate Section 803(6)(G) pursuant to Pub. L. 99-361, July 9, 1986, 100 Stat. 768. For legislative history, see H.R. 237, HOUSE REPORT No. 99-405 (Comm. on Banking, Finance and Urban Affairs). CONGRESSIONAL RECORD: Vol. 131 (1985): Dec. 2, considered and passed House. Vol. 132 (1986): June 26, considered and passed Senate.

SECTION 807, SUBSECTION (11), was amended to affect when debt collectors must state (a) that they are attempting to collect a debt and (b) that information obtained will be used for that purpose, pursuant to Pub. L. 104-208 § 2305, 110 Stat. 3009 (Sept. 30, 1996).

Glossary

annual percentage rate (APR)   The percentage rate based on a yearly basis

applicant   Any person who applies to a creditor for credit

asset   Property that can be used to repay a debt such as cash, real estate, or personal property

balance   The amount owed on an account

bankruptcy   The act of having your estate administered under the bankruptcy laws for the benefit of creditors

charge card   A card used to buy goods and services from the issuing merchant on credit and usually due in 30 days

collateral   Property offered to secure a loan or credit that becomes subject to seizure in the case of default

co-signer   A second individual who signs for a loan and assumes equal liability for the debt

credit   The promise to pay in the future in order to buy or borrow in the present; a sum of money due a person or business

credit card   A card that may be used repeatedly to borrow money or purchase goods and services on credit

credit contract   A written agreement between a creditor and debtor that enforces the terms of the contract

credit history   A record of how a person has repaid his debts

credit rating   An evaluation by a creditor or credit reporting agency that reflects a debtor's past credit history based on her payment pattern

credit reporting agency   An agency that keeps credit records on individuals

creditor   An individual or business that makes credit available by lending money or selling goods and services on credit

default   Failure to meet a financial obligation

deferred payment   A payment that can be paid at a later time

deficiency   The difference between the amount you owe a creditor who has foreclosed on your house or repossessed an item of personal property such as a car and the amount of money the sale of the property brings in, with the deficiency amount owed to the creditor

exempt   An account that can be released from obligation to pay in a bankruptcy

finance charge   The dollar amount paid to get credit

foreclosure   The right of a creditor, such as a mortgage lender that has a lien on your property, to force a sale of your property to recover what is owed if you have stopped making payments

gross income   Income of a person or business from all sources before taxes and expenses are taken out

installment contract   A written agreement to pay for goods or services that sets forth the terms, such as the payments of principal and interest, and the date of payments

joint account   An account that two or more people can use with all assuming the liability to repay the debt

judgment   The decision issued by a court at the end of a lawsuit. When a judgment is against you, the court indicates the total amount due the plaintiff (the one who sued you).

late payment   A payment made after the due date

lien   The legal right, usually placed on real estate, to hold property or have it sold or applied to the payment of a claim owed a creditor

liquidate   To convert an asset to cash

net income   The amount of income of a person or business from all sources after taxes and expenses are paid

nonpurchase money agreement   An agreement whereby an individual borrows money and pledges certain property for the loan

purchase money agreement   An agreement whereby a person pledges the property or item she is buying

quitclaim deed   A deed that must be signed, notarized, and recorded when a person who holds title on real property wishes to add or remove another person holding title

refinance   Paying old debts with a new loan

reinstate a contract   Put a contract back in force after all fees and back payments are brought current on property or an item that has been foreclosed or repossessed

repossession   A creditor's reclaiming or taking back property from a consumer who does not fulfill the terms of his contract

retail credit   Credit offered to customers by merchants that allows them to buy now and pay later

secured credit card   A credit card obtained by opening a savings account with certain banks that secure a major credit card they issue with the savings account deposit

secured debt   A debt secured (guaranteed) by using a specific item as collateral to guarantee payment and entitling the creditor to the item designated as collateral if the payments cease

security agreement   The contract a person signs when getting a secured loan that indicates what property or collateral can be taken should the debtor default

service charge   A fee charged for a particular service that is often in addition to the interest charge

unsecured debt   A debt not linked to any collateral or guaranteed specific item, making the creditor sue to collect if the debt is not paid

Index

A

Accounting bills, 53, 143
Accounts receivable, 65, 68–69
Affinity cards, 171
Airline company cards, 172–73
Alimony, 157
American Express, 172
Annual percentage rate, 11, 31
ATM cards, 73, 173
Attorney bills, 53, 143
Auto expenses, 52, 74, 115
    insurance, 55
    repayment schedules, 141

B

Bank cards, 171–72. *See also* Credit cards
Bankruptcy, 13, 157–58
    types of, 157–58
Banks
    banking charges, 74
    secured credit cards and, 176
Behavioral analysis, 15–21
    assessment worksheet, 21
Better Business Bureau, 69, 175
Beverages, 75
Budget, 111–32, 182
    net worth statement, 112, 113, 114
    personal monthly budget worksheet, 118–30
    yearly worksheet, 131–32
Business owners
    collection remedies, 65, 68–69
    credit rating, 161
    debt priorities, 56
    increasing sales, 70
    priorities, 68

C

Cable television, 74
Cambridge Credit Counseling, 156
Car expenses
    maintenance, 112
    payments, 52
Carte Blanche, 172
Cash advances, 12, 32
Cash worksheets
    cash flow, 65–67, 71
    expenditures, 78–90
    extra cash, 104–10
Chapter bankruptcies, 157–58
Charge cards. *See* Credit cards
Charitable giving, 182
ChexSystems, 168
Child care expenses, 55
Child support, 52, 157
Clothing expenses, 55, 115
Collateral, 141
Collection agencies, 69, 138–39
Collection remedies, 65, 68–69
College funds, 182–83

Commissions, 111–12
Comparison shopping, 76
Co-signers, 12
Country club memberships, 55
Credit
    cost of, 31–34
    myths, 8–14
    offers, 10–11
    payment history, 10
    purchasing behavior, analyzing, 15–21
    quiz, 3–6
    shopping for, 175
    unused, 162
    wise use of, 9
Credit card(s)
    annual fee, 171
    application incentives, 19
    cash advances, 12, 32
    chart, 151
    consolidation, 146, 149–50
    co-signers, 12
    cost of, 31–34
    credit card trackers, 22–27
    and debit cards compared, 173–74
    expenditures worksheet, 74, 91–103
    extra payments on, 150
    grace (float) period, 172
    limiting, importance of, 180
    minimum payments on, 11

Credit card(s) *continued*
 organizer worksheet, 174
 paying off, 74–75, 150
 preapproved/unsolicited,
  10–11, 178–79
 priority, 53
 recording purchases, 19
 repayment schedules, 141–42
 shopping for, 175–77
 teaser rate, 176–77
 types of, 171–74
Credit counseling, 155–57, 159
Creditors
 communications with, 134–36,
  138–39
 negotiations, 133–45
 reaging program, 138, 156
 repayment schedules, setting,
  139–45
 sample letter to, 137
Credit reporting agencies, 9, 161
Credit reports, 162–68
 bankruptcies and, 158
 dispute letters, 165–67
 repossessions and, 141
 requesting, 161–66
Credit system knowledge quiz, 3–6

D

Debit cards, 173–74
Debt
 analyzing, 15–21
 categories of, 51
 co-signers and, 12
 credit card consolidation, 146,
  149–50
 dischargeable, 157
 habits, breaking, 181–84
 installment, 32
 lower debts priority, 53–54
 monthly debt worksheets,
  38–49
 negotiation, 137–38
 prioritizing, 50–61
 sample monthly worksheet, 36
 stress, physical problems and,
  17
 survival category, 51–52, 57–58
 warning signs of, 28–37
Debt destroyer tips, 7, 14, 20, 36,
 56, 71, 76, 116, 144, 160, 169,
 180, 183
Debt-free dream list worksheet, 184
Debt ratio, 36, 37, 180
Debt Relief Clearinghouse, 156
Dentist bills, 143
Department store credit cards, 53,
 149–50, 172

Diners Club, 172
Dischargeable debts, 157
Discipline, 2
Disclosure notices, 11
Doctor bills, 143
Dun & Bradstreet, 161, 166

E

Economy, 2
Emergency credit, 9
Emergency funds, 182
 living expenses, 114
Employment, 64
Entertainment expenses, 74–75
Equifax, 9, 161, 166, 176
Equity loans, 12–13
Expenses
 average American, 32, 35
 budget-busters, 112, 115, 117
 emergency funds and, 114, 182
 incidental, 72–73
Experian, 9, 161, 166, 176

F

Fair Credit Reporting Act, 163–64,
 168
Fair Debt Collection Practices Act,
 139, 199–208
Federal repayment plan, 158
Federal Trade Commission, 69, 139
FICO scores, 162, 167–68, 170
Financial goals, 181–84
 age and, 15–16
*Financially Secure: An Easy-to-
 Follow Money Program for
 Women* (McNaughton), 76
Financial planners, 182
Food expenses, 52, 75
Foreclosure, 140

G

Garage sales, 63, 76
Gasoline charge cards, 53, 172–73
Glossary, 209–10
Goals, 182–83
Gold cards, 172
Gym memberships, 55

H

Health, debt and, 17
Health club memberships, 55, 75
Home
 buying, 182
 housing expenses, 115
 refinancing, 13
Home equity loans, 12–13, 154
Homeowners insurance, 143
Homesavers U.S.A., 140

Housing expenses, 115

I

Impulse buying, 19–20
Incentive cards, 171
Income, increasing, 63–71
 business owners and, 65, 68–71
 personal cash flow, 63–65,
  66–67
Income-to-debt ratio, 17
Installment debt, 32
Insurance, 182
 auto, 55, 143
 deductibles, 75
 homeowners, 112, 143
 life, 54–55
 medical, 52, 54, 143
 repayment schedules, 143
Interest
 prorated, 31
 rates, 11
 sample credit card chart, 33
Internal Revenue Service, 142

L

Life insurance, 54–55
Loan(s)
 consolidation, 31
 from family/friends, 158
 fraudulent, 157
 loan-to-value ratio, 154
 mortgage. *See* Mortgage
 student, 30, 142, 157, 182
 unsecured, 53

M

Marriage, debt and, 17–18
MasterCard, 171–72, 175
Medical bills/expenses, 53, 115
 insurance, 52, 54, 143
 repayment schedules, 144
 deductibles, 143
Memberships, 75, 115
Merchant cards, 171
Money calorie counter, 77
Monthly budget worksheet, 118–30
Monthly debt worksheets, 36, 38–
 49
Mortgage, 9
 biweekly, 155, 186–98
 as priority expense, 51
 refinancing, 151, 154
 repayment schedules, 140
 second, 154
Myths, of credit, 8–14

N

Net worth, calculating, 112–14

O

Office expenses, 115
Ohio State University study, 17
Overtime income, 64

P

Personal monthly budget worksheet, 118–30
Pets (expenses of), 115
Platinum cards, 172
Pledge, to self, 185
Preapproved credit cards, 10–11, 178–79
Property taxes, 112
Purchasing behavior, analyzing, 15–21

Q

Quitclaim deed, 140
Quizzes
    credit system knowledge, 3–6
    personal finance, 29
    self-owned business, 30

R

Reaging program, 138, 156
Rebates, 76
Recreation expenses, 115
Refinancing
    auto, 141
    home, 13, 151, 154
Rent repayment schedules, 140–41

Repayment strategies, 14
Repossession, 141
Retirement account, 182
Rolling late account, 136

S

Sales, increasing, 70
Savings accounts, 157
Schooling expenses, 115
Secured credit cards, tracking, 177
Secured loan payments, 52, 141
Self-employed, budgets and, 111–12
Seller credit cards, 172–73
Shopping, 55, 76
Straight bankruptcy, 157
Student loans, 30, 157, 182
    repayment schedules, 142
Subscriptions, 75, 115

T

Tax(es), 157
    deductions, 182
    repayment schedules, 142–43
    unpaid, 52
Telephone expenses, 76
TransUnion, 9, 161, 166, 176
Travel and entertainment cards, 172
Tuition, 55
Tutoring expenses, 55

U

Universal charge cards, 171–72
Unsecured credit repayment schedules, 141–42
Unsecured loans, 53
Utilities, 51–52, 74, 115

V

Visa card, 171–72, 175

W

Wage earner's plan, 158
Worksheets
    behavior assessment, 21
    budget-buster expenses, 116–17
    business owner's cash flow, 71
    cash expenditures (30-day), 78–90
    credit card expenditures (30-day), 74, 91–103
    credit card organizer, 174
    creditor communication log, 135
    debt, 147–48
    debt-free dream list, 184
    debt ratio, 37
    debt repayment, 145
    extra cash, 104–10
    increasing cash flow, 66–67
    monthly debt, 36, 38–49
    net worth, 114
    payoff strategy, 153
    personal monthly budget, 118–30
    prioritizing debt, 58–62
    secured credit cards tracking, 177
    yearly budget, 131–32, 151

Y

Yearly budget worksheet, 131–32, 151

About the Author

Deborah McNaughton is the founder of Professional Credit Counselors. She is a nationally known credit expert who has been interviewed on hundreds of radio and television talk shows. McNaughton's business offers assistance in credit consulting, mortgages, real estate purchases, automobile purchases, and financial planning. She is the author of several books on credit, including *All about Credit, The Insider's Guide to Managing Your Credit, Financially Secure: An Easy to Follow Money Program for Women, Everything You Need to Know about Credit, Fix Your Credit, Have a Good Report* (coauthored with John Avanzini), and *The Credit Repair System,* a business opportunity manual that has helped hundreds of credit counseling businesses throughout the United States get started. McNaughton conducts credit and financial strategies seminars nationally and offers a distributor program for her seminars.

McNaughton's seminar and workshop *Your Financial Future: Understanding Credit, Debt and Planning for Tomorrow!* is available in a video and workbook series. McNaughton has also produced the video *A Gift for America: How to Survive a Financial Crisis.*

In 1990, McNaughton founded Inner-Strength International, introducing her motivational workshop and book *Yes You Can* to help individuals discover their full potential in life by focusing on finances, hope, and encouragement.

To receive more information about McNaughton's seminars, products, services, and monthly *Financial Victory* newsletter, visit her Web site at <www.financialvictory.com>, call 714-541-2637, or write to:

Deborah McNaughton
1100 Irvine Blvd., #541
Tustin, CA 92780